NAVY SEALS HOME DEFENSE SURVIVAL GUIDE

The Ultimate Advanced Strategies to Build a Safe Haven for Maximum Protection and Security of Your Family and Property

CALEB J. GREYSON

GET YOUR BONUS NOW!

THE BONUS BELOW IS <u>100%</u> FREE

VIDEO TUTORIALS

TO GET IT SCAN
THE QR CODE BELOW OR GO TO

bonusbookshelf.com/caleb-greyson-hd

TABLE OF CONTENTS

BOOK 1: SEAL MINDSET & MENTAL RESILIENCE

Adopting the SEAL mindset and mental resilience is not just about physical toughness; it's a comprehensive approach that encompasses the strength of your mind, the tenacity of your spirit, and the unyielding determination to overcome any challenge. This mindset is cultivated through rigorous training, a disciplined lifestyle, and a relentless pursuit of excellence in all aspects of life. To begin this journey, one must first understand the core principles that define the SEAL mentality: discipline, mental toughness, and the ability to remain calm under pressure.

Discipline is the foundation upon which mental resilience is built. It's about setting high standards for yourself and consistently meeting them, regardless of the circumstances. This means adhering to a strict routine, committing to continuous self-improvement, and never allowing excuses to derail your progress. To incorporate discipline into your daily life, start by establishing a structured schedule that includes time for physical training, mental conditioning, and personal development. Make a commitment to stick to this schedule, even when it's challenging or inconvenient. Remember, discipline is not about occasional acts of heroism; it's about the consistent, daily grind that slowly but surely transforms you into a stronger, more resilient individual.

Mental toughness, another cornerstone of the SEAL mindset, is the ability to push through pain, fatigue, and fear to accomplish the mission. It's about controlling your thoughts and emotions, rather than being controlled by them. To develop mental toughness, practice stepping out of your comfort zone on a regular basis. This could mean taking cold showers, engaging in challenging physical activities, or even public speaking. Each time you face and overcome a fear, you build confidence in your ability to handle adversity. Additionally, practice mindfulness and meditation to improve your focus and mental clarity. These tools can help you maintain composure in stressful situations, allowing you to make rational decisions under pressure.

The ability to remain calm under pressure is perhaps the most visible trait of a Navy SEAL. In the chaos of combat or any high-stress environment, panic is your worst enemy. To cultivate calmness, practice stress inoculation. This involves gradually exposing yourself to stressful situations in a controlled manner, so you can learn to manage your reactions. Techniques such as deep breathing, visualization, and positive self-talk can be invaluable in these moments. By rehearsing your response to stress, you can train your brain to remain focused and calm, even in the face of overwhelming odds.

Building on the foundation of discipline and mental toughness, the journey towards embodying the SEAL mindset involves cultivating an unwavering focus. Focus, in this context, is the ability to direct your attention and energy towards your goals, despite distractions or setbacks. This requires not only a clear understanding of your objectives but also the resilience to pursue them with single-minded dedication. To enhance your focus, begin by setting specific, measurable, achievable, relevant, and time-bound (SMART) goals. Break these goals down into smaller, manageable tasks, and prioritize them to ensure you are always working towards your most important objectives. This methodical approach prevents overwhelm and keeps you motivated, as each completed task brings you one step closer to your ultimate goal.

Another critical aspect of the SEAL mindset is adaptability. The ability to quickly adjust to changing circumstances and think on your feet is essential for overcoming unexpected challenges. To develop adaptability, practice problem-solving in a variety of situations. Engage in activities that require quick thinking and flexibility, such as strategic games, outdoor survival exercises, or learning new skills outside of your comfort zone. These experiences teach you to view obstacles as opportunities for growth and encourage creative thinking, preparing you to handle whatever life throws your way with confidence and agility.

Teamwork and leadership are also integral to the SEAL ethos. While personal resilience and mental toughness are crucial, the strength of a team lies in its ability to work cohesively towards a common goal. To foster these skills, seek out opportunities for collaboration, whether in your professional life, through volunteer work, or in community projects. Practice active listening, clear communication, and conflict resolution. Remember, a true leader is not just someone who can take charge, but someone who can empower others, build trust, and bring out the best in their team.

Finally, the SEAL mindset is about continuous learning and growth. The world is constantly changing, and staying adaptable requires an ongoing commitment to education and self-improvement. Dedicate time to reading, attending workshops, and seeking mentorship. Be open to feedback and willing to learn from both successes and failures. This commitment to growth ensures that you are always prepared to meet the challenges of tomorrow with knowledge, skill, and confidence.

Embracing the SEAL mindset and mental resilience is a comprehensive approach to life that goes beyond mere physical endurance. It's about developing a strong character, honed through discipline, focus, adaptability, teamwork, and a commitment to continuous improvement. By integrating these principles into your daily life, you can build a resilient safe haven not just in a physical sense, but also within yourself, capable of withstanding any storm. This journey is demanding, but the rewards of living with the strength, confidence, and integrity of a Navy SEAL are immeasurable.

CHAPTER 1: DEVELOPING THE SEAL MENTALITY

Building on the established foundation of discipline and mental toughness, the journey toward mastering the SEAL mentality introduces the critical element of situational awareness. Situational awareness is the ability to identify, process, and comprehend the critical elements of information about what is happening around you. It's akin to having a 360-degree understanding of your environment, enabling you to anticipate potential threats and opportunities. To develop this skill, start by practicing observation in your daily life. Pay attention to the details of your surroundings, the behavior of people around you, and any anomalies that break the pattern of normal activity. This practice can be as simple as noting which cars are parked in your neighborhood as you walk down the street, observing the mood and body language of people in a room, or keeping track of the exits whenever you enter a new building.

Enhancing your situational awareness also involves honing your intuition. Intuition is that gut feeling or sixth sense that often alerts you to danger before you're consciously aware of it. To sharpen this instinct, listen to your gut feelings in various situations and reflect on their accuracy afterward. Did you feel uneasy about a person or situation that later proved to be problematic? Learning to trust and act on your intuition can be a powerful tool in developing the SEAL mentality.

Another aspect of situational awareness is the ability to adapt quickly to changing circumstances. This requires not only a keen observation of your surroundings but also the flexibility to modify your plans based on new information. Practice this by setting up scenarios where you must make quick decisions. For example, while driving, take a different route than planned when you encounter a roadblock or heavy traffic, and observe how quickly you can come up with an alternative plan. Or, during a workout, change your routine unexpectedly and notice how you adapt to the new exercises. These exercises will improve your ability to think on your feet, a crucial component of the SEAL mentality.

Critical thinking is another skill that complements situational awareness. It involves analyzing information objectively and making reasoned judgments. Start by questioning the information you receive daily, whether from news sources, social media, or conversations. Evaluate the credibility of the sources, look for biases, and consider alternative viewpoints. This practice will enhance your ability to discern truth from misinformation and make informed decisions, a key aspect of mental resilience.

To further develop your critical thinking skills, engage in activities that challenge your problem-solving abilities. Puzzles, strategy games, and brain teasers are excellent tools for this purpose. They not only sharpen your mind but also provide a fun and engaging way to build your mental acuity. Additionally, try to approach problems in your life from multiple perspectives. When faced with a challenge, list out all possible solutions, weigh their pros and cons, and consider the potential outcomes. This methodical approach to problem-solving will strengthen your critical thinking skills and prepare you for the unpredictable nature of crisis situations. Remember, the goal of developing situational awareness and critical thinking is not to live in a state of constant paranoia but to cultivate a sharp, prepared mind that can navigate challenges with confidence and agility. These skills are essential for anyone looking to adopt the SEAL mentality, as they enable you to anticipate and react to threats more effectively, making you a stronger, more resilient individual.

Building on the established foundation of discipline and mental toughness, the journey toward mastering the SEAL mentality introduces the critical element of situational awareness. Situational awareness is the ability to identify, process, and comprehend the critical elements of information about what is happening around you. It's akin to having a 360-degree understanding of your environment, enabling you to anticipate potential threats and opportunities. To develop this skill, start by practicing observation in your daily life. Pay attention to the details of your surroundings, the behavior of people around you, and any anomalies that break the pattern of normal activity. This practice can be as simple as noting which cars are parked in your neighborhood as you walk down the street, observing the mood and body language of people in a room, or keeping track of the exits whenever you enter a new building.

Enhancing your situational awareness also involves honing your intuition. Intuition is that gut feeling or sixth sense that often alerts you to danger before you're consciously aware of it. To sharpen this instinct, listen to your gut feelings in various situations and reflect on their accuracy afterward. Did you feel uneasy about a person or situation that later proved to be problematic? Learning to trust and act on your intuition can be a powerful tool in developing the SEAL mentality.

Another aspect of situational awareness is the ability to adapt quickly to changing circumstances. This requires not only a keen observation of your surroundings but also the flexibility to modify your plans based on new information. Practice this by setting up scenarios where you must make quick decisions. For example, while driving, take a different route than planned when you encounter a roadblock or heavy traffic, and observe how quickly you can come up with an alternative plan. Or, during a workout, change your routine unexpectedly and notice how you adapt to the new exercises. These exercises will improve your ability to think on your feet, a crucial component of the SEAL mentality.

Critical thinking is another skill that complements situational awareness. It involves analyzing information objectively and making reasoned judgments. Start by questioning the information you receive daily, whether from news sources, social media, or conversations. Evaluate the credibility of the sources, look for biases, and consider alternative viewpoints. This practice will enhance your ability to discern truth from misinformation and make informed decisions, a key aspect of mental resilience.

To further develop your critical thinking skills, engage in activities that challenge your problem-solving abilities. Puzzles, strategy games, and brain teasers are excellent tools for this purpose. They not only sharpen your mind but also provide a fun and engaging way to build your mental acuity. Additionally, try to approach problems in your life from multiple perspectives. When faced with a challenge, list out all possible solutions, weigh their pros and cons, and consider the potential outcomes. This methodical approach to problem-solving will strengthen your critical thinking skills and prepare you for the unpredictable nature of crisis situations.

Remember, the goal of developing situational awareness and critical thinking is not to live in a state of constant paranoia but to cultivate a sharp, prepared mind that can navigate challenges with confidence and agility. These skills are essential for anyone looking to adopt the SEAL mentality, as they enable you to anticipate and react to threats more effectively, making you a stronger, more resilient individual.

Mental Toughness in High-Stress Environments

Mental toughness is a critical attribute in high-stress environments, a trait that Navy SEALs must possess to successfully navigate the challenges they face. This quality is not inherent; it is cultivated through rigorous training and experience, designed to fortify the mind against the pressures and unpredictability of combat situations. For civilians looking to adopt this aspect of the SEAL mentality, understanding the importance of mental toughness in high-stress environments is the first step toward building a resilient mindset capable of withstanding any crisis.

High-stress environments, whether in a military operation, emergency situations, or daily life challenges, test our mental fortitude and our ability to remain composed, make decisions, and act effectively under pressure. Mental toughness enables individuals to face these challenges head-on, with a clear mind and a steadfast purpose. It involves a combination of focus, confidence, control, and perseverance, qualities that allow one to push through the barriers of fear, fatigue, and uncertainty that high-stress situations often present.

To begin developing mental toughness, start by recognizing the triggers that cause stress and anxiety in your life. Once identified, you can work on strategies to manage these triggers. For example, if public speaking induces stress, gradually exposing yourself to speaking engagements can help desensitize and build confidence in your abilities. This approach, known as stress inoculation, is a technique used by Navy SEALs to prepare for the psychological demands of their missions. By gradually exposing themselves to the stressors they will face, SEALs learn to manage their reactions and maintain composure under pressure. Another method to enhance mental toughness is through the practice of visualization. Visualization is a powerful tool that involves mentally rehearsing scenarios you might encounter in a high-stress environment. By vividly imagining yourself successfully navigating these situations, you can build confidence and reduce anxiety when faced with the real thing. Navy SEALs often use visualization to mentally prepare for missions, picturing themselves executing their tasks with precision and calmness. This mental rehearsal not only prepares them for the task at hand but also reinforces their belief in their ability to overcome challenges.

Building mental toughness also requires a commitment to physical fitness. The connection between physical and mental resilience is well-documented, with regular exercise proving to be an effective stress reliever. Physical fitness challenges your limits and teaches discipline, perseverance, and the importance of pushing through discomfort, lessons that are directly transferable to mental challenges. By incorporating a rigorous physical fitness regimen into your routine, you can strengthen your mental fortitude alongside your physical endurance.

Furthermore, developing a strong support system is crucial in building mental toughness. Surrounding yourself with individuals who encourage and challenge you can provide the motivation and accountability needed to persevere through difficult times. Navy SEALs rely heavily on their teams, drawing strength from the collective resilience and camaraderie of their unit. In civilian life, a support system can come from family, friends, or community groups who share similar goals and values.

The journey to developing mental toughness is ongoing, with each challenge faced serving as an opportunity to strengthen this vital attribute. By adopting the strategies used by Navy SEALs to prepare for high-stress environments, individuals can cultivate a mindset that thrives under pressure, characterized by resilience, confidence, and an unwavering determination to overcome any obstacle.

Embracing challenges as opportunities for growth is a hallmark of mental toughness. This mindset shift is essential for effectively dealing with high-stress environments. Instead of viewing difficult situations as insurmountable obstacles, see them as chances to develop resilience and adaptability. This perspective not only reduces the impact of stress but also empowers you to approach challenges with a proactive mindset. For instance, rather than avoiding a challenging project at work, tackle it head-on, viewing it as a chance to enhance your problem-solving skills and expand your expertise. This approach mirrors the Navy SEALs' method of confronting challenges, where every mission is seen as an opportunity to test and refine their skills.

Journaling is another powerful tool for building mental toughness. By regularly recording your thoughts, feelings, and experiences, you can gain insights into how you react to stress and identify patterns in your behavior that may need adjustment. This self-reflection process can help you understand your strengths and weaknesses, allowing you to develop strategies to leverage your strengths and address your weaknesses. Navy SEALs often debrief after missions, analyzing what went well and what didn't, to improve future performance. Similarly, journaling provides a personal debriefing mechanism, enabling you to learn from your experiences and make more informed decisions in the future.

Setting and achieving small, incremental goals is also crucial for developing mental toughness. These goals should challenge you, yet be attainable with effort and dedication. Achieving these goals provides a sense of accomplishment and boosts your confidence, reinforcing your belief in your ability to overcome challenges. This practice is akin to the Navy SEALs' training philosophy, where recruits are faced with progressively more difficult tasks, each designed to push their limits and build their resilience. By applying this principle in your life, you can gradually increase your mental toughness, preparing you for more significant challenges ahead.

Practicing gratitude is another aspect of mental toughness often overlooked. Focusing on the positive aspects of your life, even in the midst of adversity, can shift your mindset from one of scarcity and fear to one of abundance and optimism. This shift is crucial in high-stress environments, where a negative mindset can exacerbate the situation. Navy SEALs are trained to maintain a positive outlook, focusing on the mission's objectives rather than the dangers that lie ahead. By incorporating gratitude into your daily routine, you can cultivate a positive mindset that enhances your resilience and mental toughness.

Lastly, seeking out mentors who embody the mental toughness you aspire to can provide guidance and inspiration. These individuals can offer valuable advice, share their experiences, and provide feedback on your progress. Just as young SEALs learn from more experienced operators, you can benefit from the wisdom of those who have navigated the path you're on. Their support can be instrumental in helping you develop the mental toughness needed to thrive in high-stress environments.

Incorporating these strategies into your life can help you build the mental toughness characteristic of Navy SEALs, enabling you to face high-stress environments with confidence, resilience, and a positive mindset. Each challenge becomes a stepping stone to greater mental fortitude, preparing you to handle whatever life throws your way with grace and determination.

Controlling Stress and Fear in Critical Moments

When faced with critical moments that test our limits, controlling stress and fear becomes paramount to maintaining clarity, making sound decisions, and executing actions with precision. Navy SEALs, trained to operate in some of the most high-pressure environments imaginable, utilize specific techniques to manage these intense emotions. These methods, grounded in both psychology and physiology, can be adapted for civilian use to navigate the stresses of daily life or emergency situations.

The first technique involves focused breathing, also known as combat or tactical breathing. This method is designed to calm the nervous system and can be employed in any situation, from the battlefield to a stressful day at the office. To practice focused breathing, inhale slowly through your nose for a count of four, hold the breath for a count of four, exhale slowly through your mouth for a count of four, and then hold the empty breath for another count of four. This square breathing technique helps to reset your stress response and brings your attention back to the present moment, allowing for clearer thought processes and decision-making.

Another critical technique is the use of positive self-talk, a strategy that involves replacing negative, fear-inducing thoughts with affirming, empowering ones. Navy SEALs are trained to monitor their internal dialogues and consciously shift them towards positivity, especially under stress. This practice is based on the principle that our thoughts can influence our emotions and behaviors, and by controlling them, we can reduce fear and anxiety. Start by identifying common negative thoughts that arise in stressful situations and create a list of positive counterstatements. For example, replace "I can't handle this" with "I've faced challenges before and emerged stronger."

Visualization is another powerful tool for managing stress and fear. This technique involves mentally rehearsing a task or scenario in detail, imagining oneself performing it successfully. Navy SEALs use visualization to prepare for missions, picturing each step of their operation and visualizing their success. This practice not only enhances confidence but also primes the brain and body to perform the envisioned actions more effectively. To apply visualization, take a few moments before a stressful event to close your eyes and picture yourself navigating the situation with calmness and competence. Focus on the sensations, actions, and positive outcomes, making the mental rehearsal as vivid as possible.

Progressive muscle relaxation (PMR) is a method that reduces physical tension and the psychological stress that accompanies it. Stress and fear often manifest physically in the form of tightened muscles, and by consciously relaxing these muscles, we can signal to our brain that we are not in immediate danger, thereby reducing our overall stress level. Begin by tensing a group of muscles, such as your fists, as tightly as possible for a few seconds, and then release the tension, noticing the contrast. Work through different muscle groups in your body, from your feet to your head, tensing and then relaxing each one. This technique not only helps in the moment but, with regular practice, can improve your overall stress resilience.

Lastly, establishing a routine of regular physical exercise is essential for stress and fear management. Physical activity releases endorphins, the body's natural stress relievers, and improves overall physical health, making the body more resilient to stress. Navy SEALs maintain rigorous physical training regimens, not only for the physical benefits but also for the mental discipline and stress relief it provides. Incorporating a mix of cardiovascular exercise, strength training, and flexibility work into your routine can help manage stress and fear by improving your physical condition and providing a healthy outlet for stress release.

By integrating these techniques into your daily life, you can develop a toolkit for managing stress and fear in critical moments, enhancing your ability to remain calm, make clear decisions, and act effectively under pressure.

Adopting a mindset of preparedness and acceptance is another pivotal strategy for controlling stress and fear in critical moments. This approach involves acknowledging the reality of a situation while mentally and physically preparing oneself to face it head-on. Navy SEALs are trained to accept the possibility of danger and discomfort as part of their operations, which in turn, reduces the power of fear over their actions. To cultivate this mindset, focus on accepting that stress and fear are natural responses to challenging situations. Then, engage in mental and physical preparations that enhance your readiness to confront these challenges. This could involve regularly reviewing emergency plans, practicing skills relevant to potential scenarios, or simply conditioning your mind to accept discomfort as a temporary state that you have the power to navigate through.

Another technique that complements the SEAL approach to stress and fear management is the establishment of small, achievable goals within the larger context of a high-pressure situation. Breaking down a daunting task into smaller, manageable parts can help maintain focus and reduce feelings of overwhelm. For each small goal achieved, a sense of progress and control is reinforced, which can significantly diminish the impact of stress and fear. Start by identifying the overall objective, then break it down into a series of steps or milestones that are clear and attainable. As you accomplish each step, acknowledge your progress to bolster your confidence and maintain momentum.

The practice of grounding techniques can also be invaluable in moments of acute stress or fear. Grounding techniques are designed to divert your focus from the source of stress or fear to the present moment, often through sensory engagement or cognitive exercises. One simple yet effective method is the 5-4-3-2-1 technique, which involves identifying five things you can see, four things you can touch, three things you can hear, two things you can smell, and one thing you can taste. This technique helps anchor your mind in the present, reducing the intensity of stress and fear by shifting your attention away from distressing thoughts or future anxieties.

Incorporating mindfulness and meditation into your daily routine can also build a foundation of mental resilience that stands strong in the face of stress and fear. Mindfulness meditation encourages an attentive awareness of the present moment, along with a non-judgmental acceptance of one's thoughts and feelings. Regular practice can enhance your ability to remain centered and calm, even when external circumstances are chaotic or threatening. Start with just a few minutes each day, focusing on your breath or a mantra, and gradually increase the duration as you become more comfortable with the practice.

Finally, fostering a sense of community and support plays a crucial role in managing stress and fear. Navy SEALs operate as part of a tightly knit team, relying on each other for support, motivation, and accountability. In civilian life, building a network of friends, family, or colleagues who understand and share your commitment to resilience can provide emotional support and practical assistance in times of need. Engage with your community, participate in group activities that promote bonding and cooperation, and don't hesitate to reach out for help when you need it. Knowing you have a support system can significantly reduce feelings of isolation and helplessness in stressful situations.

By weaving these techniques into the fabric of your daily life, you can cultivate a robust set of skills for managing stress and fear. Like the Navy SEALs, who train relentlessly to perform under pressure, you too can develop the mental fortitude to face life's challenges with confidence and composure. Each technique, from focused breathing to fostering community support, contributes to a comprehensive strategy for resilience that empowers you to navigate critical moments with grace and determination.

Building Confidence with Discipline and Focus

Building unshakeable confidence through discipline and focus begins with setting clear, achievable goals. These goals act as the roadmap for your journey, guiding each step and decision you make. Start by identifying what you want to achieve in both the short term and the long term. Be specific in your goal setting; instead of a vague aim like "I want to be more confident," pinpoint exact areas you wish to improve, such as "I want to confidently lead meetings at work" or "I want to feel more secure in emergency situations at home." Once your goals are set, break them down into smaller, actionable steps. For instance, if your goal is to lead meetings confidently, your first step might be to improve your public speaking skills by practicing in front of friends or attending a workshop.

Discipline is the bridge between goals and accomplishment, and it requires consistency. Consistency in your actions transforms them into habits, and it's these habits that build the foundation of confidence. Establish a daily routine that aligns with your goals. If you're working on becoming more physically fit to handle emergency situations with confidence, incorporate regular physical training into your schedule. This could mean setting aside time each morning for a run or dedicating specific days to strength training. The key is to stick to your routine, even on days when motivation wanes. Remember, discipline is choosing between what you want now and what you want most.

Focus, on the other hand, is about channeling your energy and attention to the task at hand. In a world filled with distractions, maintaining focus can be challenging, but it's essential for achieving your goals. Enhance your focus by creating an environment conducive to concentration. This might involve decluttering your workspace, using apps that block distracting websites during work hours, or setting specific times of the day for checking emails and social media. When working on a task, use techniques like the Pomodoro Technique, which involves working for a set period, typically 25 minutes, followed by a short break. This method can help keep your mind fresh and maintain a high level of focus throughout the day.

Another critical aspect of building confidence through discipline and focus is the practice of mindfulness. Mindfulness involves being fully present in the moment, aware of where we are and what we're doing, without being overly reactive or overwhelmed by what's going on around us. Start incorporating mindfulness exercises into your daily routine, such as deep breathing, meditation, or even mindful walking. These practices can help reduce stress, enhance concentration, and improve your overall mental clarity, contributing to a stronger, more confident mindset.

As you work on building your confidence through discipline and focus, it's important to track your progress. Keep a journal or log where you can note your achievements, no matter how small they may seem. Celebrating these victories not only boosts your morale but also reinforces the belief in your ability to achieve your goals. Whether it's successfully leading a meeting without feeling nervous or completing a challenging workout, acknowledging your progress is crucial in building and maintaining confidence.

Remember, confidence doesn't develop overnight. It's the result of consistent, focused effort over time. By setting clear goals, practicing discipline, maintaining focus, embracing mindfulness, and celebrating your progress, you're on the path to building unshakeable confidence. As you continue to work on these areas, you'll find that your confidence grows, not just in your ability to handle specific tasks or situations, but in your overall belief in yourself and your capabilities.

Building unshakeable confidence through discipline and focus also involves seeking feedback and learning from it. Feedback, whether it comes from a mentor, colleague, or even your own self-assessment, is invaluable for personal growth. It provides a different perspective on your performance and areas for improvement. Approach feedback with an open mind and a willingness to adapt. For example, if you receive constructive criticism about your public speaking skills, use it as a stepping stone to enroll in a speaking course or join a local Toastmasters club. This proactive approach not only enhances your skills but also solidifies your confidence through the knowledge that you are capable of growth and improvement.

Engaging in continuous learning is another cornerstone of building confidence. The world is constantly evolving, and staying informed and skilled is crucial. Dedicate time to read books, attend workshops, or take online courses related to your goals. This commitment to learning not only broadens your knowledge base but also keeps your mind sharp and adaptable. For instance, if your goal is to feel more secure in emergency situations, taking a first aid course or a self-defense class can provide you with the knowledge and skills to act confidently should the need arise.

Surrounding yourself with a supportive community plays a significant role in bolstering confidence. Connect with individuals who share similar goals and values, and who encourage your growth. This could be a professional network, a fitness group, or an online community. Being part of a community provides a sense of belonging and support, making the journey towards your goals less daunting. It also offers opportunities for collaboration and learning from others' experiences, further enhancing your confidence.

Practicing self-care is crucial for maintaining the mental and physical energy needed to pursue your goals with discipline and focus. Ensure you're getting enough sleep, eating nutritious foods, and engaging in activities that relax and rejuvenate you. Self-care is not selfish; it's an essential part of the process. When you take care of your well-being, you're in a better position to face challenges with confidence.

Finally, embracing failure as part of the learning process is key to building unshakeable confidence. Failure is not the opposite of success; it's a stepping stone towards it. When you attempt something and fail, you gain valuable insights into what doesn't work, which is as important as knowing what does. Instead of viewing failure as a setback, see it as an opportunity to learn, grow, and come back stronger. Each failure brings you closer to your goals, as long as you're willing to learn from it and keep moving forward.

By integrating these practices into your life—seeking feedback, engaging in continuous learning, surrounding yourself with support, practicing self-care, and embracing failure—you create a robust framework for building confidence. This confidence is not just about believing in your ability to achieve specific tasks; it's a deep-rooted belief in your overall capability and worth. With discipline and focus as your guiding principles, you'll find that confidence becomes not just something you do, but something you are.

CHAPTER 2: TRAINING FOR MENTAL ENDURANCE

Training for mental endurance is akin to preparing for a marathon rather than a sprint. It's about cultivating a mindset that can withstand not just the immediate pressures and challenges but also the long, often unpredictable journey ahead. This process begins with understanding that mental endurance, much like physical strength, is built over time through consistent practice and exposure to stressors in a controlled and manageable way. The goal is to stretch your limits gradually, without overwhelming yourself, to increase your capacity for stress and adversity.

One effective method to start enhancing your mental endurance is through setting and pursuing progressively challenging goals. Begin with small, achievable objectives that slightly push your comfort zone. For instance, if you're looking to improve your ability to focus under pressure, you might start by completing a complex task with minor distractions, gradually increasing the level of distraction over time. This could involve solving puzzles with the television on in the background, moving on to more complex tasks in noisier environments. The key is incremental progression; each step should be just slightly more challenging than the last, ensuring continuous growth without causing undue stress.

Another crucial aspect of training for mental endurance involves the practice of mindfulness and meditation. These practices help in developing a keen awareness of the present moment, allowing you to recognize and manage stressors as they arise. Begin with just a few minutes each day, focusing on your breath or a simple mantra. The objective is not to clear your mind of thoughts but to observe them without judgment and bring your focus back to the present moment whenever it wanders. This practice enhances your ability to remain calm and focused amidst chaos, a vital component of mental endurance.

Journaling is another powerful tool in the arsenal for building mental endurance. It serves as a reflective practice, allowing you to process experiences, thoughts, and emotions. By regularly writing down your challenges, successes, and the emotions associated with them, you create a personal account of your journey towards greater mental resilience. This not only helps in tracking your progress but also in identifying patterns in your responses to stress and adversity. Over time, you'll be able to pinpoint areas for improvement and develop strategies to address them. Physical exercise cannot be overlooked when training for mental endurance. Engaging in regular physical activity, especially aerobic exercises like running, swimming, or cycling, has been shown to reduce stress, improve mood, and enhance cognitive function. The discipline required to maintain a regular exercise regimen also translates into mental toughness. By setting fitness goals and working towards them, you're not just building physical strength but also cultivating the perseverance and resilience needed to tackle mental and emotional challenges.

Lastly, the practice of continuous learning plays a significant role in developing mental endurance. By constantly challenging your brain with new information and skills, you keep it engaged and flexible, ready to adapt to change. This could involve learning a new language, picking up a musical instrument, or even engaging in new hobbies that require problem-solving and critical thinking. The key is to choose activities that are both enjoyable and challenging, ensuring that you're engaged and motivated to continue learning.

As you embark on this journey to build mental endurance, remember that progress is often slow and incremental. There will be setbacks and challenges along the way, but with persistence and a commitment to continuous self-improvement, you'll develop the mental resilience akin to that of a Navy SEAL. This resilience will not only serve you in high-stress situations but will also empower you to navigate the complexities of daily life with confidence and composure. Building on the foundation of setting progressively challenging goals, practicing mindfulness, and engaging in physical exercise, it's essential to incorporate stress inoculation training into your regimen for enhancing mental endurance. Stress inoculation training involves exposing yourself to stress in a controlled and gradual manner, allowing you to build up your tolerance to stress over time. Start by identifying stressors that you can control and gradually expose yourself to these stressors in a way that allows you to practice coping mechanisms. For example, if public speaking is a stressor, begin by speaking in front of a mirror, progress to speaking in front of a small group of friends, and eventually, participate in larger public speaking engagements. This methodical approach allows you to become accustomed to the stressor, reducing its impact over time and increasing your mental resilience.

Another key strategy is to develop a strong support network. Surrounding yourself with individuals who understand your goals and can provide encouragement and feedback is invaluable. This network can include family, friends, mentors, or even colleagues who share a common interest in building mental endurance. Having a support system not only provides you with a sounding board for your challenges and successes but also offers different perspectives and strategies for coping with stress. Engage in regular discussions with your support network about your progress and challenges, and be open to their suggestions and support.

Time management skills also play a crucial role in building mental endurance. Effective time management allows you to prioritize tasks, reduce stress, and increase productivity. Start by creating a daily schedule that allocates time for work, exercise, relaxation, and personal development. Use tools like calendars, planners, or digital apps to track your tasks and deadlines. Learning to say no to non-essential tasks and delegating when possible can also help manage your workload and reduce stress. By controlling your time effectively, you can ensure that you're not only meeting your obligations but also dedicating time to activities that support your mental endurance training.

Nutrition should not be overlooked in its importance for mental endurance. Consuming a balanced diet rich in fruits, vegetables, lean proteins, and whole grains can provide the energy and nutrients necessary for cognitive function and stress management. Consider incorporating foods high in omega-3 fatty acids, such as salmon or walnuts, which have been shown to reduce stress levels and improve mood. Additionally, staying hydrated and limiting intake of caffeine and sugar can help maintain stable energy levels and focus throughout the day.

Finally, adopting a positive mindset is crucial for overcoming the inevitable challenges and setbacks you will encounter. Practice reframing negative thoughts into positive ones and view challenges as opportunities for growth and learning. Celebrate your successes, no matter how small, and learn from your failures without allowing them to diminish your self-esteem. Cultivating gratitude by acknowledging the good in your life can also shift your perspective from one of scarcity to one of abundance, further enhancing your mental resilience.

By integrating these strategies into your daily routine, you can build and maintain the mental endurance necessary to face life's challenges with strength, agility, and confidence. Remember, the journey to developing mental endurance is unique for everyone, and what works for one person may not work for another. Be patient with yourself, and remain flexible in your approach, adjusting your strategies as needed to find what best supports your growth and resilience.

Stress Inoculation for Resilience

Developing resilience through controlled exposure to stress, often referred to as stress inoculation, is a technique that can significantly enhance your ability to manage and withstand stressors when they arise. This process involves gradually and systematically exposing yourself to stress in a manageable way, allowing you to build up your tolerance over time. The concept is akin to immunization against a disease; by introducing a small amount of the stressor into your system, you give your mind and body the chance to develop coping mechanisms and resilience against it. Here's how you can implement stress inoculation in your daily life to fortify your mental endurance.

1. **Identify Your Stressors**: Begin by making a list of situations that induce stress in your life. These can range from public speaking and meeting tight deadlines to managing personal conflicts or facing fears such as heights. Prioritize these stressors based on how frequently you encounter them and their impact on your life.

2. **Start Small**: Choose a stressor that is lower on your list, something that causes mild stress but is manageable. The idea is to start with scenarios that are slightly uncomfortable but not overwhelming.

3. **Develop a Controlled Exposure Plan**: For each stressor, develop a plan for how you can expose yourself to it in a controlled manner. For instance, if public speaking is a stressor, you might start by speaking to a small, familiar group before gradually increasing the audience size or the complexity of the topics you're discussing.

4. **Implement Coping Strategies**: Before you begin your exposure, equip yourself with coping strategies. These can include deep breathing exercises, positive self-talk, visualization techniques, or any other method that helps you maintain composure. Practice these strategies regularly so they become second nature.

5. **Gradually Increase Exposure**: Once you feel comfortable managing your stress response in the initial scenario, gradually increase the intensity of the exposure. This could mean extending the duration of the exposure, introducing more complex elements, or reducing the amount of preparation time you have, depending on the specific stressor.

6. **Reflect and Adjust**: After each exposure, take time to reflect on the experience. What did you learn? How did you feel? Did your coping strategies work as expected? Use this information to adjust your approach for the next exposure, whether that means choosing a different coping strategy, increasing the stress level more slowly, or even repeating the same level of exposure until you feel more comfortable.

7. **Seek Feedback**: Where possible, seek feedback from others on your performance and your handling of the stressor. This can provide valuable insights and encouragement, reinforcing your progress and highlighting areas for further growth.

8. **Maintain Regular Practice**: Stress inoculation is not a one-time activity but a continuous process. Regularly practicing and exposing yourself to stressors in a controlled manner can help maintain and enhance your resilience.

9. **Expand Your Stressor List**: As you become more comfortable with initial stressors, begin to incorporate more challenging ones from your list into your stress inoculation practice. This will help you build resilience across a wider range of scenarios.

10. **Incorporate Real-Life Applications**: Look for opportunities to apply your stress inoculation training in real-life situations. This could mean volunteering for projects that push you out of your comfort zone, seeking out new experiences that challenge you, or simply changing your approach to daily stressors with the techniques you've learned.

By following these steps, you can gradually increase your tolerance to stress, enhancing your mental resilience. This process not only prepares you to handle specific stressors more effectively but also improves your overall confidence and ability to navigate the complexities of life with a calm and composed mindset. Remember, the goal of stress inoculation is not to eliminate stress from your life, which is an unrealistic expectation, but to equip you with the tools and confidence to manage stress proactively and effectively.

Effective Visualization for Adversity

Visualization is a powerful technique that can significantly impact one's ability to overcome adversity. This practice involves creating a detailed mental image of a desired outcome or the process of performing a specific task successfully. It's a technique used by Navy SEALs to prepare for missions, allowing them to experience success before the mission begins. Here's how to implement effective visualization practices in your life to build resilience and overcome challenges.

1. Choose a Quiet Space: Start by finding a quiet and comfortable space where you won't be interrupted. This could be a room in your home, a secluded spot in a park, or any place that feels peaceful to you. The key is to be in an environment where you can relax and focus without external distractions.

2. Use Deep Breathing to Relax: Before you begin the visualization process, take a few deep breaths to relax your body and mind. Inhale slowly through your nose, allowing your abdomen to expand, and then exhale slowly through your mouth. Repeat this several times until you feel calm and centered.

3. Define Your Objective: Clearly define the objective of your visualization. Whether it's overcoming a specific challenge, improving your performance in a particular task, or simply building your resilience, having a clear goal in mind is crucial. This objective will guide your visualization and help you focus on the details that matter most.

4. Create a Vivid Mental Image: Close your eyes and start constructing a vivid mental image of your objective. Imagine the scenario in as much detail as possible, including the environment, the sounds, the smells, and even the emotions you would feel. For instance, if your goal is to remain calm during a public speaking event, visualize yourself standing on the stage, feeling confident, speaking clearly, and receiving positive feedback from the audience.

5. Incorporate All Senses: To make your visualization more effective, incorporate all your senses into the mental image. What do you see? What sounds are present? Is there a particular smell? How do you feel physically and emotionally? Engaging all your senses makes the visualization more realistic and impactful.

6. Practice Positive Self-Talk: Throughout the visualization, practice positive self-talk. Encourage yourself with affirmations and remind yourself of your ability to overcome adversity. Phrases like "I am capable," "I can handle this," and "I am strong" can reinforce your confidence and resilience.

7. Repeat the Visualization Regularly: Like any skill, visualization becomes more effective with practice. Dedicate time each day to repeat the visualization process, gradually refining the details and the emotions involved. Consistency is key to embedding these positive outcomes in your subconscious, making it easier to access this resilience in real-life situations.

8. Reflect on the Experience: After each visualization session, take a moment to reflect on the experience. Consider what felt most real, what emotions you experienced, and how you can enhance the visualization next time. This reflection can provide insights into your resilience and areas for growth.

9. Apply Lessons Learned to Real Life: Finally, apply the confidence, strategies, and emotions from your visualization to real-life situations. When faced with adversity, recall the mental images and emotions from your visualization practice. This can help you access a state of calm and confidence, enabling you to navigate challenges more effectively.

By incorporating these visualization practices into your routine, you can harness the power of your mind to build resilience, overcome adversity, and achieve your goals with the determination and strength characteristic of a Navy SEAL. Visualization is not just about seeing success; it's about feeling and believing in that success deeply enough that it becomes a part of who you are, ready to be called upon when faced with real-world challenges.

Controlling Panic Under Pressure

In high-pressure situations, maintaining composure and controlling panic are critical skills that can significantly impact outcomes. Navy SEALs are trained to handle extreme stress, and their techniques can be adapted for civilian use to enhance mental resilience and emotional control. One effective strategy is focused breathing, a method that involves deep, deliberate breaths to calm the nervous system and reduce the physiological symptoms of stress. Start by inhaling slowly through your nose for a count of four, hold the breath for a count of four, then exhale slowly through your mouth for a count of four. This technique, known as the 4-4-4 breathing method, can be practiced anywhere, anytime you feel panic rising. It serves to anchor your mind in the present moment and regain control over runaway thoughts and emotions.

Another strategy is positive self-talk, which involves replacing negative, panic-inducing thoughts with reassuring, empowering statements. This technique starts with awareness—recognizing when your thoughts are spiraling into negativity. Once you've identified these thoughts, consciously challenge and replace them with positive affirmations. For example, if you find yourself thinking, "I can't handle this," actively replace that thought with, "I am prepared and can work through any challenge." This shift in mindset can reduce feelings of panic and increase feelings of control and competence.

Visualization is also a powerful tool for maintaining composure under pressure. This involves mentally rehearsing how you want to respond in a stressful situation. Spend time visualizing yourself handling a crisis calmly and effectively, focusing on the details of your actions, the environment, and the successful outcome. This mental rehearsal can build confidence and reduce anxiety when faced with the actual situation, as your mind and body feel 'prepared' for the challenge.

Progressive muscle relaxation (PMR) is another technique that can be used to control panic. PMR involves tensing each muscle group in the body tightly, but not to the point of strain, and then slowly relaxing them. Start from the toes and work your way up to the head. This process not only helps in identifying areas of tension in the body but also serves in reducing overall stress and anxiety levels, making it easier to maintain composure in stressful situations.

Each of these strategies—focused breathing, positive self-talk, visualization, and progressive muscle relaxation—can be practiced and refined over time. They are not only useful in crisis situations but also beneficial in daily life to manage stress, improve emotional regulation, and enhance overall mental resilience. By incorporating these techniques into your routine, you can build a strong foundation of mental endurance and composure, ready to face high-pressure situations with confidence.

Physical exercise, while primarily known for its benefits to physical health, plays a crucial role in managing stress and maintaining mental composure under pressure. Engaging in regular physical activity, such as running, swimming, or even brisk walking, triggers the release of endorphins, the body's natural painkillers and mood elevators. These biochemical changes in the brain contribute to a state of well-being and can significantly reduce the perception of stress. To effectively utilize physical exercise as a tool for stress management, it's recommended to establish a routine that includes at least 30 minutes of moderate-intensity exercise most days of the week. This not only aids in building physical resilience but also prepares the mind to handle stress more effectively.

Journaling is another technique that offers a way to process emotions and stress in a constructive manner. By putting thoughts and feelings onto paper, individuals can gain clarity on their situations, identify patterns in their thinking, and work through challenges. The act of writing can serve as a form of release, allowing for a reduction in the mental burden of stress. To incorporate journaling into your stress management toolkit, set aside a few minutes each day to write about your experiences, thoughts, and feelings. This practice can enhance self-awareness and provide a sense of control over one's emotional state.

Building a support system is also essential in managing stress and maintaining composure. Having a network of friends, family, or colleagues to turn to can provide emotional support, practical advice, and a different perspective on stressful situations. Sharing your experiences with others can help in diffusing the intensity of your emotions, offering relief, and sometimes even solutions to the problems at hand. To strengthen your support system, make an effort to maintain regular contact with your network, offer your support to them, and be open to seeking help when needed.

Lastly, embracing challenges as opportunities for growth is a mindset shift that can significantly impact how stress is perceived and managed. Viewing difficult situations as chances to learn and develop resilience can transform the emotional response to stress from one of fear and avoidance to one of engagement and determination. This approach encourages a proactive stance towards challenges, fostering a sense of empowerment and confidence in one's ability to overcome adversity.

Incorporating these strategies into your daily life—physical exercise, journaling, building a support system, and viewing challenges as opportunities—can equip you with a comprehensive set of tools for managing stress and maintaining composure under pressure. These practices, when combined with focused breathing, positive self-talk, visualization, and progressive muscle relaxation, form a robust framework for developing mental endurance and resilience, enabling you to navigate high-pressure situations with grace and confidence.

CHAPTER 3: ACHIEVING EMOTIONAL CONTROL

Emotional control, especially during crises, is not just about managing your feelings in the moment but also about preparing your mind and body to handle stress before it happens. One of the most effective ways to achieve this state of readiness is through the practice of mindfulness meditation. Mindfulness meditation involves sitting quietly and paying attention to thoughts, sounds, the sensations of breathing, or parts of the body, bringing your attention back whenever your mind starts to wander. This practice trains your brain to focus on the present, reducing the tendency to react impulsively to stressful situations. To start, find a quiet space where you won't be disturbed.

Sit in a comfortable position, close your eyes, and focus on your breath. Inhale deeply through your nose, feeling your chest and belly rise, then exhale slowly through your mouth. If your mind wanders, gently redirect your focus back to your breath. Begin with five minutes a day, gradually increasing the time as you become more comfortable with the practice.

Another technique to enhance emotional control is the practice of gratitude. Focusing on gratitude can shift your perspective from what is lacking or stressful to what is abundant and positive in your life. Each night, write down three things you are grateful for. These can be as simple as a warm cup of coffee in the morning, a kind word from a friend, or the comfort of your bed at night. This practice can help rewire your brain to focus more on positivity, which is crucial for maintaining emotional control during challenging times.

Creating a routine that incorporates physical activity is also vital. Exercise not only strengthens the body but also reduces

Staying Calm in Emergencies

In emergencies, the ability to remain calm is paramount, not just for your safety but also for those around you. The chaos and unpredictability of such situations demand a clear head and a steady heart, qualities that can be cultivated through specific, actionable techniques. Here, we delve into methods that can help stabilize your emotions and maintain clarity when every second counts.

Firstly, adopt the 'Grounding Technique,' a powerful tool to anchor yourself in the present and prevent your mind from being overwhelmed by the situation. This method involves engaging all five senses to bring your focus back to the here and now. Start by naming five things you can see around you, no matter how insignificant. Next, identify four things you can touch; it could be the fabric of your clothes or the coolness of the ground beneath you. Then, acknowledge three things you can hear, which might be the distant sound of traffic or the wind rustling through trees. Move on to recognizing two things you can smell, perhaps the faint scent of rain in the air or the aroma of your own skin. Finally, identify one thing you can taste, even if it's just the lingering flavor of your last meal. This technique effectively diverts your attention from the source of panic to your immediate environment, helping to reduce stress levels.

Secondly, engage in 'Tactical Breathing,' a method used by military personnel and first responders to control their physiological response to stress. This involves inhaling deeply through your nose for a count of four, holding the breath for a count of four, exhaling slowly through your mouth for a count of four, and then pausing for another count of four before repeating the cycle. This controlled breathing helps slow your heart rate, allowing you to think more clearly and make rational decisions in the heat of the moment.

Another crucial technique is the 'AWARE' strategy, an acronym that stands for Acknowledge, Wait, Act, Repeat, and Evaluate. Begin by acknowledging the emergency and your initial reactions to it, whether it's fear, panic, or confusion. Then, wait and give yourself a moment to breathe and assess the situation without rushing into action. After taking this brief pause, act by deciding on the most logical step to take next. Repeat the process as necessary, continuously evaluating the situation and your response to it. This methodical approach encourages a more measured and effective response to emergencies.

Incorporating these techniques into your daily routine can significantly improve your ability to remain calm during emergencies. Practice the Grounding Technique and Tactical Breathing regularly, so they become second nature when you truly need them. Familiarize yourself with the AWARE strategy and visualize applying it in various emergency scenarios. By preparing your mind and body through these methods, you'll be better equipped to handle crises with composure and resilience, embodying the mental fortitude of a Navy SEAL.

Managing Emotional Fatigue in Crises

Managing emotional fatigue during prolonged crises requires a multifaceted approach that encompasses both the mind and body. Emotional fatigue, a state of feeling emotionally drained or overwhelmed, can significantly impact one's ability to think clearly and make decisions, especially in high-stress environments. To effectively combat this, it's essential to adopt strategies that Navy SEALs use to maintain psychological resilience and emotional stamina over extended periods.

Firstly, establish a routine that includes regular physical exercise. Exercise acts as a natural stress reliever, promoting the release of endorphins which can improve mood and decrease feelings of anxiety and depression. Aim for at least 30 minutes of moderate to vigorous activity daily, such as jogging, cycling, or even brisk walking. Incorporating strength training exercises twice a week can also enhance your physical resilience, making you better equipped to handle stress.

Secondly, prioritize sleep and rest. Sleep is crucial for cognitive function, emotional regulation, and overall mental health. Strive for 7-9 hours of quality sleep per night. Create a sleep-conducive environment by minimizing exposure to blue light from screens at least an hour before bedtime, maintaining a cool, dark, and quiet bedroom, and establishing a consistent sleep schedule even on weekends.

Thirdly, practice mindfulness and deep breathing exercises. Mindfulness meditation can help center your thoughts and reduce the rumination that often accompanies stress. Dedicate a few minutes each day to sit quietly, focusing on your breath or a mantra. This practice can help ground you in the present moment, providing a break from stressors. Deep breathing exercises, such as the 4-7-8 technique—inhaling for 4 seconds, holding the breath for 7 seconds, and exhaling for 8 seconds—can also help reduce stress and promote relaxation.

Fourthly, maintain a balanced diet rich in nutrients that support brain health and emotional well-being. Incorporate foods high in omega-3 fatty acids, such as salmon and walnuts, which have been shown to reduce symptoms of anxiety and depression. Additionally, ensure adequate intake of fruits, vegetables, and whole grains to provide the vitamins and minerals necessary for maintaining energy levels and resilience.

Fifthly, cultivate a strong support network. Sharing your experiences and feelings with trusted friends, family members, or a support group can provide emotional relief and a sense of belonging. Don't hesitate to seek professional help if you find it challenging to manage emotional fatigue on your own. A therapist or counselor can offer strategies and tools tailored to your specific needs.

Sixthly, engage in activities that bring you joy and relaxation. Whether it's reading, gardening, painting, or listening to music, dedicating time to hobbies and interests can serve as a valuable counterbalance to stress. These activities not only provide an outlet for creative expression but also help distract from worries, contributing to a more positive outlook.

Seventhly, set realistic goals and break them down into manageable tasks. This approach can help mitigate feelings of being overwhelmed and foster a sense of accomplishment as you progress. Celebrate small victories and practice self-compassion, recognizing that it's okay to not always meet expectations, especially under challenging circumstances.

Eighthly, limit exposure to news and social media if you find that it exacerbates your stress or anxiety. Stay informed but set boundaries to protect your mental health. Choose specific times to check updates and prefer reputable sources to avoid misinformation, which can fuel anxiety.

By integrating these strategies into your daily life, you can build resilience against emotional fatigue, enabling you to navigate long-term crises with greater composure and strength. Remember, managing emotional fatigue is not about eliminating stress but rather developing the tools and mindset to cope with it effectively, ensuring you remain mentally and emotionally prepared for the challenges ahead.

Quick Recovery After Mental Strain

Recovering quickly from mental strain is essential for maintaining resilience and emotional control in high-stress environments. This process involves a series of deliberate actions and lifestyle adjustments aimed at rejuvenating the mind and restoring mental energy. Here, we delve into specific methods that facilitate rapid recovery from mental strain, ensuring you can return to a state of readiness and maintain performance under pressure.

1. **Structured Decompression Time**: Allocate a specific period each day dedicated solely to unwinding and mentally decompressing. This could involve activities that you find relaxing and enjoyable, such as reading, taking a leisurely walk, or engaging in a hobby. The key is to engage in these activities without any goal other than relaxation. It's not the time for multitasking or productivity; it's time for your mind to rest and reset.

2. **Tech Detox**: Implement a daily tech-free period, especially before bedtime, to reduce cognitive stimulation caused by screens. The blue light emitted by phones, tablets, and computers can interfere with your sleep cycle and keep your mind in a heightened state of alertness. Choose a cutoff time each evening, such as 8 PM, after which you avoid all electronic devices. This practice can help your mind unwind and improve sleep quality, which is crucial for mental recovery.

3. **Mindful Breathing Exercises**: Incorporate short, mindful breathing sessions throughout your day to help reset your stress levels. This can be as simple as taking a few minutes to focus solely on your breath, inhaling deeply through the nose for a count of four, holding for a count of four, and exhaling slowly through the mouth for a count of six. This exercise helps activate the body's relaxation response, reducing immediate stress and aiding in quicker mental recovery.

4. **Nature Immersion**: Spend time in natural settings as often as possible. Research has shown that being in nature, or even viewing scenes of nature, reduces anger, fear, and stress and increases pleasant feelings. Exposure to nature not only makes you feel better emotionally, it contributes to your physical wellbeing, reducing blood pressure, heart rate, muscle tension, and the production of stress hormones. Even a short walk in a park can significantly contribute to mental recovery.

5. **Nutritional Support**: Optimize your diet to support brain health and stress recovery. Incorporate foods rich in omega-3 fatty acids, antioxidants, and vitamins. For example, salmon, blueberries, nuts, and leafy green vegetables can have a profound impact on improving your mood and reducing stress levels. Additionally, staying hydrated is crucial; even mild dehydration can affect your mood and energy levels.

6. **Physical Activity**: Engage in regular physical exercise tailored to your fitness level and interests. Exercise is a powerful stress reliever. It can help lower your body's stress hormones, such as cortisol, over time. It also stimulates the production of endorphins, chemicals in the brain that are the body's natural painkillers and mood elevators. Consistent participation in aerobic exercise has been shown to decrease overall levels of tension, elevate and stabilize mood, improve sleep, and improve self-esteem.

7. **Sleep Hygiene**: Prioritize sleep and establish a consistent sleep routine. Aim for 7-9 hours of quality sleep per night. Develop a pre-sleep ritual to help signal your body it's time to wind down. This could include

reading, taking a warm bath, or gentle stretching. Keeping a regular sleep schedule, even on weekends, helps regulate your body's clock and can help you fall asleep and stay asleep for the night.

8. **Social Connections**: Maintain strong social connections and communicate regularly with friends and family. Social interaction can provide a sense of belonging, improve your mood, and offer support during stressful times. Even when you're busy, try to carve out time for social activities or simply to catch up with loved ones over the phone.

9. **Skillful Distractions**: Engage in activities that require focus and concentration, such as puzzles, games, or learning a new skill. These activities can act as a temporary distraction, allowing your mind to break away from stressors and recharge through engagement in a non-stressful challenge.

10. **Professional Support**: If you find that your strategies for mental recovery are not enough, consider seeking professional help. A mental health professional can provide personalized strategies and support to manage stress and recover from mental strain effectively.

By integrating these methods into your lifestyle, you can enhance your ability to recover from mental strain swiftly, ensuring you remain mentally agile and resilient in the face of challenges.

BOOK 2: PHYSICAL READINESS & FITNESS

Building core physical strength is a cornerstone of Navy SEAL training and a critical component of overall physical readiness and fitness. Core strength is not just about having a toned abdomen; it involves developing the muscles around your entire trunk and pelvis area. This includes the abdominals, lower back, hips, and glutes. A strong core enhances balance and stability, which can prevent falls and injuries during physical activities. It also plays a pivotal role in performing everyday tasks and movements more efficiently. Here, we will delve into specific strength training exercises designed to fortify your core, providing a solid foundation for resilience and stamina.

Start with the plank exercise, a fundamental core strengthening workout. Begin by lying face down on the floor or a mat. Prop yourself up onto your elbows and toes, keeping your elbows directly under your shoulders. Your body should form a straight line from your head to your heels. Engage your core muscles by pulling your belly button towards your spine and tighten your glutes. Hold this position for 20 to 30 seconds initially, gradually increasing the duration as your strength improves. Ensure your hips do not sag or lift too high, as maintaining a neutral spine is crucial. The plank exercise targets a wide range of core muscles, including the transverse abdominis, rectus abdominis, and the obliques, as well as the muscles in your back.

Next, incorporate the Russian twist into your routine to engage and strengthen the oblique muscles. Sit on the floor with your knees bent and feet flat. Lean back slightly, keeping your back straight, and lift your feet off the floor until your shins are parallel to the floor. This is your starting position. Clasp your hands together or hold a weight if you prefer an added challenge. Twist your torso to the right, bringing your hands or the weight beside your right hip. Return to the center and then twist to the left. This completes one repetition. Perform 10 to 15 repetitions for 2 to 3 sets. The Russian twist not only strengthens the core but also enhances rotational mobility, which is beneficial for various physical activities and sports.

The bird dog exercise is another excellent workout for core stability and strength. Begin on all fours in a tabletop position, with your hands directly under your shoulders and knees under your hips. Engage your core and simultaneously extend your right arm forward and your left leg backward until they are both in line with your body. Keep your hips and shoulders square to the ground, avoiding any rotation. Hold this position for a few seconds, then slowly return to the starting position. Repeat with the opposite arm and leg. Aim for 10 to 12 repetitions on each side for 2 to 3 sets. The bird dog exercise targets the lower back, abdominals, and glutes while improving balance and coordination.

Incorporating these core strength training exercises into your fitness routine can significantly enhance your physical readiness and overall fitness. Not only do they build a strong and stable core, but they also contribute to improved posture, reduced risk of injuries, and better performance in both daily activities and more demanding physical tasks. As you progress, gradually increase the intensity and complexity of the exercises to continue challenging your muscles and building endurance.

For an effective core workout, the dead bug exercise is a must-include for enhancing core stability and reducing lower back pain. Lie on your back with your arms extended towards the ceiling directly above your shoulders. Bend your knees to a 90-degree angle and lift your feet off the ground. This is your starting position. Slowly lower your right arm behind your head and extend your left leg out straight, just above the floor, simultaneously. Keep your lower back pressed firmly into the floor to engage your core. Return to the starting position and repeat on the opposite side. This alternating pattern mimics the movements of a bug on its back, hence the name. Aim for 8 to 10 repetitions on each side, for 2 to 3 sets. The dead bug exercise targets the deep abdominal muscles and helps in stabilizing the spine, crucial for preventing injuries and enhancing performance in physical activities.

Another key component of a comprehensive core strengthening program is the hanging leg raise, which focuses on the lower abdominals and hip flexors. Begin by hanging from a pull-up bar with your hands shoulder-width apart and your legs straight down. Brace your core and slowly raise your legs in front of you until they are parallel to the ground, keeping them straight. Avoid swinging or using momentum to lift your legs. Slowly lower them back to the starting position. If you're a beginner, you may start with knee raises, bending your knees and lifting them towards your chest. Perform 8 to 12 repetitions for 2 to 3 sets. This exercise not only strengthens the core but also improves grip strength and overall upper body endurance.

To further challenge your core and enhance functional fitness, incorporate the side plank into your routine. Lie on your side with your legs straight and prop your upper body up on your elbow, aligning it directly under your shoulder. Stack your feet on top of each other and lift your hips off the ground, forming a straight line from your head to your feet. Hold this position, keeping your hips elevated and your core engaged. Aim to hold for 20 to 30 seconds, then switch sides. The side plank targets the obliques, which are crucial for side-to-side movements, rotational strength, and overall stability.

Lastly, the stability ball pike is an advanced exercise that targets the entire core, emphasizing the upper abdominals and the hip flexors. Start in a plank position with your feet on a stability ball and your hands on the ground, shoulder-width apart. Keep your back straight and your core engaged. Slowly roll the ball towards your hands by piking your hips up towards the ceiling and keeping your legs straight. Your body should form an inverted V shape at the top of the movement. Hold for a moment, then carefully roll back to the starting position. Perform 6 to 8 repetitions for 2 to 3 sets. This exercise not only strengthens the core but also challenges your balance and stability, making it an excellent addition to your fitness regimen.

Incorporating these exercises into your core training routine will provide a solid foundation for building strength, stability, and endurance. Regularly challenging your core with a variety of exercises ensures balanced muscle development and contributes to overall physical readiness and peak performance. Remember to focus on form and gradually increase the intensity of your workouts to continue making progress and avoid plateaus. With dedication and consistency, you'll build a strong, resilient core that will support you in all your physical endeavors.

CHAPTER 1: BUILDING CORE PHYSICAL STRENGTH

To effectively build core physical strength, a key exercise to incorporate into your routine is the bicycle crunch, which targets the rectus abdominis and the obliques, providing a comprehensive core workout. Begin by lying flat on your back on a mat with your hands placed behind your head, elbows wide. Lift your knees to a 90-degree angle and elevate your shoulder blades off the ground without pulling on your neck. Bring your right elbow towards your left knee while straightening your right leg out in front of you, hovering above the floor. Quickly switch sides, bringing your left elbow towards your right knee while extending your left leg. Continue alternating sides in a pedaling motion for 1 to 2 minutes, focusing on the quality of movement rather than speed. Ensure that you are engaging your core throughout the exercise and not relying on momentum to carry you through the movements.

Another fundamental exercise for core development is the reverse crunch, which emphasizes the lower abdominals, a region often neglected in standard crunches. To perform a reverse crunch, lie on your back with your hands at your sides or underneath your glutes for added support. Lift your legs off the ground and bend your knees at a 90-degree angle. Pressing your lower back into the mat, use your core muscles to bring your knees towards your chest by lifting your hips off the floor. Then, slowly lower your legs back to the starting position without letting your feet touch the ground. Aim for 3 sets of 10 to 15 repetitions, focusing on controlled movements to maximize engagement of the lower abdominal muscles.

For those looking to further challenge their core and incorporate balance and stability into their routine, the Swiss ball rollout is an excellent choice. This exercise not only targets the core muscles but also engages the shoulders and back, providing a full-body workout with a focus on core stability. Begin by kneeling on a mat with a Swiss ball in front of you. Place your forearms on the ball with your hands clasped. Keeping your back straight and your core engaged, slowly roll the ball away from you, extending your body as far as you can without allowing your back to sag or arch. Use your core muscles to pull the ball back towards your knees, returning to the starting position. Perform 2 to 3 sets of 8 to 12 repetitions, ensuring that you maintain a slow and controlled pace throughout the exercise.

In addition to these targeted exercises, it's crucial to incorporate functional movements that mimic everyday activities or specific sports movements. This not only helps in building a strong core but also ensures that the strength gained is applicable and beneficial in real-world scenarios. One such functional exercise is the farmer's walk, which simulates the act of carrying heavy loads over a distance. This exercise engages the entire core, as well as the shoulders, arms, and legs, making it an effective full-body workout. To perform a farmer's walk, stand straight with a weight in each hand at your sides. This could be dumbbells, kettlebells, or any heavy object that is challenging to hold. Keep your core engaged, shoulders back, and gaze forward as you walk forward for a set distance or time. Start with lighter weights to focus on form and gradually increase the weight as your core strength improves. Aim for 2 to 3 sets of walks, each lasting between 30 seconds to 1 minute.

By integrating these exercises into your fitness regimen, you can build a strong, stable, and functional core that will enhance your performance in physical activities, reduce the risk of injuries, and improve your overall fitness level. Remember, consistency is key to seeing progress, so ensure that you are regularly challenging your core with these exercises and gradually increasing the intensity as your strength improves.

To further enhance core strength and stability, incorporating the mountain climber exercise into your routine offers a dynamic and cardiovascular approach. This exercise not only targets the core muscles but also boosts heart rate, contributing to improved aerobic fitness. Start in a high plank position with your hands placed directly under your shoulders and your body forming a straight line from head to heels. Drive your right knee towards your chest, then quickly switch, driving your left knee towards your chest, while keeping your hips down and your core engaged. Alternate legs rapidly as if running in place, focusing on the movement originating from your core. Aim for 3 sets of 30 seconds to 1 minute, increasing the duration as your endurance and core stability improve.

Another exercise that targets the core while also challenging the upper body is the push-up with side plank. This combination exercise works the rectus abdominis, obliques, shoulders, chest, and triceps. Begin in a standard push-up position. Perform a push-up, and as you return to the starting position, rotate your body to the right, extending your right arm towards the ceiling, transitioning into a side plank. Hold the side plank for a few seconds before returning to the push-up position and repeating on the left side. This exercise not only strengthens the core but also promotes shoulder stability and balance. Perform 2 to 3 sets of 8 to 10 repetitions on each side, ensuring proper form and alignment throughout the movement.

For those seeking to intensify their core workouts, the V-sit hold is an advanced exercise that targets the entire abdominal region. Sit on the floor with your legs extended in front of you and lean back slightly to find your balance on your sit bones. Engage your core and lift your legs off the ground, keeping them straight, while also lifting your arms so they are parallel to the ground. Your body should form a V shape. Hold this position for 15 to 30 seconds, focusing on keeping your core tight and your body stable. Perform 2 to 3 sets, gradually increasing the hold time as your core strength improves.

Incorporating a variety of core exercises into your fitness routine is essential for developing a well-rounded and resilient core. Each exercise targets different aspects of core strength and stability, from the deep abdominal muscles to the muscles supporting the spine. Regularly challenging your core with these exercises not only enhances physical performance but also contributes to better posture and reduces the risk of back pain.

To maximize the benefits of your core training, pay close attention to your form and breathing. Ensure that you are engaging your core muscles throughout each exercise and using controlled, deliberate movements. Breathing correctly—exhaling on the effort and inhaling on the return—can also help in maximizing engagement and effectiveness of the core muscles.

Remember, building a strong core is a gradual process that requires consistency and dedication. By incorporating these exercises into your routine and progressively increasing the intensity and complexity, you can achieve a strong, stable, and functional core that supports a wide range of physical activities and enhances your overall fitness and well-being.

Navy SEAL Fitness Training Essentials

Navy SEAL fitness training is renowned for its intensity and effectiveness, focusing on building a high level of physical readiness that encompasses strength, endurance, agility, and mental toughness. At the heart of this regimen are core elements that push the human body to its limits while ensuring a holistic approach to fitness and well-being. Understanding these core elements can provide valuable insights into developing a comprehensive fitness program that prepares individuals for any physical challenge.

The first core element is functional strength training. This involves exercises that improve the strength and coordination of muscles used during everyday activities and operational tasks. Unlike traditional weightlifting, which often isolates specific muscles, functional strength training focuses on movements that engage multiple muscle groups simultaneously. For example, a Navy SEAL's routine might include exercises like deadlifts, kettlebell swings, and sandbag lifts. These exercises mimic real-world activities, such as lifting heavy objects or carrying equipment, ensuring that the strength developed is practical and directly transferable to operational needs.

Endurance training forms the second core element, designed to build stamina and cardiovascular health. Running is a staple in this category, with SEALs often engaging in both long-distance runs and sprints to improve their aerobic and anaerobic capacities. Swimming, another critical component of SEAL training, enhances endurance while also preparing candidates for water-based operations. Incorporating interval training, where high-intensity bursts of activity are followed by periods of lower intensity or rest, can significantly boost cardiovascular endurance, closely mirroring the unpredictable demands of field operations.

The third core element is agility and speed training, which enhances a SEAL's ability to move quickly and efficiently, crucial for navigating hazardous environments and reacting to sudden threats. Exercises like shuttle runs, cone drills, and obstacle courses improve coordination, balance, and reaction times. These activities not only increase physical agility but also require mental focus and adaptability, reinforcing the mind-body connection that is vital for operational success.

Bodyweight exercises constitute the fourth core element, emphasizing the ability to control and maneuver one's own body weight in various situations. Pull-ups, push-ups, sit-ups, and burpees are heavily featured in SEAL training, promoting muscle endurance, strength, and flexibility. These exercises can be performed anywhere, making them ideal for maintaining fitness levels when access to gym equipment is limited or when deployed in the field.

Finally, recovery and resilience are integral to the Navy SEAL fitness regimen. SEAL training is as much about pushing limits as it is about knowing when to rest and recover. Techniques such as active recovery, stretching, foam rolling, and adequate sleep are emphasized to prevent injury and ensure long-term physical and mental health. Nutrition also plays a crucial role, with a focus on a balanced diet rich in proteins, carbohydrates, fats, and hydration to support intense physical activity and recovery.

Incorporating these core elements into a fitness program requires careful planning and a commitment to pushing personal boundaries. Start by integrating functional strength and bodyweight exercises into your routine, gradually increasing intensity and complexity. Add endurance and agility training, focusing on improving your cardiovascular health and movement efficiency. Remember, recovery is just as important as the workouts themselves; prioritize rest, nutrition, and recovery techniques to maintain overall health and prevent burnout.

By adopting the core elements of Navy SEAL fitness training, individuals can build a solid foundation of physical readiness and resilience. Whether preparing for military service or simply seeking to improve personal fitness, these principles offer a roadmap to achieving peak physical and mental performance.

Strength Training for Resilience

To build resilience and core physical strength, incorporating specific strength training exercises into your routine is essential. These exercises, inspired by Navy SEAL training, focus on enhancing your body's endurance, power, and ability to withstand the physical demands of high-stress situations. Let's delve into a series of exercises designed to fortify your resilience, providing step-by-step guidance to ensure you execute each movement with precision for maximum effectiveness.

1. **Deadlifts**: Begin with the barbell on the ground. Stand with your feet hip-width apart, bending at the hips and knees to grip the bar. Your grip should be shoulder-width, with palms facing you or one palm facing you and the other facing away for a mixed grip. Keep your back flat, chest up, and look straight ahead as you lift the bar by straightening your hips and knees to a standing position. The bar should be close to your body throughout the lift. Slowly lower the bar to the ground by bending at the hips and controlling its descent. Deadlifts target your lower back, glutes, hamstrings, and core, providing a solid foundation for resilience. Perform 3 sets of 5-8 reps.

2. **Squats**: Start by standing with your feet shoulder-width apart and a barbell across your shoulders. Lower your body by bending your knees and pushing your hips back as if sitting in a chair, keeping your chest up and your gaze forward. Lower down until your thighs are at least parallel to the floor, then push through your heels to return to the starting position. Squats engage your core, quads, hamstrings, and glutes, crucial for overall strength. Aim for 3 sets of 8-10 reps.

3. **Pull-Ups**: Grip a pull-up bar with your palms facing away from you, hands slightly wider than shoulder-width. Hang from the bar with your arms fully extended. Pull yourself up by pulling your elbows down to the floor until your chin is above the bar. Lower yourself back to the starting position with control. Pull-ups strengthen the back, shoulders, and arms, enhancing your upper body resilience. If you're unable to perform a pull-up initially, start with assisted pull-ups or negative pull-ups. Work towards completing 3 sets of as many reps as possible.

4. **Push-Ups**: Begin in a plank position with your hands slightly wider than shoulder-width apart and your body forming a straight line from your head to your heels. Lower your body towards the floor by bending your elbows, keeping them close to your body. Push through your hands to return to the starting position. Push-ups target the chest, shoulders, triceps, and core. For added difficulty, elevate your feet or try wearing a weighted vest. Perform 3 sets of 12-15 reps.

5. **Planks**: Start in a push-up position but rest on your forearms instead of your hands, with elbows directly beneath your shoulders. Keep your body in a straight line from head to heels, engaging your core and squeezing your glutes. Hold this position for time, starting with 30 seconds and working up to 2 minutes. Planks are excellent for building core strength and stability, essential for resilience.

6. **Farmer's Walk**: Grab a heavy dumbbell or kettlebell in each hand, stand tall, and walk a specified distance, such as 50 feet. Keep your shoulders back, chest up, and core engaged. This exercise improves grip strength, endurance, and overall body resilience. Perform 2-3 sets, walking back and forth in a designated area.

Incorporate these exercises into your fitness routine 2-3 times per week, allowing for rest and recovery between sessions. Each exercise contributes to building a resilient body capable of handling the physical demands of emergency situations, mirroring the strength and endurance developed through Navy SEAL training. Remember to focus on form and gradually increase the weight or resistance to continue challenging your body and building resilience.

Endurance Exercises for Stamina Building

To effectively build stamina, incorporating targeted endurance exercises into your fitness regimen is crucial. These exercises are designed to increase your cardiovascular capacity, allowing you to sustain physical activity over longer periods, which is essential for maintaining peak performance during high-stress situations. Here, we detail a series of endurance exercises, inspired by Navy SEAL training, to enhance your stamina.

1. **Running**: Start with a moderate pace for a distance of 1 to 2 miles, three times a week. Focus on maintaining a steady pace that challenges you but is sustainable. Gradually increase the distance by 10% each week to progressively build your endurance. Choose routes with varying elevations to simulate different terrains. Wear a quality pair of running shoes designed for your foot type and running style to prevent injuries.

2. **Swimming**: Begin with 10 to 20 laps in a standard-sized pool, focusing on freestyle stroke for efficiency and speed. Incorporate interval training by alternating between fast-paced laps and slower, recovery laps. This not only builds endurance but also improves your breathing technique and overall swimming efficiency. Aim to swim at least twice a week, gradually increasing the number of laps as your stamina improves.

3. **Cycling**: Start with a 30-minute session at a moderate pace on flat terrain or a stationary bike. Use a gear that provides enough resistance to challenge your leg muscles but allows you to maintain a consistent pedaling speed. Incorporate interval training by alternating between high-intensity sprints and lower-intensity recovery periods. Over time, extend your cycling sessions to 1 hour or more and explore more challenging terrains with hills.

4. **Rowing**: Begin with a 15-minute session on a rowing machine, focusing on maintaining a consistent stroke rate. Aim for a stroke rate that challenges your cardiovascular system while allowing you to sustain the activity for the entire session. Gradually increase the duration of your rowing sessions by 5 minutes each week. Incorporate interval training by rowing at a high intensity for 1 minute followed by a 1-minute period of moderate intensity.

5. **Jump Rope**: Start with 1-minute intervals of jumping rope, followed by 30 seconds of rest. Aim for 10 intervals per session, focusing on maintaining a consistent pace and using proper form to maximize efficiency and minimize the risk of injury. As your stamina improves, increase the duration of each interval and decrease the rest period. Jumping rope not only builds cardiovascular endurance but also improves coordination and agility.

6. **Stair Climbing**: Find a set of stairs or use a stair-climbing machine. Begin with a session lasting 10 to 15 minutes, focusing on maintaining a steady pace. As your endurance improves, increase the duration of your stair-climbing sessions and incorporate intervals of increased speed or double-step climbing for added intensity. Stair climbing is an excellent way to build lower body strength and cardiovascular endurance simultaneously.

For all these exercises, it's important to stay hydrated, maintain proper form, and listen to your body to prevent overtraining and injuries. Incorporating these endurance exercises into your routine 2-3 times per week, along with adequate rest and recovery, will significantly enhance your stamina, preparing you for the physical demands of any situation.

CHAPTER 2: SEAL FITNESS TRAINING METHODS

Improving flexibility and mobility is crucial for enhancing your ability to respond effectively in crisis situations. Flexibility, the ability of your muscles to stretch, and mobility, the ability of your joints to move freely, together play a significant role in your overall physical readiness. These elements are vital for performing a wide range of movements with precision and efficiency, reducing the risk of injury, and maintaining physical performance under stress. Here we will delve into specific exercises and techniques inspired by Navy SEAL training to improve your flexibility and mobility, ensuring you can move with agility and adaptability in any scenario.

1. **Dynamic Stretching Routine**: Begin your workout with a dynamic stretching routine to prepare your body for physical activity. Dynamic stretches involve moving parts of your body and gradually increasing reach, speed of movement, or both. This type of stretching improves flexibility, warms up your muscles, and enhances range of motion. Examples include leg swings, arm circles, and lunges with a twist. Perform each dynamic stretch for 30 seconds to 1 minute, focusing on smooth, controlled movements.

2. **Yoga for Mobility**: Incorporate yoga sessions into your weekly fitness regimen, aiming for 2-3 times per week. Yoga is an effective way to enhance both flexibility and mobility through a series of poses that stretch and strengthen the body. Focus on poses that target key areas for mobility, such as the hips, shoulders, and spine. Poses like the pigeon pose, downward-facing dog, and the warrior series are particularly beneficial. Hold each pose for 30 seconds to 1 minute, breathing deeply to maximize the stretch.

3. **Foam Rolling**: Utilize a foam roller for self-myofascial release, a technique that helps release muscle tightness and improve blood flow. Foam rolling can be done before or after your workouts to aid in recovery and increase flexibility. Target major muscle groups such as the calves, quads, hamstrings, back, and shoulders. Roll each area for 30 seconds to 2 minutes, applying moderate pressure and pausing on tender spots.

4. **Mobility Drills**: Incorporate specific mobility drills that focus on joint health and range of motion. Examples include shoulder pass-throughs using a PVC pipe or resistance band, hip circles, and ankle mobility exercises. These drills are designed to enhance the movement capacity of your joints, allowing for smoother and more efficient motion. Perform each drill for 30 seconds to 1 minute, focusing on controlled, deliberate movements.

5. **Active Isolated Stretching (AIS)**: AIS involves extending a muscle, holding the stretch for 2 seconds, then relaxing and repeating. This technique allows for a deeper stretch without triggering the muscle's protective stretch reflex, leading to improved flexibility. Use a strap or towel to assist with stretches for hard-to-reach areas like the hamstrings or back. Perform 10-15 repetitions of each stretch, gently increasing the range of motion with each rep.

6. **Breathing Techniques**: Proper breathing plays a crucial role in maximizing your flexibility and mobility efforts. Focus on deep, diaphragmatic breathing during stretching and mobility exercises. This type of breathing helps to relax the muscles, allowing for deeper stretches and greater range of motion. Inhale deeply through the nose, filling your abdomen with air, then exhale slowly through the mouth. Use the rhythm of your breath to guide your movements, deepening the stretch with each exhale.

Incorporating these exercises and techniques into your fitness routine will significantly improve your flexibility and mobility, key components of physical readiness and resilience. By dedicating time to these practices, you'll enhance your ability to perform a wide range of movements more effectively and with less risk of injury, a critical advantage in high-stress situations. Remember, consistency is key to seeing progress, so make these exercises a regular part of your training regimen.

HIIT for Survival Scenarios

High-intensity interval training, or HIIT, is a powerful method to enhance your physical readiness for survival scenarios, drawing on the rigorous conditioning techniques used by Navy SEALs. This training approach alternates between short bursts of intense activity and periods of lower intensity or rest, effectively pushing the body to adapt and improve both aerobic and anaerobic fitness levels. Here's how to implement a HIIT regimen tailored for survival preparedness, ensuring you're equipped to handle the physical demands of any crisis.

First, select exercises that target a broad range of muscle groups and mimic movements you might encounter in survival situations. Examples include sprints, burpees, push-ups, and bodyweight squats. The goal is to choose activities that elevate your heart rate quickly and can be performed with minimal equipment.

Begin your HIIT session with a thorough warm-up to prepare your body and reduce the risk of injury. A five to ten-minute dynamic stretching routine, incorporating movements like leg swings and arm circles, will increase your heart rate and loosen up your muscles.

For the workout structure, start with a high-intensity exercise, such as sprinting at full effort for 30 seconds. The key is to push yourself to the maximum level of exertion possible during these intervals. Following the sprint, shift to a lower-intensity exercise or rest period for a duration of one to two minutes. This could involve walking or performing slow, controlled air squats. The contrast between high exertion and recovery is the essence of HIIT, stimulating improvements in cardiovascular health, endurance, and muscle strength.

Aim for a total workout time of 20 to 30 minutes, alternating between your chosen high and low-intensity exercises. As your fitness level improves, you can adjust the duration of both the high-intensity intervals and the recovery periods. Decreasing the rest time or increasing the length of the intense bursts will continuously challenge your body and lead to greater fitness gains.

Incorporate HIIT workouts into your fitness routine two to three times per week, allowing for adequate recovery between sessions. Overtraining can lead to injuries and diminish the effectiveness of your workouts, so listen to your body and rest as needed.

To maximize the benefits of your HIIT training for survival scenarios, simulate conditions you might face in a real-world crisis. For instance, if you're training for resilience in wilderness survival, include exercises that mimic climbing, lifting, or carrying heavy loads. This not only enhances your physical preparedness but also your mental toughness, as you learn to push through fatigue and discomfort.

Remember, the goal of HIIT in a survival context is not just to improve physical fitness but to prepare your body and mind to handle the unexpected. By incorporating these intense, varied workouts into your regimen, you'll build the stamina, strength, and resilience needed to face any challenge with confidence.

Functional Fitness for Practical Strength

Functional fitness exercises are designed to prepare your body for real-life movements and scenarios, focusing on strength, endurance, and mobility. These exercises simulate common physical activities you might encounter, ensuring that your body is adept at handling practical tasks with ease and efficiency. By incorporating functional fitness into your routine, you're not just training to improve your physical appearance but also enhancing your capability to perform everyday tasks and meet unexpected challenges with resilience. Here, we detail a series of functional fitness exercises that are pivotal for developing practical strength, mirroring the rigorous training and adaptability of Navy SEALs.

1. **Sandbag Lifts**: Start by selecting a sandbag of moderate weight, aiming for something that challenges you without compromising your form. Stand with your feet shoulder-width apart, squat down, and grip the

sandbag with both hands. Engage your core and lift the sandbag by extending your hips and knees, bringing it to chest height before lowering it back to the ground. This exercise mimics lifting heavy objects, engaging multiple muscle groups including your legs, back, and arms. Perform 3 sets of 8-12 reps.

2. **Farmer's Carry**: Grab a pair of heavy dumbbells or kettlebells, one in each hand. Stand up straight with your shoulders back and walk a specified distance, such as 50 to 100 feet. Keep your core engaged and maintain an upright posture throughout the walk. This exercise improves grip strength, core stability, and overall endurance, essential for carrying heavy loads over distances. Complete 2-3 sets, resting between each set.

3. **Tire Flips**: Find a large, heavy tire typically used for tractor or large machinery. Stand facing the tire with your feet wider than shoulder-width apart. Squat down and grip the underside of the tire with both hands. In a powerful motion, lift the tire by extending your legs and hips while pushing up with your arms. Flip the tire over and repeat. Tire flips develop explosive power, strength, and endurance, simulating the lifting and moving of heavy objects. Aim for 3 sets of 5-8 flips.

4. **Box Jumps**: Use a sturdy box or platform that can support your weight. Stand in front of the box with your feet shoulder-width apart. Lower into a semi-squat, then explode upwards, jumping onto the box with both feet. Step back down and repeat. Box jumps enhance lower body strength and improve explosive power, critical for jumping and climbing movements. Perform 3 sets of 10-12 jumps.

5. **Battle Ropes**: Anchor a heavy battle rope at a fixed point. Stand facing the anchor point with your feet shoulder-width apart, holding the end of the rope in each hand. Begin by rapidly alternating your arms up and down, creating waves in the rope. Increase the intensity by incorporating jumps, squats, or lunges while moving the ropes. This exercise boosts upper body strength, endurance, and coordination, essential for tasks requiring sustained upper limb activity. Continue for 30 seconds to 1 minute, completing 3-4 sets.

6. **Sled Push/Pull**: Load a sled with a weight that is challenging yet allows you to maintain proper form. For the push, grip the sled at shoulder height and drive it forward using your legs and core, keeping your back straight. For the pull, attach a rope or harness to the sled, walk forward to create tension, then walk or run backward, pulling the sled towards you. This exercise simulates pushing or dragging heavy loads, vital for developing leg strength, endurance, and core stability. Perform 3 sets of 20-30 feet for both push and pull.

Incorporating these functional fitness exercises into your training regimen will not only enhance your physical strength and endurance but also prepare you for a wide range of practical, real-world scenarios. By focusing on movements that mimic everyday tasks, you're ensuring that your body remains versatile, resilient, and capable of handling whatever challenges come your way, much like the rigorous and adaptable nature of Navy SEAL training. Remember, the key to functional fitness is consistency and gradually increasing the intensity or weight of the exercises to continue challenging your body and improving your overall physical readiness.

Improving Flexibility for Crisis Response

Improving your flexibility and mobility is not just about stretching your muscles; it's about enhancing your body's ability to move freely and efficiently in any situation, especially during high-stress scenarios where quick and adaptable movements can make a significant difference. To achieve this, a comprehensive approach that includes dynamic stretching, targeted mobility exercises, and consistent practice is essential. Here's how to incorporate these elements into your routine to improve your crisis response capabilities.

Dynamic stretching should be the first step in your mobility routine. Unlike static stretching, which involves holding a stretch for a prolonged period, dynamic stretching is about moving through a range of motion with control. This type of stretching prepares your body for physical activity, reduces the risk of injury, and improves overall mobility. Start with movements such as leg swings, where you gently swing your leg forward and backward, gradually increasing the height and speed of the swing. Perform 10 swings per leg. Next, incorporate arm circles by extending your arms and rotating them in large circles, 10 times forward and 10 times backward. These exercises warm up the joints, increase blood flow to the muscles, and enhance your range of motion.

Incorporating mobility drills specifically designed to target the joints can significantly improve your movement efficiency. Begin with shoulder pass-throughs using a PVC pipe or a resistance band. Hold the pipe or band in front of you with a wide grip, then lift it over your head and down behind your back as far as comfortable, keeping your arms straight. This exercise opens up the shoulders and improves the range of motion. Perform 10-15 pass-throughs. For hip mobility, try hip circles. Stand with your hands on your hips and feet shoulder-width apart. Move your hips in a circular motion, 10 times clockwise and 10 times counterclockwise. This drill helps to loosen the hip joints and improve flexibility in the lower body.

Foam rolling is another critical component of improving flexibility and mobility. It involves using a foam roller to apply pressure to specific muscles and tissues, helping to break up knots and increase blood flow. Focus on major muscle groups like the calves, quads, hamstrings, and back. Roll each area slowly, spending about 30 seconds to 2 minutes on each muscle group. When you find a tender spot, hold the pressure for a few moments to help release the tightness. This self-myofascial release technique aids in recovery, reduces muscle soreness, and improves flexibility.

Active Isolated Stretching (AIS) is a method that helps to effectively increase flexibility by stretching the muscles in a specific, isolated manner. For example, to stretch the hamstrings, lie on your back and lift one leg as high as possible while keeping the other leg flat on the ground. Use a towel or strap around the foot of the lifted leg to gently pull it towards you, holding the stretch for 2 seconds before releasing. Repeat 10-15 times for each leg. This technique allows for a deeper stretch without triggering the muscle's protective reflex, promoting better flexibility.

Breathing techniques play a vital role in enhancing flexibility and mobility. Proper breathing helps to relax the muscles and allows for deeper stretches. Focus on deep, diaphragmatic breathing, inhaling deeply through the nose to fill the abdomen with air, and exhaling slowly through the mouth. This type of breathing not only aids in relaxation but also increases oxygen flow to the muscles, facilitating better movement and flexibility.

By integrating these exercises and techniques into your daily routine, you'll notice significant improvements in your flexibility and mobility. These improvements will enable you to move more freely and efficiently, crucial for responding effectively in crisis situations. Dedicate time each day to practice these exercises, and remember, consistency is key to achieving and maintaining optimal flexibility and mobility.

CHAPTER 3: FITNESS UNDER STRESS

Maintaining fitness under stress requires a strategic approach that not only focuses on physical conditioning but also on adapting your training to the unique challenges posed by high-stress environments. This part of the chapter will delve into the initial steps and considerations necessary to ensure that your fitness regimen remains effective and sustainable, even when faced with the pressures and uncertainties of stressful situations.

First and foremost, it's crucial to recognize the impact of stress on the body and mind. Stress can manifest physically in the form of increased heart rate, muscle tension, and fatigue, as well as mentally, through anxiety, decreased concentration, and sleep disturbances. These symptoms can significantly hinder your ability to maintain a regular fitness routine. Therefore, the first step in maintaining fitness under stress is to develop a comprehensive stress management strategy. This strategy should include techniques such as deep breathing exercises, meditation, and time management skills to help mitigate the effects of stress on your body and mind.

Once you have a stress management plan in place, the next step is to adapt your fitness routine to the realities of your stressful environment. This means being flexible with your workout schedule and locations, and being prepared to modify your exercises based on the resources available to you. For instance, if you find yourself unable to access a gym, look for bodyweight exercises or outdoor activities that can serve as effective alternatives. Push-ups, sit-ups, running, or even brisk walking are excellent ways to keep fit without the need for specialized equipment.

In addition to adapting your routine, it's also important to set realistic fitness goals. Stressful situations can disrupt your normal routines and make it difficult to adhere to ambitious training schedules. By setting achievable, short-term goals, you can maintain a sense of progress and motivation, which is crucial for staying on track with your fitness under stress. For example, instead of aiming for a specific weight loss or muscle gain within a short period, focus on maintaining consistency in your workouts or gradually increasing your endurance.

Another key aspect of maintaining fitness under stress is to prioritize recovery and self-care. High-stress environments can take a toll on your body, making recovery an essential component of your fitness regimen. Ensure you're getting enough sleep, staying hydrated, and incorporating rest days into your schedule. Techniques such as foam rolling, stretching, and yoga can also aid in muscle recovery and help reduce stress levels, making them valuable additions to your fitness routine.

Lastly, nutrition plays a vital role in maintaining fitness under stress. Stressful situations can lead to unhealthy eating habits, which can negatively impact your fitness goals and overall health. Focus on consuming a balanced diet rich in fruits, vegetables, lean proteins, and whole grains to support your body's needs during stressful times. Additionally, consider meal prepping or having healthy snacks on hand to avoid resorting to fast food or processed snacks when under stress.

By incorporating these strategies into your approach to fitness, you can create a resilient and adaptable regimen that supports your physical and mental well-being, even in the face of significant stress. Remember, the key is to be flexible, realistic, and compassionate with yourself as you navigate the challenges of maintaining fitness under stress.

Understanding the nuances of your body's response to stress is paramount in crafting a fitness regimen that not only withstands the pressures of stress but thrives in spite of them. It's essential to listen to your body and recognize when to push forward and when to scale back. This intuitive approach to training under stress ensures that you're not exacerbating stress-related symptoms through overexertion. For instance, if you're experiencing heightened anxiety, a high-intensity workout might further increase your cortisol levels, the body's stress hormone. In such cases, opting for a moderate or low-intensity activity like a long walk or a gentle yoga session can provide the physical benefits of exercise without overwhelming your system.

Adapting your fitness routine to include stress-reducing activities is another crucial step. Activities such as tai chi, qigong, and certain forms of yoga are not only beneficial for physical fitness but also for mental tranquility. These practices emphasize breath control, mindfulness, and gentle movements, all of which are effective in lowering stress levels and enhancing mental clarity. Incorporating these activities two to three times a week can serve as a counterbalance to the rigors of more intense training, providing a holistic approach to fitness that nurtures both body and mind.

The role of community and social support in maintaining fitness under stress cannot be overstated. Engaging in group fitness classes, whether virtually or in person, can offer a sense of camaraderie and accountability that is especially valuable during stressful times. If group settings are not accessible, consider enlisting a workout buddy or joining online fitness communities where you can share goals, celebrate achievements, and navigate challenges together. This social aspect of fitness not only bolsters your motivation but also provides a network of support, reminding you that you're not alone in your fitness journey.

Incorporating variety into your fitness regimen is also key to staying engaged and motivated under stress. Routine can become monotonous, leading to a plateau in both interest and results. By varying your workouts, you introduce new challenges and stimuli, keeping both your mind and body engaged. This could mean trying out different fitness disciplines, altering your workout environment, or setting new and varied fitness challenges for yourself. The novelty can reignite your enthusiasm for exercise and prevent the stagnation that often accompanies prolonged stress.

Finally, tracking your progress can be incredibly motivating and provide a tangible sense of achievement. Use a journal, app, or any tracking method that resonates with you to log your workouts, note any improvements in your physical and mental state, and reflect on how exercise is helping you manage stress. This record not only serves as a motivational tool but also as a reminder of the powerful role fitness plays in your overall well-being.

By weaving these strategies into the fabric of your fitness approach, you create a dynamic and responsive regimen capable of supporting you through the ebbs and flows of stress. This adaptive strategy ensures that your pursuit of physical fitness remains a constant and supportive pillar, regardless of the stressors you face. Remember, the goal of maintaining fitness under stress is not about adhering to a rigid schedule or achieving peak performance but about fostering a resilient and healthy relationship with your body that supports your well-being through all of life's challenges.

Adapting Fitness to Challenging Environments

Adapting fitness routines to challenging environments requires creativity, flexibility, and a willingness to leverage the unique aspects of any setting to maintain physical readiness. Whether you find yourself in a cramped apartment, a bustling city without open spaces, or in a remote area with no gym equipment, the key is to use your surroundings to your advantage and keep your body in peak condition. Here's how to adapt your fitness routine to virtually any environment, ensuring you can stay fit and prepared, no matter the circumstances.

First, assess your available space and any potential tools or objects at your disposal. In a small indoor space, furniture can become an invaluable resource. Chairs or sturdy tables can substitute for workout benches, supporting exercises like step-ups, dips, or incline push-ups. For resistance training, filled water bottles or heavy books can serve as makeshift dumbbells. The limited space might restrict movement, but exercises such as burpees, sit-ups, push-ups, and yoga can be performed effectively in tight quarters.

When outdoor space is accessible but equipment is not, utilize the natural and architectural elements around you. Parks offer open areas for running, brisk walking, or bodyweight circuits, and playground equipment can be repurposed for pull-ups and hanging leg raises. Benches are perfect for tricep dips and step-ups, while hills can provide the resistance needed for a challenging cardio workout. Always be mindful of your surroundings to ensure safety and respect for public spaces and property.

For those in remote or natural environments, the landscape itself offers a wealth of fitness opportunities. Logs can be lifted for strength training, rocks can be carried for endurance, and trees can serve as anchors for resistance bands. Trail running or hiking not only improves cardiovascular health but also enhances agility and balance as you navigate uneven terrain. Swimming in natural bodies of water, where safe and permitted, can be an excellent full-body workout, combining strength and endurance training.

Incorporating bodyweight exercises is a universally effective strategy for adapting fitness routines to any environment. Develop a circuit that includes squats, lunges, push-ups, planks, and burpees to target all major muscle groups with minimal space and no equipment. To increase the difficulty, experiment with variations like one-legged squats, decline push-ups, or plank reaches. These exercises rely solely on your body weight for resistance, making them incredibly versatile and adaptable.

Flexibility and mobility exercises are also crucial and can be practiced anywhere. Stretching routines, yoga sequences, and mobility drills require no equipment and little space, focusing instead on movement quality and range of motion. These practices not only aid in recovery and injury prevention but also improve overall physical performance by enhancing flexibility and joint health.

For those looking to maintain cardiovascular fitness, interval training can be an effective method in any setting. High-intensity interval training (HIIT) sessions, combining short bursts of intense activity with periods of rest, can be customized to any environment. Running on the spot, high knees, mountain climbers, and shadow boxing are just a few examples of cardio exercises that can be performed in a confined space or outdoors.

Creativity in your approach to fitness is essential when adapting to challenging environments. Use everyday objects as equipment, see your surroundings as a gym, and remember that consistency and intensity can compensate for a lack of traditional workout resources. Always prioritize safety, especially when improvising with non-standard equipment or training in new or uneven terrains. Listen to your body, adjust your workouts to match your current environment, and maintain a focus on achieving a balanced and comprehensive fitness routine. By embracing the challenge of adapting your fitness routine to your environment, you not only keep your body in top condition but also sharpen your problem-solving and adaptability skills, which are invaluable in any high-stress situation.

SEAL Recovery Techniques

In the demanding world of Navy SEALs, rapid physical recuperation is not just a goal; it's a necessity. The techniques used by these elite operators to recover quickly from physical exertion can be adapted for anyone looking to enhance their fitness resilience. One of the most effective strategies for rapid recovery involves a combination of active recovery, nutrition, hydration, sleep, and stress management. Each of these components plays a crucial role in helping the body bounce back from stress and strain, ensuring you're ready for the next challenge.

Active recovery is the first step in the SEAL approach to recuperation. Instead of complete rest or sitting still, engaging in low-intensity activities such as walking, cycling on a stationary bike for 20-30 minutes, or performing dynamic stretching can significantly enhance blood flow. This increased circulation helps to flush out metabolic waste products accumulated during intense physical activity. Incorporate movements that target the whole body, ensuring each major muscle group is gently stretched and mobilized.

Nutrition immediately post-exercise is critical. Focus on consuming a balanced meal or snack rich in proteins and carbohydrates within a 45-minute window after rigorous activity. A ratio of 3:1 carbohydrates to protein can significantly aid in muscle repair and glycogen replenishment. For instance, a smoothie made with whey protein, a banana, and a handful of berries, blended with almond milk, provides an optimal mix of nutrients for post-workout recovery.

Hydration cannot be overstated in its importance. Replacing fluids lost through sweat is essential. The SEALs' guideline suggests drinking 16 to 24 ounces of water for every pound lost during exercise. Monitoring the color of your urine is a practical way to gauge hydration levels; aim for a pale yellow color. Adding electrolytes to your water can also aid in faster recovery, especially after prolonged or intense sessions.

Sleep is the cornerstone of recovery. Aim for 7-9 hours of quality sleep per night. The body undergoes most of its healing and repair work during sleep, including muscle growth and psychological recovery. Creating a pre-sleep routine that promotes relaxation, such as reading or meditative breathing, can enhance sleep quality. Ensure your sleeping environment is conducive to rest, keeping it cool, dark, and quiet.

Stress management is the final piece of the recovery puzzle. Chronic stress can impede recovery by affecting sleep quality and hormonal balance. Techniques such as deep breathing exercises, yoga, or even spending time in nature can mitigate stress levels. Allocating time for hobbies or activities that you find enjoyable and relaxing is also beneficial.

Incorporating these SEAL recovery techniques into your fitness regimen can significantly enhance your ability to recover rapidly from physical exertion. By paying close attention to active recovery, nutrition, hydration, sleep, and stress management, you're not just improving your fitness levels but also adopting a holistic approach to health and well-being that is sustainable in the long term.

Peak Physical Performance Under Stress

To maintain peak physical performance under prolonged stress, it's essential to adopt a comprehensive approach that encompasses not only physical training but also nutritional strategies, rest, and psychological resilience. This section delves into actionable strategies that can be seamlessly integrated into daily routines, ensuring that individuals can sustain high levels of physical performance even when faced with ongoing stressors.

Firstly, prioritize consistency in your physical training regimen. Incorporate a balanced mix of cardiovascular exercises, strength training, and flexibility workouts. For cardiovascular health, consider interval running where you alternate between sprinting for one minute and jogging for two minutes, aiming for a total of 30 minutes. This method enhances both aerobic and anaerobic fitness. In strength training, focus on compound movements such as deadlifts, using a barbell with a weight that allows for 8-12 repetitions for three sets, ensuring a 48-hour rest period for muscle recovery. Incorporate yoga twice a week for flexibility, targeting a 60-minute session that includes poses like downward dog and pigeon pose to enhance mobility and reduce injury risk.

Nutrition plays a pivotal role in sustaining energy levels and facilitating recovery. Structure your diet around whole foods, prioritizing lean proteins like grilled chicken breast, complex carbohydrates such as sweet potatoes, and healthy fats found in avocados. Aim for five to six small meals spread throughout the day to maintain steady energy levels. Post-workout, a recovery shake containing 20 grams of whey protein and 40 grams of simple carbohydrates can expedite muscle repair.

Hydration is another critical factor. Drink at least 64 ounces of water daily, increasing intake on training days or in hot climates. Utilize electrolyte solutions or tablets to replenish minerals lost through sweat during intense or prolonged exercise sessions.

Adequate rest is indispensable for recovery and performance. Aim for 7-9 hours of sleep nightly, establishing a consistent sleep schedule even on weekends. Utilize relaxation techniques such as progressive muscle relaxation or guided imagery to improve sleep quality, especially during periods of high stress.

Psychological resilience can significantly impact physical performance. Develop mental toughness through practices like mindfulness meditation, which can be done for 10-20 minutes daily to enhance focus and reduce stress. Regularly set and review personal fitness goals to stay motivated and track progress, adjusting your plan as needed to overcome plateaus or challenges.

Lastly, recovery strategies are essential to maintain peak performance. Incorporate active recovery days where you engage in low-impact activities like walking or swimming at a leisurely pace. Utilize foam rolling for 10-15 minutes daily to alleviate muscle tightness, focusing on major muscle groups such as the calves, quads, and back. Implement cold water immersion or contrast water therapy post-exercise once a week to reduce inflammation and enhance recovery. For contrast water therapy, alternate between 1 minute of cold water (around 50-59°F) and 2 minutes of warm water (about 98-104°F) for a total of 15 minutes.

By integrating these detailed strategies into your routine, you can effectively maintain peak physical performance even under prolonged stress, embodying the resilience and endurance characteristic of Navy SEALs training and operations.

BOOK 3: HOME FORTIFICATION AND SECURITY

When it comes to fortifying your home against potential threats, the first line of defense is often the physical barriers that stand between your family and the outside world. Drawing from the expertise of Navy SEALs, who are trained to secure and defend in the most challenging environments, this guide will walk you through the process of strengthening your home defenses, starting with the critical entry points: doors and windows.

Doors, being the primary entry and exit points, require particular attention. The material of your door plays a significant role in its resilience against forced entry. Solid wood doors or those made from steel are preferable for exterior doors due to their durability and resistance to impact. However, even the strongest door can be compromised by weak hinges and locks. To enhance security, install grade 1 deadbolt locks, which offer the highest level of residential security. These locks have a 1-inch long bolt that resists sawing and heavy blows. For hinges, ensure they are secured with 3-inch screws that go into the door frame and wall stud, providing additional strength against forceful attempts to break the door down. Another often overlooked aspect of door security is the door frame itself, which can be the weakest link. Reinforce the door frame using a door reinforcement kit, which typically includes a metal plate that extends the length of the door frame.

This plate distributes the force of a blow more evenly, making it significantly harder for an intruder to kick the door in. Additionally, consider installing a door barricade or a security bar for an extra layer of protection, especially at night or when you're away for extended periods.

Windows, on the other hand, are the eyes of your home but can also be vulnerable points of entry. The first step in reinforcing windows is to ensure they are made from impact-resistant glass. Tempered glass, while more expensive than traditional glass, is designed to withstand heavy impacts. For those living in areas prone to hurricanes or other high-risk scenarios, installing storm shutters can provide an additional layer of security and protection against flying debris.

Beyond the glass itself, window locks should not be overlooked. Standard window locks can be easily forced open or broken. Replace them with keyed locks or pin locks for a more secure locking mechanism. For ground-level windows or those accessible from a flat roof, consider installing window bars or grills. Ensure these barriers are designed with a quick-release mechanism from the inside to allow for an emergency exit if necessary.

Creating multiple layers of home defense doesn't stop at reinforcing doors and windows. The concept of 'defensive depth' involves setting up several layers of security that an intruder would have to bypass to gain entry. This includes motion sensor lighting around the perimeter of your home, which can deter intruders by illuminating them as they approach, and a well-maintained landscape that eliminates potential hiding spots near windows and doors. Remember, the goal of home fortification is not just to make your home impenetrable but to create enough deterrents and obstacles that would-be intruders find it too difficult or risky to attempt a break-in. By starting with the strengthening of doors and windows, you lay a solid foundation for a comprehensive home defense strategy that prioritizes the safety and security of your family.

To further enhance your home's security, integrating advanced security systems plays a crucial role. Surveillance cameras, when strategically placed around the perimeter of your property, can provide real-time monitoring of all activities. Opt for high-definition cameras that offer night vision capabilities to ensure round-the-clock surveillance. Position cameras at entry points, such as front and back doors, and areas where intruders might attempt to gain access, like ground-level windows. It's also advisable to have cameras covering the garage and driveway areas to monitor any vehicles approaching or leaving the premises.

In addition to cameras, a robust alarm system serves as a critical component of your home defense strategy. Modern alarm systems can be connected to your mobile device, allowing you to receive instant alerts if any sensors are triggered. Ensure your system includes door and window sensors, motion detectors, and glass break sensors to cover a broad range of potential breach points. For added security, consider integrating smoke and carbon monoxide detectors into the system, providing comprehensive protection against various threats.

Effective communication systems within the home can significantly enhance your security protocol. In the event of an intrusion or emergency, having a reliable method for family members to communicate is essential. Install a home intercom system that allows for easy communication between different rooms and floors. For situations where traditional communication networks might be down, consider having backup options like satellite phones or two-way radios that can operate independently of cellular networks.

The exterior lighting of your home is another area that requires careful consideration. Motion-activated floodlights can be a deterrent to intruders by exposing their presence as they approach your property. Place these lights around the perimeter, focusing on entry points and dark corners where an intruder might hide. Ensure the lighting is bright enough to illuminate the area effectively but positioned in a way that does not disturb neighbors or create blind spots.

Landscaping can also play a significant role in your home's security. Maintain a clear line of sight from the house to the street by trimming bushes and trees that could provide cover for intruders. Use thorny plants under windows as a natural barrier. Gravel paths around the home can create noise when walked on, serving as an audible alert to movement outside.

Finally, establishing a neighborhood watch program can extend your security efforts beyond your property lines. Collaborating with neighbors to report suspicious activities and share information about potential threats can enhance the safety of the entire community. Regular meetings can foster a sense of camaraderie and ensure everyone is informed about best practices for home security.

By adopting these comprehensive measures, you create a multi-layered defense system for your home that not only deters potential intruders but also provides peace of mind knowing your family and property are well-protected. Each layer of security complements the others, creating a robust and resilient home defense strategy inspired by the principles and tactics of Navy SEALs.

CHAPTER 1: STRENGTHENING HOME DEFENSES

To further bolster your home's defenses beyond the sturdy doors and reinforced windows, it's essential to consider the role of advanced technological systems and the strategic placement of physical barriers. These elements work in tandem to create a comprehensive security network that can alert you to potential threats and deter intruders before they can gain access to your home.

Starting with technological advancements, the installation of a high-quality surveillance system is paramount. Opt for cameras equipped with high-definition resolution and night vision capabilities to ensure clear footage day and night. When positioning cameras, aim to cover all angles of your property, focusing on entry points, perimeters, and any blind spots where an intruder might attempt to hide or gain entry undetected. It's advisable to choose cameras with motion detection technology that can send real-time alerts to your smartphone or tablet, allowing you to monitor your home remotely. For added security, consider cameras that offer two-way audio communication, enabling you to challenge intruders verbally without having to confront them physically.

Incorporating smart locks into your home security system offers another layer of protection and convenience. These locks can be controlled remotely through your smartphone, allowing you to lock and unlock doors from anywhere, check the status of your locks, and receive notifications whenever a door is opened. Some smart locks also feature keypad entry, providing a keyless option for family members and guests, and eliminating the risk associated with lost or stolen keys. For maximum security, select smart locks that integrate with your home's Wi-Fi network and are compatible with other smart home devices, such as your surveillance system and alarm system, creating a unified security ecosystem.

The significance of a robust alarm system cannot be overstated. Modern alarm systems can be customized to fit the specific needs of your home, including motion sensors that cover interior spaces and entry points, glass break sensors that detect the sound of breaking glass, and door and window sensors that alert you when doors or windows are opened. To ensure comprehensive coverage, your alarm system should also include smoke and carbon monoxide detectors. Choose an alarm system that offers professional monitoring services, ensuring that in the event of a break-in or other emergency, the monitoring center is notified immediately and can dispatch law enforcement or emergency services to your home.

Transitioning from technological measures to physical barriers, the strategic use of landscaping can play a crucial role in home defense. While maintaining aesthetic appeal, your landscaping should be designed to minimize hiding spots for potential intruders and maximize visibility from inside the house. Keep shrubs and bushes trimmed and low to the ground, especially near windows and entryways, and consider using gravel or other noisy materials for pathways leading to your home, which can alert you to someone's approach. Additionally, strategic placement of thorny plants under windows can act as a natural deterrent.

Lighting is another critical aspect of home defense, serving both as a deterrent to potential intruders and as a way to enhance visibility around your property. Install motion-activated floodlights around the perimeter of your home, focusing on entry points and dark areas where an intruder might attempt to hide. Ensure that these lights are bright enough to illuminate the area effectively but positioned in such a way as to avoid light pollution and disturbance to neighbors. For added security, consider integrating your outdoor lighting with your home automation system, allowing you to control lights remotely and set schedules for lights to turn on and off automatically, simulating occupancy even when you're away.

By integrating advanced security technologies with strategic physical defenses, you create a multi-layered security strategy that not only deters potential intruders but also provides you with the tools and information needed to respond effectively to any threat. This approach to home fortification, inspired by the principles and tactics of Navy SEALs, ensures that your home remains a safe haven for you and your family, protected against a wide range of potential threats.

To enhance the effectiveness of your home's security measures, the integration of a comprehensive alarm system plays a pivotal role. This system should be equipped with a variety of sensors, including those for motion detection within the home and at entry points, as well as glass break sensors that can identify the sound of shattering glass, a common sign of an intrusion attempt. Additionally, incorporating door and window sensors that trigger alerts when unauthorized openings occur is crucial for immediate awareness of potential breaches. For a truly robust defense, your alarm system should extend its protective reach to include smoke and carbon monoxide detectors, thereby safeguarding against a broader spectrum of threats. Opting for an alarm system that provides professional monitoring services ensures that any alerts are promptly addressed, with the monitoring center capable of dispatching law enforcement or emergency services to your residence swiftly in the event of a confirmed emergency.

Beyond technological enhancements, the strategic deployment of physical barriers and natural deterrents can significantly bolster your home's security. Effective landscaping plays a dual role in this regard, enhancing the aesthetic appeal of your property while simultaneously removing potential hiding spots for intruders. By keeping shrubbery and bushes well-trimmed and ensuring they remain low to the ground around windows and entryways, you effectively eliminate concealment opportunities for would-be intruders. Incorporating gravel or similarly noisy materials in pathways leading to your home can serve as an audible alert mechanism, signaling the approach of visitors. The use of thorny plants placed strategically under windows adds a natural layer of defense, deterring any attempts to breach these vulnerable points.

Illumination around your property is not just a matter of visibility; it serves as a critical deterrent to unauthorized entry. The installation of motion-activated floodlights around your home's perimeter, especially focusing on potential entry points and shadowed areas, can startle and ward off intruders. These lights should be sufficiently bright to ensure effective area coverage but positioned thoughtfully to prevent any disturbance to neighboring properties. For an added layer of security and convenience, integrating your outdoor lighting system with your home automation setup allows for remote control of lighting fixtures. This capability enables you to activate or schedule lighting patterns that mimic occupancy, an effective strategy for deterring potential intruders during periods when the house is unoccupied.

By adopting a holistic approach to home security that combines state-of-the-art technology with strategic physical defenses, you establish a formidable barrier against intrusions. This comprehensive strategy, inspired by the meticulous and proactive defense tactics of Navy SEALs, transforms your home into a fortified sanctuary. It not only deters potential threats but also equips you with the necessary tools and systems to respond swiftly and effectively to any security challenges. Through the diligent application of these principles, your home security setup becomes a dynamic shield, ensuring the safety and peace of mind for you and your family against a wide array of potential threats.

Advanced Locks and SEAL Entry Tactics

When it comes to installing advanced locks and securing entry points using SEAL tactics, the focus is on creating a barrier that is both formidable and intelligent. The process begins with selecting the right type of lock. For exterior doors, a Grade 1 deadbolt is recommended due to its proven resistance to tampering and forced entry. This type of lock features a solid, one-inch-long bolt that extends deep into the doorframe, providing a strong physical barrier. When shopping for a deadbolt, look for one that meets the American National Standards Institute (ANSI) Grade 1 designation, ensuring it has passed rigorous testing for durability and strength.

The installation of a Grade 1 deadbolt requires precise measurements and tools. Start by marking the position of the deadbolt on the door and the doorframe. The center of the deadbolt should be at least 6 inches above the doorknob to minimize the risk of being compromised. Using a hole saw attachment on your drill, create a hole through the door for the deadbolt. Ensure the hole is level and straight to allow the deadbolt to extend and retract smoothly. For the strike plate on the doorframe, use a chisel to carve out a recess that matches the thickness of the plate. This allows the strike plate to sit flush with the doorframe, providing a clean and secure fit. Secure the strike plate with 3-inch screws that penetrate into the wooden doorframe and wall stud, offering additional resistance against force.

Beyond the lock itself, reinforcing the door's physical structure is crucial. A door reinforcement kit can be employed to fortify the door and its frame. These kits typically include metal plates that attach to the doorjamb and hinges, distributing the force of any attempted break-in across a wider area, thus making the door much harder to kick in or break down. For the door itself, consider installing a door edge guard, a metal strip that runs along the door edge, to prevent the door from splitting under force.

Windows present a unique challenge as they can be fragile entry points. To secure windows, start by replacing standard latches with keyed locks or pin locks, which provide a higher level of security. For accessible windows, especially those on the ground floor, installing window security film can make the glass harder to break. This clear film adheres to the glass, holding it together even when shattered, delaying or deterring an intruder. Additionally, consider installing window bars or grates on particularly vulnerable windows, ensuring they come with an internal release mechanism to allow for a quick exit in case of an emergency.

The concept of layered security is integral to SEAL tactics, emphasizing the importance of not relying on a single defense mechanism. Motion sensor lights should be installed around the perimeter of your home to illuminate any approach at night, serving as both a deterrent and an alert system. The positioning of these lights should cover all potential entry points and dark areas where an intruder might hide. Opt for LED bulbs for their longevity and brightness, ensuring that the sensors are adjusted to avoid false alarms caused by small animals or passing cars.

Finally, the integration of technology can significantly enhance your home's security. Smart locks offer the convenience of remote control and monitoring, allowing you to lock and unlock doors from anywhere via a smartphone app. These locks can also send alerts if a door is left unlocked or opened unexpectedly, providing real-time security updates. When selecting a smart lock, choose one that can be integrated with your home's existing security system for a unified approach to home defense.

By meticulously selecting and installing advanced locks, reinforcing entry points, and adopting a layered approach to security, you can significantly enhance the safety and security of your home. These measures, inspired by the rigorous standards and tactics of Navy SEALs, ensure that your home becomes a stronghold against potential threats, providing peace of mind and protection for you and your family.

Reinforcing Windows and Doors

To effectively reinforce windows and doors against forced entry, it's essential to focus on both the strength of the materials and the integrity of the installation. Starting with doors, the core material should be either solid wood, metal, or a metal-clad exterior. A solid core door offers much more resistance to being kicked in or broken down compared to hollow-core doors commonly found inside homes. When selecting a solid wood door, look for hardwood varieties such as oak or maple which provide additional strength. For metal doors, ensure the door is made from steel with a gauge of 16 or lower, as the lower the gauge, the thicker and more resistant the metal.

The door frame is equally, if not more, important than the door itself. A weak frame can easily be compromised even with a strong door. To reinforce the frame, use a door frame reinforcement kit, which typically includes steel plates that attach to the door jamb and hinges. These plates should be installed with long screws, at least 3 inches in length, that anchor into the wall studs around the frame, not just into the door jamb. This significantly increases the door's resistance to being kicked in or forced open.

For the door's locking mechanism, install a grade 1 deadbolt lock along with a reinforced strike plate. The deadbolt should have a throw (the part of the lock that extends into the door frame) of at least one inch. The strike plate, which is the metal plate affixed to the door frame that the deadbolt extends into, should be secured with long screws that reach the wall studs similar to the reinforcement kit. For added security, consider installing a smart lock with built-in alarms that trigger upon forced entry attempts, providing an additional layer of security.

Turning attention to windows, the first step in reinforcement is to upgrade the glass. Install impact-resistant glass designed to withstand blows from objects or attempts at shattering. This type of glass is made by bonding a layer of tough plastic between two layers of glass, making it much harder to break. For areas particularly vulnerable to break-ins or severe weather, consider exterior window shutters that can be locked from the inside.

Window locks are often the weakest point in window security. Replace standard window locks with keyed locks or pin locks for a more secure locking mechanism. For sliding windows, a simple but effective reinforcement is a dowel or a metal bar placed in the track to prevent the window from being opened from the outside.

For ground-floor windows or those accessible from a flat roof, installing window bars or grills provides a significant deterrent. Ensure these bars have a quick-release mechanism accessible from the inside to allow for emergency exits. Another option for window reinforcement is the application of security film. This film makes the window glass harder to break and can hold the glass together even if shattered, delaying entry and potentially deterring the intruder.

In addition to reinforcing the physical structures of windows and doors, integrating them into a broader home security system enhances overall protection. This includes connecting door and window sensors to an alarm system that alerts homeowners to unauthorized entry attempts. Motion sensors and security cameras placed strategically around entry points can also provide early warning of an intrusion attempt, allowing for a quicker response.

By meticulously selecting materials and employing strategic reinforcement techniques, homeowners can significantly enhance the security of their windows and doors. This not only deters potential intruders but also provides peace of mind, knowing that the home's entry points are fortified against forced entry.

Layered Home Defense Strategies

Creating multiple layers of home defense is akin to building a fortress around your family, ensuring that each layer serves as a deterrent or a barrier to potential intruders. This strategy is not about turning your home into a military base but about implementing sensible, practical measures that enhance security while maintaining the comfort and aesthetics of your living space. The first layer involves the perimeter of your property. Start by assessing the boundary lines of your home, whether it's a fence, a hedge, or simply the edge of your yard. For those with fences, consider the material and height. A fence made of solid wood or metal that stands at least 6 feet tall provides a physical barrier as well as a psychological one. However, ensure that the design of the fence does not provide easy handholds or footholds. Smooth, vertical boards without horizontal rails on the outside deter climbers. For added security, top the fence with a lattice or spikes that make climbing over more challenging.

Beyond the physical barrier, the perimeter should be equipped with motion-sensor lighting. Choose LED floodlights that cover a wide area and are triggered by movement. Position these lights to illuminate dark corners of the yard, pathways, and entry points into the home. The sudden illumination not only startles intruders but also alerts you and your neighbors to potential activity outside.

The next layer focuses on the immediate exterior of your home. Start with the landscaping. Keep bushes and trees trimmed so they cannot be used as hiding spots or obscure windows and doors. Use gravel in landscaping near windows; the noise of someone walking on it can be a deterrent. Thorny plants under windows add an extra layer of natural security.

For windows, apply security film that makes the glass harder to break, delaying an intruder's entry and possibly deterring them altogether. Install window locks that require a key, and for sliding doors, use a security bar or a wooden dowel in the track to prevent them from being forced open. For doors, upgrade to solid-core or metal-clad doors with deadbolts. Add a strike plate lock to reinforce the door frame and prevent it from being kicked in.

The interior of your home constitutes the next layer. Use smart home technology to your advantage. Install a security system that includes door and window sensors, motion detectors, and a central monitoring system that can alert you and the authorities to a breach. Smart locks can be programmed to lock automatically at certain times and can be monitored and controlled remotely. Cameras placed inside can monitor activity and be accessed remotely, giving you visual confirmation of your home's status.

Finally, the personal layer of defense involves the people within the home. Educate your family members about security practices, such as locking doors and windows, not opening the door to strangers, and having a plan in case of an emergency. Regularly discuss and practice what to do in different scenarios, whether it's a break-in, a fire, or a natural disaster. Establish a safe room that can be secured from the inside and equipped with a means of communication to the outside world.

Each of these layers, from the perimeter of your property to the personal safety practices of your family, works together to create a comprehensive defense strategy. By implementing these measures, you not only make your home a harder target for potential intruders but also provide peace of mind knowing that you've taken proactive steps to protect your home and loved ones.

CHAPTER 2: ADVANCED SECURITY SYSTEMS INTEGRATION

Integrating advanced security systems into your home requires a strategic approach to ensure maximum protection and efficiency. The process begins with selecting the right components that work together seamlessly to create a comprehensive security network. Here's how to effectively integrate advanced security systems into your home defense strategy.

First, choose a central security system that serves as the brain of your home security operation. Look for a system that supports a wide range of devices, including door and window sensors, motion detectors, security cameras, and smart locks. The central hub should be capable of connecting both wired and wireless devices, offering flexibility in system design and expansion.

A system with a user-friendly interface, accessible via smartphone or computer, allows for real-time monitoring and control from anywhere.

Next, focus on the installation of high-definition security cameras. Position cameras to cover all entry points and key areas around the perimeter of your property. Cameras should offer night vision capability to ensure clear footage 24/7. Opt for cameras with motion detection features that can send alerts to your smartphone when activity is detected. To maximize coverage, consider a mix of fixed and pan-tilt-zoom (PTZ) cameras.

Fixed cameras provide constant coverage of specific areas, while PTZ cameras can be remotely controlled to follow movement or investigate specific areas of interest. For door and window sensors, select models that are discreet yet effective. These sensors should be installed on all exterior doors and windows, especially those hidden from view or easily accessible. The sensors will alert the central hub if a door or window is opened or tampered with, triggering an alarm and notifying you of a potential breach.

Motion detectors play a crucial role in identifying movement within your property. Install motion detectors in high-traffic areas and potential entry points. Look for models with pet immunity to avoid false alarms triggered by your pets. Strategic placement is key; ensure detectors cover the main pathways through your home without being easily avoided by intruders. Smart locks enhance security by allowing you to control access to your home remotely. Choose smart locks that integrate with your central security system for seamless operation.

These locks can be programmed with temporary access codes for visitors or service personnel, eliminating the need for physical keys. Receive notifications when the lock is engaged or disengaged, providing insight into who is entering or leaving your home.

The integration of a professional monitoring service adds an additional layer of security. In the event of an alarm, the monitoring service can assess the situation and dispatch emergency services if necessary. This ensures a rapid response to break-ins, fires, or medical emergencies, even if you're unable to act.

Finally, ensure your security system includes backup power solutions to maintain operation during power outages. Battery backups or a generator can keep your system running, ensuring continuous protection.

To integrate these components effectively, start by mapping out your home's layout and identifying potential vulnerabilities. Work with a professional installer who can recommend the best devices and placement based on your specific needs. Regularly test and maintain your system to ensure all components are functioning correctly.

By following these detailed steps, you can create a robust and integrated home security system that leverages advanced technology to protect your home and family. This approach, inspired by Navy SEAL tactics, emphasizes the importance of preparation, adaptability, and the use of cutting-edge technology to create a safe haven.

Setting up motion detectors and security lighting around key areas

Project Introduction (Description - Benefits - Challenges)

This project focuses on enhancing home security through the strategic placement of motion detectors and security lighting around key areas of your property. The primary benefit of this setup is to deter potential intruders by increasing visibility and alerting homeowners to movement in sensitive areas. Challenges include selecting the optimal locations for detectors and lights, ensuring all components are weatherproof and compatible, and configuring the system for maximum efficiency and minimal false alarms.

Required Materials

- Motion detectors (preferably with adjustable sensitivity and range, capable of covering 180 to 360 degrees)
- Outdoor security lights (LED lights recommended for their long life and energy efficiency, with a brightness of at least 700 lumens)
- Weatherproof electrical boxes and conduit for outdoor wiring
- Electrical wire (14/2 or 12/2 outdoor-rated, depending on local code requirements)
- Wire nuts and electrical tape
- Mounting hardware (screws, wall anchors, mounting brackets)

Required Tools

- Drill with drill bits (for mounting hardware and creating openings for wiring)
- Screwdriver set
- Wire stripper/cutter
- Ladder
- Voltage tester

Detailed Instructions

1. **Planning Placement**: Identify key areas that require monitoring, such as walkways, driveways, side entrances, and dark corners of your yard. Ensure that the motion detectors have a clear line of sight and are not obstructed by landscaping or decor. Consider the field of view of the detectors, which typically ranges from 90 to 180 degrees, and ensure they cover the entire area without blind spots. Use a measuring tape to determine the optimal distance for detection, which can vary from 30 to 100 feet depending on the model

2. **Mounting Motion Detectors**: Install motion detectors at a height of 6 to 10 feet above the ground to optimize the detection range and minimize false triggers from small animals. Use a drill and mounting hardware to secure the detectors in place. Ensure that the detectors are mounted at an angle that maximizes their coverage area, typically tilting them slightly downward. Check the manufacturer's specifications for the recommended mounting height and angle for your specific model

3. **Installing Security Lights**: Position the lights so they illuminate the detected area without causing light pollution to neighbors. Angle the lights downward to focus the illumination on the intended area and prevent glare. Choose LED security lights with a lumen output of at least 800 to 1,200 lumens for effective illumination. Consider using adjustable fixtures that allow you to change the angle and direction of the light after installation

4. **Wiring**: Run outdoor-rated electrical wire from the power source to the motion detectors and from the detectors to the lights. Use weatherproof electrical boxes and conduit to protect the connections. Ensure all

wiring complies with local electrical codes, typically using 14-gauge wire for standard installations. If your system requires a transformer, ensure it is rated for outdoor use and can handle the total wattage of the lights

5. **Connecting and Testing**: Connect the wires using wire nuts, following the manufacturer's instructions for the motion detectors and lights. Use electrical tape to secure the connections. Test the system by walking through the monitored areas to ensure the lights activate as expected. Adjust the sensitivity settings on the motion detectors to reduce false triggers from pets or passing vehicles, and ensure the lights remain on for the desired duration after activation, typically adjustable from 10 seconds to 10 minutes.

Safety

- Always turn off the power at the circuit breaker before starting any electrical work.
- Use a voltage tester to confirm that the power is off before handling wires.
- Follow all manufacturer instructions for installing and configuring motion detectors and lights.
- Ensure all outdoor electrical components are rated for outdoor use to prevent electrical hazards.

Cost of the Project

Approximately $200-$500, depending on the quality and quantity of motion detectors and lights selected.

Preparation Time

4-6 hours, including planning, installation, and testing.

Maintenance and Care

- Regularly check and clean the motion detectors and lights to ensure they remain functional and free from obstructions.
- Replace bulbs as needed (if not using LED lights).
- Periodically test the system to ensure all components are operational.

FAQ or Common Issues

- **Q: What if the lights trigger too frequently?**
- **A:** Adjust the sensitivity settings on the motion detectors to reduce false triggers.
- **Q: Can the system work during the day?**
- **A:** Yes, most motion detectors can be adjusted to operate 24/7 or only during the night.

Difficulty Rating

★★★☆☆

Variations

- Solar-powered lights can be used for areas without easy access to power.
- Smart motion detectors and lights can be integrated into a home automation system for remote monitoring and control.

Troubleshooting

- **Motion Detector Not Activating**: Check the power source to ensure the unit is receiving electricity. Inspect the sensor for obstructions such as dirt, debris, or spider webs that may block its view. Verify the sensitivity settings; they may need adjustment to detect movement effectively

- **False Alarms**: Review the placement of the motion detector; it should not be aimed at areas with frequent movement from pets or trees swaying in the wind. Adjust the sensitivity settings to a lower level to reduce the likelihood of false triggers

- **Security Lighting Not Turning On**: Confirm that the light bulbs are functioning and properly installed. Check the wiring connections for any loose or damaged wires. Ensure the light sensor is not obstructed and is set to the correct sensitivity level for ambient light

- **Inconsistent Performance**: If the motion detector activates sporadically, examine the installation angle; it may need repositioning to cover the intended area more effectively. Look for environmental factors such as heat sources or reflective surfaces that could interfere with the sensor's operation

- **Remote Control Issues**: If using a remote control for your security lighting, replace the batteries and ensure there are no obstructions between the remote and the receiver. Test the remote from different distances to determine if the issue is with the remote or the lighting system itself

- **Integration with Home Security System**: If the motion detectors are not communicating with your home security system, check the compatibility of the devices. Ensure that all components are properly paired and that the system is updated with the latest firmware

- **Battery-Powered Units**: For battery-operated motion detectors, regularly check and replace batteries to prevent failure. Monitor the battery life indicator if available, and consider using rechargeable batteries for sustainability

- **Environmental Factors**: Be aware of seasonal changes that may affect performance, such as heavy snowfall or rain that could obstruct sensors. Regularly inspect and maintain the area around the detectors to ensure optimal functionality

Installing Surveillance Systems

To effectively install a surveillance system for continuous monitoring, it's crucial to approach the task with precision and attention to detail. Begin by assessing the perimeter of your property to identify strategic locations for camera placement. These locations should offer a clear, unobstructed view of entry points, including doors and ground-level windows, as well as any pathways or fences. Opt for weather-resistant, high-definition cameras that provide both day and night vision capabilities to ensure 24/7 monitoring. Cameras with motion detection features can offer additional security by alerting you to any activity in real-time.

Once you've identified the optimal locations for your cameras, the next step involves mounting them securely. Use sturdy mounting brackets and ensure that each camera is positioned at a height that is out of easy reach to prevent tampering. The ideal height is around 8 to 10 feet above the ground. Angle the cameras to maximize the field of view and minimize blind spots. Each camera should cover as much ground as possible, with overlapping fields of view between cameras to ensure comprehensive coverage of your property.

For the wiring process, consider using conduit to protect the cables from weather elements and potential damage. Running cables through the attic or crawlspace can provide a hidden path that keeps your setup discreet and reduces the risk of tampering. When connecting the cameras to the power source and recording device, follow the manufacturer's instructions closely to ensure a secure connection. If using a wireless system, ensure your home Wi-Fi network has sufficient bandwidth and range to maintain a stable connection to all cameras.

The recording device, or Digital Video Recorder (DVR) for analog systems and Network Video Recorder (NVR) for IP systems, should be placed in a secure, locked location to prevent unauthorized access. Ensure it has enough storage capacity to retain footage for your desired retention period, with many experts recommending at least two weeks of storage. Adjust the settings according to your needs, setting up motion detection alerts and scheduling recording times if desired.

Finally, regularly test the system to ensure all cameras are functioning correctly and that the recording device is capturing and storing footage as expected. Keep the system's firmware and software updated to protect against vulnerabilities and ensure the highest level of security.

By meticulously selecting the right equipment, strategically placing cameras, and ensuring a secure installation, you can establish a robust surveillance system that provides continuous monitoring and enhances the security of your home.

Crisis-Proof Communication Systems

In the event of an intrusion, having a crisis-proof communication system in place is paramount for ensuring the safety and security of your home and family This system should enable you to alert authorities and communicate with family members quickly and efficiently, even if standard communication networks are compromised Here's how to set up a robust communication system tailored for such critical situations

Project: Setting Up a Crisis-Proof Communication System

Objective
To establish a reliable communication system that ensures safety and security during a home intrusion

Materials

1. Two-Way Radios
- FRS/GMRS radios for short-range communication
- Extra batteries or solar chargers for extended use

2. Satellite Phone
- Satellite phone with a reliable service plan
- Spare battery and charging equipment

3. Emergency Communication Device
- Hand-crank or solar-powered emergency radio
- NOAA weather band capability for alerts

4. Signal Mirrors
- High-visibility signal mirror for visual communication over long distances

5. Whistles
- Durable, high-decibel whistles for signaling in emergencies

6. Notebooks and Writing Instruments
- Waterproof notebooks for jotting down important information
- Permanent markers or pencils for writing in various conditions

7. Communication Plan
- Printed copies of your family communication plan
- Maps of the local area with marked meeting points

8. Backup Power Sources
- Portable power banks for charging devices
- Generator for extended power outages

9. Cellular Signal Booster

- Signal booster to enhance mobile phone reception in low-signal areas

10. Emergency Contact List
- Printed list of important contacts, including family, friends, and local emergency services

11. Visual Signaling Devices
- Colored flags or reflective tape for marking locations or signaling

12. Internet Communication Tools
- Pre-installed apps for secure messaging and video calls
- Backup internet connection options, such as a mobile hotspot

13. Training Materials
- Guides or manuals on effective communication during crises
- Practice drills for family members to ensure everyone knows the plan

14. Storage Containers
- Waterproof and durable containers for storing communication equipment and supplies

15. First Aid Kit
- Comprehensive first aid kit to address any injuries during communication efforts

16. Emergency Lighting
- Flashlights or headlamps with extra batteries for visibility during power outages

17. Personal Locator Beacons (PLBs)
- PLBs for emergency location signaling in remote areas

18. Community Communication Network
- Contact information for local community groups or neighborhood watch programs

19. Ham Radio Equipment
- Basic ham radio setup for long-distance communication
- Licensing materials and study guides for obtaining a ham radio license

20. Survival Manual
- A comprehensive survival manual that includes communication strategies and techniques
Preparation
1. Assess your home layout to determine optimal locations for communication devices, focusing on areas that are easily accessible yet discreet
2. Research and select the best equipment based on your family's needs and budget, considering factors like range, durability, and ease of use
3. Create a family emergency communication plan that includes all communication methods, ensuring everyone understands their roles and responsibilities

Tools
- High-quality two-way radios: Look for models with a minimum range of 5 miles and features like weather alerts and emergency channels
- Smartphones with secure messaging apps (Signal or Telegram): Ensure devices are compatible with the chosen apps and have sufficient storage for updates
- Hard-wired landline phone: Choose a corded model for reliability during power outages
- VoIP system with battery backup: Select a system that offers clear voice quality and can function without internet during emergencies
- Basic tools for installation (screwdriver, drill, etc.): Have a toolkit ready for any mounting or setup needs

Crisis-Proof Communication Systems

In times of crisis, maintaining effective communication is crucial for ensuring the safety and coordination of your household. Here are step-by-step instructions to establish a robust communication system that can withstand emergencies

1. Assess Your Communication Needs
- Identify the number of family members and their locations during a crisis
- Determine the types of emergencies you may face, such as natural disasters or civil unrest
- Consider the communication methods that will be most effective for your situation, such as radios, walkie-talkies, or mobile phones

2. Choose Reliable Communication Devices
- Research and select devices that are durable and have a long battery life
- Opt for two-way radios or walkie-talkies with a range suitable for your area
- Ensure that all family members are familiar with the devices and their functions

3. Establish a Communication Plan
- Create a plan that outlines how family members will communicate during a crisis
- Designate a primary and secondary method of communication
- Establish a meeting point where family members can regroup if separated

4. Create a Contact List
- Compile a list of important contacts, including family members, friends, and emergency services
- Ensure that each family member has a copy of the contact list stored in a waterproof bag
- Regularly update the list to include new contacts or remove outdated information

5. Practice Regular Drills
- Conduct regular communication drills to ensure everyone knows how to use the devices and follow the plan
- Simulate different emergency scenarios to test the effectiveness of your communication system
- Encourage feedback from family members to improve the plan and address any concerns

6. Stay Informed
- Invest in a battery-powered or hand-crank emergency radio to receive updates during a crisis
- Follow local news and weather reports to stay informed about potential threats
- Share important information with family members to keep everyone on the same page

7. Backup Power Solutions
- Prepare backup power sources, such as portable chargers or solar-powered devices, to keep communication devices operational
- Store extra batteries for radios and other essential devices in an easily accessible location
- Regularly check and replace batteries to ensure they are functional when needed

By following these steps, you can create a crisis-proof communication system that enhances your family's safety and preparedness during emergencies

Safety Measures
- Ensure all devices are stored in secure, yet accessible locations, such as a designated emergency drawer or safe
- Regularly check the functionality of all communication devices, testing them monthly to confirm they are operational
- Educate family members on the importance of maintaining silence during an intrusion, practicing scenarios to reinforce this behavior

Cost Estimate
- Two-way radios: $50 - $200 (depending on quality and features)
- Smartphones: $0 - $1,000 (if not already owned)
- Landline phone: $20 - $100
- VoIP system: $50 - $300 (plus monthly service fees)
- Total estimated cost: $120 - $1,600

Time Estimate
- Research and purchase equipment: 2-4 hours
- Installation and setup: 1-2 hours
- Family training session: 1 hour
- Total estimated time: 4-7 hours

Safety Tips
- Keep communication devices charged and in working order, establishing a routine for checking battery levels
- Regularly practice the emergency communication plan with family members, conducting drills to ensure everyone is familiar with the process
- Ensure that all family members know how to use each communication method, providing hands-on training for less tech-savvy individuals

Troubleshooting
- If two-way radios are not functioning, check battery levels and ensure they are on the correct channel, also verify that the antenna is properly extended
- For smartphones, ensure the secure messaging app is updated and functioning properly, checking for any app-specific settings that may need adjustment
- If the landline phone is not working, check the connection and ensure it is plugged into a working outlet, also consider testing with a different phone if available

Maintenance
- Regularly test all communication devices to ensure they are operational, setting reminders for monthly checks
- Update the family emergency communication plan as needed, especially after any changes in family dynamics or living situations
- Replace batteries in two-way radios and ensure the VoIP system has a functioning backup battery, keeping spare batteries on hand

Difficulty Rating
(3 stars - moderate difficulty)

Variations
- Consider adding a satellite phone for communication in remote areas, especially if you live in a location prone to natural disasters
- Explore the use of mesh networking devices for local communication without internet access, which can be particularly useful in urban settings
- Implement a community communication network with neighbors for added security and support, establishing a group chat or regular meetings to discuss safety strategies

By meticulously selecting the right equipment, establishing secure channels, and ensuring all family members are trained on the emergency communication plan, you can create a crisis-proof communication system that enhances your home's security and provides peace of mind in high-stress situations.

CHAPTER 3: SECURING FAMILY DURING CRISIS

In times of crisis, ensuring the safety and security of your family becomes paramount. One of the most effective ways to achieve this is by establishing a designated safe room within your home. This space serves as a last-resort sanctuary where your family can retreat during an emergency situation, such as a home invasion or natural disaster. The selection and preparation of your safe room require careful consideration and meticulous planning to maximize its effectiveness.

Firstly, choose a room that has few or no windows, making it harder for intruders to gain access or even be aware of your family's presence inside. Basements often make ideal choices due to their below-ground location, providing natural protection. However, if a basement is not available, an interior room on the ground floor, preferably without external walls, can serve as a suitable alternative. The key is to select a space that is not easily accessible from the outside.

Once you have selected the appropriate room, reinforce the door to withstand attempts at forced entry. Replace standard interior doors with solid core or metal doors that offer higher resistance to being kicked in or breached. Install deadbolt locks, and if possible, consider adding a steel security door frame for added reinforcement. Remember, the strength of a door is not just in the material but also in its frame and locking mechanisms.

For the interior of the safe room, stock it with essential supplies to support your family for at least 72 hours. This includes bottled water, non-perishable food items, a first aid kit, flashlights with extra batteries, and a battery-powered or hand-crank radio to stay informed about the situation outside. Additionally, include blankets, a change of clothes for each family member, and basic sanitation supplies to maintain hygiene.

Communication tools are vital in a crisis, so ensure that your safe room includes a charged cell phone with an external battery pack or a landline telephone. The cell phone should have important contact numbers pre-saved, including local law enforcement, emergency services, and relatives or friends who can assist in an emergency. A whistle or air horn can also be useful to signal for help without revealing your exact location to an intruder.

Another critical component of your safe room is a comprehensive first aid kit. This should include not only basic supplies such as bandages, antiseptic wipes, and over-the-counter pain relievers but also any prescription medications that family members may require. Consider taking a basic first aid course to familiarize yourself with how to use these supplies effectively in an emergency.

Lastly, maintain a folder or waterproof container in your safe room that contains copies of important documents. This should include identification for each family member, insurance policies, bank account records, and contact information for all relevant service providers. These documents can be crucial in the aftermath of a crisis for rebuilding and recovery efforts.

By following these steps to select and equip your safe room, you provide a secure environment for your family during the most critical times. The peace of mind that comes from knowing you have a plan in place is invaluable, allowing you to respond calmly and effectively in an emergency situation. Ensuring the safe room remains hidden and secure is also paramount. To achieve this, consider installing a false wall or a bookshelf that swings open to reveal the entrance. This not only keeps the location of your safe room discreet but also adds an additional layer of security. The mechanism for opening should be simple yet not obvious to anyone who is not aware of its existence, such as a hidden latch or a book that acts as a lever. In addition to physical preparations, it's crucial to train all family members on how to use the safe room effectively. This includes practicing how to quickly and quietly move to the safe room from various parts of the house. Establish a code word or signal that indicates when it's time to retreat to the safe room, ensuring even the youngest family members understand its importance without causing undue alarm.

Within the safe room, set up a system for monitoring the exterior of your home. This can be achieved through a secure, hardwired surveillance system with a monitor inside the safe room, allowing you to keep an eye on the situation without exposing yourself to danger. Ensure this system is separate from the main house network to prevent it from being disabled or hacked.

Lighting in the safe room should be controlled and include options for both complete darkness and low-level lighting, allowing you to remain unseen while still being able to navigate and manage tasks within the space. Opt for blackout curtains or paint the windows black if the room has any, ensuring no light can escape and give away your position at night.

Ventilation is another critical aspect to consider. If possible, the safe room should have an independent air supply or an air filtration system to protect against smoke or chemical attacks. This system should be discreetly integrated into the room to prevent tampering from the outside. For defense, while the primary goal of a safe room is to provide a secure place to hide until help arrives, it may also be necessary to defend yourself if an intruder attempts to breach the room. Securely store a defensive tool, such as pepper spray or a stun gun, in an easily accessible location within the room. Ensure all adult and responsible family members are trained in their safe and effective use.

Regular maintenance checks are essential to ensure the safe room remains functional and ready at a moment's notice. This includes checking the integrity of the door and locks, ensuring all supplies are within their use-by dates, and testing communication devices and surveillance equipment.

By integrating these advanced preparations and practices, your safe room will serve as a formidable bastion of safety for your family during a crisis. The key is not just in having a safe room but in the details of its setup, concealment, and the training of your family to use it effectively. This comprehensive approach to home security, inspired by Navy SEAL tactics, ensures that you are prepared to protect your loved ones in any situation.

Emergency Security Protocols

Creating an emergency security protocol for your household is a critical step in ensuring the safety and preparedness of your family during a crisis. This protocol should be comprehensive, covering all aspects of security, communication, and emergency response, tailored to the unique layout of your home and the specific needs of your family members. Here's how to develop a robust emergency security protocol step by step.

1. **Assessment of Potential Threats**: Begin by identifying potential threats specific to your area and household. This could range from natural disasters like earthquakes and floods to human threats such as home invasions or burglaries. Understanding these risks will guide the development of your protocol.

2. **Designation of Safe Zones**: Choose a room or area in your home that will serve as a safe zone during an emergency. This should be a space with limited windows and doors, preferably without external walls, to minimize points of entry. Basements or interior rooms are ideal choices. Ensure this space is stocked with emergency supplies including water, non-perishable food, a first aid kit, flashlights, and a battery-powered radio.

3. **Secure and Reinforce Entry Points**: Inspect all doors and windows, reinforcing them to prevent unauthorized entry. This may involve installing deadbolts, security bars, or upgrading to more secure door and window frames. Consider the use of security film on windows to prevent them from shattering easily.

4. **Emergency Communication Plan**: Establish a clear communication plan for your family. This should include emergency contact numbers, a designated out-of-area contact person, and the use of encrypted

messaging apps for secure communication. Ensure every family member knows how to send distress signals through these channels.

5. **Evacuation Routes and Meeting Points**: Map out multiple evacuation routes from your home and designate a meeting point outside the house that is safe and easily accessible for all family members. Practice evacuating the home using these routes to ensure everyone is familiar with them.

6. **Emergency Drills**: Conduct regular emergency drills that simulate different scenarios. This will help family members understand their roles and actions during a crisis, reducing panic and confusion when faced with a real emergency.

7. **Documentation and Information**: Keep a secure but accessible file containing important documents such as identification, insurance policies, medical records, and bank account information. This file should be easily grabbable in case of an evacuation.

8. **First Aid and Self-Defense Training**: Provide basic first aid and self-defense training for all capable family members. Knowing how to respond to injuries or defend oneself can be critical in a crisis situation.

9. **Maintenance and Review of Security Systems**: Regularly check and maintain all security systems, including alarms, locks, and surveillance cameras. Ensure they are in working order and update them as necessary to cover any new vulnerabilities.

10. **Community Networking**: Engage with your local community for broader security initiatives. This can include neighborhood watch programs or community emergency response teams. Sharing information and resources can enhance security for everyone involved.

11. **Customization for Special Needs**: Tailor your emergency protocol to accommodate any family members with special needs, whether they are elderly, have disabilities, or young children. This may involve specific evacuation tools or additional medical supplies.

12. **Resource Management**: Keep an inventory of all emergency supplies, checking expiration dates and replenishing as needed. This includes food, water, batteries, and medical supplies.

13. **Mental Health Considerations**: Recognize the importance of mental health during a crisis. Include strategies for managing stress and anxiety, such as breathing exercises or designated quiet spaces.

By meticulously crafting an emergency security protocol with these steps, you can ensure that your household is prepared to face various crises with confidence. The key is regular review and practice of this protocol, ensuring that all family members are familiar with their roles and responsibilities, and adapting the plan as needed to address new threats or changes in the household.

Lockdown Procedures for Immediate Threats

When an immediate threat looms, such as a home invasion or a natural disaster, implementing a lockdown procedure swiftly and efficiently can be the difference between safety and peril. A lockdown procedure is designed to secure the household quickly, minimizing vulnerability and protecting all family members until the threat has passed or help arrives. Here's a step-by-step guide to executing a lockdown procedure tailored for immediate threats.

1. **Alert Notification**: The first step in a lockdown is to alert all household members without causing panic. Use a pre-established signal, whether it's a specific phrase, sound, or a silent alarm system, to communicate the need for immediate action. This signal should be understood by all, including children, without causing undue stress.

2. **Secure Individuals**: Quickly gather all family members into the pre-designated safe room. This room should have been chosen in advance for its few entry points and its ability to be fortified. It's essential that this room also contains your emergency supplies, communication devices, and any self-defense tools you have prepared.

3. **Lockdown Entry Points**: As you move to the safe room, ensure that all doors and windows are locked. If time and safety permit, close blinds or curtains to block visibility into your home. Doors should have deadbolts that can be secured from the inside, and windows should have locks and, ideally, security film to prevent easy entry.

4. **Communicate Externally**: Once secured in your safe room, use your predetermined communication method to alert authorities. This could be via a cell phone, landline, or a distress signal through a security system. Provide all necessary information to the dispatcher, including the nature of the threat, your address, and the fact that you are locked down in a safe room. Do not end the call until instructed to do so by the dispatcher.

5. **Maintain Silence and Stay Informed**: After alerting authorities, maintain silence to avoid detection by the intruder. Use a battery-powered or hand-crank radio to stay informed about the situation outside if the threat is a natural disaster. If the threat is a home invasion, listen carefully to any sounds that can inform you about the intruder's location and intentions, without taking any action that would reveal your presence.

6. **Self-Defense Preparedness**: While the primary goal is to avoid confrontation, be prepared to defend yourself if necessary. Ensure that any self-defense tools are accessible and that adult family members know how to use them safely and effectively. This is a last resort measure and should only be considered if the intruder attempts to enter your safe room.

7. **Wait for Help**: Remain in your safe room until help arrives. Do not leave the room until you have verified the identity of those at the door. Authorities will have protocols for safely clearing a house and rescuing occupants. Wait for a clear signal or direct communication from them before ending the lockdown.

8. **Post-Incident Protocol**: Once the immediate threat has been neutralized, follow the instructions of the authorities for leaving the safe room and your home if necessary. Have a plan for where to go if you cannot stay in your home due to damage or ongoing danger. This might include staying with relatives, friends, or at a designated community shelter.

9. **Review and Improve**: After the situation has been resolved and all family members are safe, take the time to review the effectiveness of your lockdown procedure. Discuss what worked well and what could be improved. Make adjustments to your plan based on this review to ensure better preparedness for any future threats.

By meticulously following these steps, you can create a robust defense against immediate threats, ensuring the safety and security of your family. Regularly review and practice your lockdown procedure to ensure that when seconds count, everyone knows their role and can act quickly and efficiently to secure their safety.

Developing community-based defense networks for additional protection

Project Introduction (Description - Benefits - Challenges)

Creating a community-based defense network involves organizing and coordinating with neighbors to enhance the overall security of your area. The benefits include increased surveillance, shared resources for crisis management, and a stronger sense of community. Challenges may include coordinating schedules, establishing effective communication channels, and ensuring privacy and trust among participants.

Required Materials

- Walkie-talkies or two-way radios with a minimum range of 1 mile, preferably models with a frequency of 462-467 MHz for optimal clarity and minimal interference, and consider units with weather alerts and rechargeable batteries for extended use

- Community map highlighting each household's location, emergency exits, and safe zones, created using GIS software to ensure accuracy, with printed copies distributed to all members and digital versions shared via a secure online platform

- Signage for neighborhood watch program, including reflective materials for visibility at night, with clear messaging such as "Neighborhood Watch" and contact information for local law enforcement, placed at strategic entry points to the community

- Emergency contact list for all participating households, formatted in a shared document accessible via cloud storage, including names, addresses, phone numbers, and any special medical needs or considerations for each family member

- Shared online platform or mobile app for real-time communication and alerts, utilizing secure messaging services like Signal or WhatsApp, with designated group leaders to manage information flow and ensure timely updates during emergencies

Required Tools

- Computer and printer for creating maps and contact lists
- Laminator for weather-proofing maps and signage

Detailed Instructions

1. **Organize an Initial Meeting**: Invite neighbors to discuss the concept, benefits, and logistics of forming a defense network. Use a community space or online meeting platform.

2. **Assign Roles and Responsibilities**: Identify volunteers for coordination, communication, surveillance, and emergency response roles based on skills and availability.

3. **Distribute Communication Tools**: Provide each household with a two-way radio or walkie-talkie, ensuring everyone knows how to use them.

4. **Create and Distribute a Community Map**: Include the location of each participating household, designated emergency exits, and safe zones. Laminate the map for durability.

5. **Set Up a Shared Communication Platform**: Choose an online platform or mobile app where participants can share alerts, updates, and emergency information in real-time.

6. **Install Signage**: Place neighborhood watch program signs in visible locations around the community to deter potential intruders.

7. **Conduct Regular Meetings and Drills**: Schedule monthly meetings to discuss updates, challenges, and strategies. Organize quarterly drills to practice emergency response and communication.

8. **Establish an Emergency Contact List**: Compile a list of all participants' contact information, along with local emergency services. Distribute copies and store it on the shared platform.

Safety

- Ensure all participants respect privacy and confidentiality agreements.
- Use secure channels for communication to protect sensitive information.
- Regularly check and maintain communication devices for reliability.

Cost of the Project

Approximately $50-$100 per household, depending on the cost of communication devices and materials for signage.

Preparation Time

2-4 weeks for initial setup and coordination. Ongoing participation required.

Maintenance and Care

- Regularly test communication devices and replace batteries as needed.
- Update the community map and contact lists annually or as new members join.
- Review and refresh roles and responsibilities during regular meetings.

FAQ or Common Issues

- **Q: What if some neighbors don't want to participate?**
- **A:** Focus on building a core group of participants and demonstrate the benefits. Over time, more neighbors may choose to join.
- **Q: How can we ensure privacy while using shared communication platforms?**
- **A:** Use platforms with end-to-end encryption and establish clear guidelines on what information can be shared.

Difficulty Rating

★★★☆☆

Variations

- For larger communities, consider dividing the area into zones, each with its own coordinator and communication channel.
- Incorporate technology such as shared surveillance cameras or motion-sensor lighting in common areas, with community consent.

To effectively develop community-based defense networks for additional protection, consider the following troubleshooting steps:

- **Identify Key Community Members**: Reach out to neighbors and local leaders who are willing to participate in a defense network. Establish a list of individuals with various skills, such as medical training, security experience, or emergency preparedness knowledge

- **Assess Vulnerabilities**: Conduct a thorough assessment of your community's vulnerabilities. Identify areas that may be prone to threats, such as poorly lit streets or isolated homes, and discuss these findings with your network

- **Establish Communication Channels**: Set up reliable communication methods among network members. This could include group messaging apps, walkie-talkies, or a community bulletin board to ensure everyone stays informed

- **Create a Response Plan**: Develop a clear plan of action for various scenarios, such as natural disasters or security threats. Ensure all members understand their roles and responsibilities within the plan

- **Conduct Regular Drills**: Organize training sessions and drills to practice the response plan. This will help build confidence and ensure everyone knows what to do in an emergency

- **Build Trust and Relationships**: Foster strong relationships among network members. Regular meetings and social events can help build camaraderie and trust, which are essential for effective collaboration

- **Evaluate and Adapt**: After drills or real-life incidents, gather feedback from network members to evaluate the effectiveness of your strategies. Be open to making adjustments based on lessons learned

- **Engage Local Authorities**: Establish a relationship with local law enforcement and emergency services. They can provide valuable resources and support for your community defense efforts

- **Promote Awareness and Education**: Share information about personal safety, emergency preparedness, and community resources with all members. This will empower everyone to take an active role in their own safety and the safety of the community

By following these troubleshooting steps, you can create a robust community-based defense network that enhances the safety and security of your neighborhood

DIY Chapter: Home Defense Projects

Project Introduction (Description - Benefits - Challenges)

Enhancing home security by installing reinforced doors and window bars. This project aims to significantly increase the difficulty for potential intruders to gain entry into your home, creating a safer environment for your family. The benefits include a heightened sense of security and a physical barrier against break-ins. Challenges involve ensuring proper installation without compromising the home's aesthetic appeal or emergency egress.

Required Materials

- Solid core or metal exterior doors, with a minimum thickness of 1-3/4 inches
- Window bars or grilles, made of steel or wrought iron, with spacing narrow enough to prevent a person from passing through
- Heavy-duty, four-screw, strike plate with 3-inch long screws
- Deadbolt locks with at least a 1-inch throw
- Tamper-proof screws and bolts for securing window bars
- Masonry anchors for attaching bars to brick or concrete surfaces

Required Tools

- Drill with bits suitable for wood, metal, and masonry
- Screwdriver set
- Tape measure
- Level
- Hammer drill (for masonry)
- Metal saw or grinder (for cutting window bars to size)
- Safety glasses and gloves

Detailed Instructions

1. **Door Replacement**: Begin by removing the existing door from its frame, taking care to unscrew the hinges and gently pulling the door away. Select a solid core door made of either solid wood or steel, as these materials provide superior resistance to forced entry. Ensure the door swings outward, which adds an extra layer of security by making it harder for intruders to kick it in. Use a level to check that the door is properly aligned within the frame, adjusting the hinges as necessary to achieve a perfect fit. Consider adding a door sweep at the bottom to prevent drafts and enhance security

2. **Strike Plate Installation**: Remove the standard strike plate and replace it with a heavy-duty version made of steel, which is significantly more robust. Use the provided 3-inch screws to secure the strike plate into the wall framing, ensuring that at least two screws penetrate the framing studs for maximum strength. This installation will help prevent the door from being forced open, as the longer screws will resist pulling out from the frame

3. **Deadbolt Installation**: If a deadbolt lock is not already present, select a high-quality deadbolt with a minimum 1-inch throw bolt, which extends deep into the door frame for added security. Position the deadbolt at a height of 48 inches from the floor, as this is generally out of reach from windows while still being accessible for adults. Follow the manufacturer's instructions for drilling the necessary holes, ensuring that the bolt aligns perfectly with the strike plate for smooth operation

4. **Window Bars Installation**: Measure the dimensions of each window carefully, and cut the steel bars to fit snugly within the window frame, leaving no more than 4 inches of space around the perimeter to prevent leverage points for intruders. Use a drill to create holes in the window frame or surrounding masonry, ensuring that you use a masonry bit if drilling into brick or concrete. Secure the bars using tamper-proof screws or masonry anchors, which are designed to resist removal and provide a strong hold

5. **Checking for Safety**: After completing all security enhancements, conduct a thorough check to ensure that they do not impede quick egress in the event of an emergency. Test each window to confirm that they can still be opened easily or are equipped with a quick-release mechanism from the inside, allowing for a swift exit if necessary. Additionally, consider installing a secondary escape route, such as a window ladder, to further enhance safety in emergencies.

Safety

- Wear safety glasses and gloves, especially when cutting metal or drilling into masonry.
- Double-check measurements before cutting or drilling to avoid mistakes that could weaken the structure or leave gaps.
- Ensure that all modifications comply with local building codes, especially regarding egress requirements.

Cost of the Project

Approximately $500-$1500, depending on the quality of materials chosen and whether professional installation is required for certain elements.

Preparation Time

8-12 hours, spread over a couple of days to allow for careful measurement, fitting, and installation.

Maintenance and Care

- Regularly inspect door hinges, locks, and window bars for signs of wear or tampering.
- Lubricate locks and hinges annually to ensure smooth operation.
- Check that window bars remain firmly attached and free from rust or corrosion, applying rust-inhibitor paint as needed.

FAQ or Common Issues

- **Q: What if my door frame is not strong enough to support a solid core or metal door?**
- **A:** Reinforce the door frame with metal plates or replace the frame with a more durable material.
- **Q: How can I ensure window bars don't make my home feel like a prison?**
- **A:** Choose decorative window bars or grilles that complement your home's aesthetic. Many designs provide security without sacrificing style.

Difficulty Rating

★★★★☆

Variations

- For homes in hurricane-prone areas, consider installing impact-resistant doors and windows that provide both security and protection against severe weather.
- Smart locks can be added to doors for keyless entry and remote monitoring.

Troubleshooting Home Defense Projects

1. Inadequate Lighting
- Check if all bulbs are functioning and replace any burnt-out bulbs
- Ensure motion sensors are properly calibrated and not obstructed
- Consider adding additional lighting fixtures in dark areas

2. Weak Entry Points
- Inspect doors and windows for any signs of wear or damage
- Reinforce door frames with metal plates or additional locks
- Ensure all windows have secure locks and consider adding window film for extra protection

3. Faulty Security Systems
- Test all components of your security system regularly, including alarms and cameras
- Ensure batteries in wireless systems are charged and replaced as needed
- Review the placement of cameras to cover all vulnerable areas

4. Poor Communication Plans
- Establish a clear communication plan with family members in case of an emergency
- Ensure everyone knows how to use any communication devices, such as walkie-talkies or cell phones
- Regularly practice emergency drills to reinforce the plan

5. Insufficient Emergency Supplies
- Regularly check and update your emergency supply kit, ensuring it includes food, water, and first aid supplies
- Rotate supplies to keep them fresh and usable
- Consider adding additional items based on specific family needs, such as medications or pet supplies

6. Lack of Community Awareness
- Engage with neighbors to establish a neighborhood watch program
- Share information about suspicious activities and encourage open communication
- Organize community meetings to discuss safety concerns and strategies

7. Unclear Escape Routes
- Map out multiple escape routes from your home and practice them with your family
- Ensure all exits are clear of obstructions and easily accessible
- Consider creating a safe meeting point outside the home in case of an emergency

8. Neglected Landscaping
- Trim back any overgrown bushes or trees that could provide cover for intruders
- Use gravel or other materials to create noise-making pathways around your home
- Consider planting thorny bushes near windows for added natural security

9. Inconsistent Maintenance
- Schedule regular maintenance checks for all security features, including locks and alarms
- Keep a checklist of tasks to ensure nothing is overlooked
- Address any repairs promptly to maintain the integrity of your home defense system

Installing reinforced doors and window bars for extra protection - be very detailed

Project Introduction (Description - Benefits - Challenges)

Enhancing home security through the installation of reinforced doors and window bars provides a robust barrier against potential intruders, significantly increasing the safety of your home and family. The primary benefit of this upgrade is the substantial improvement in home defense, creating a physical deterrent that can prevent break-ins. Challenges include ensuring the installation does not compromise the aesthetic appeal of your home, adhering to local building codes, and selecting materials that offer the best balance between strength and cost.

Required Materials

- Solid core or steel exterior doors, minimum thickness of 1-3/4 inches
- High-quality deadbolt locks, ANSI Grade 1
- Heavy-duty, four-screw, strike plates with 3-inch long screws
- Window bars or grilles, made of steel or wrought iron, designed to fit individual window sizes
- Tamper-proof screws and bolts for securing window bars
- Masonry anchors for attaching bars to brick or concrete surfaces

Required Tools

- Drill with bits suitable for wood, metal, and masonry
- Screwdriver set
- Tape measure
- Level
- Hammer drill (for installations into masonry)
- Metal saw or grinder (for custom-fitting window bars)
- Safety glasses and gloves

Detailed Instructions

1. **Measuring for Door Replacement**: Measure the existing door frame and select a solid core or steel replacement door that matches these dimensions. Pay special attention to the door's swing direction to ensure it opens outward, increasing resistance to forced entry.

2. **Installing the Reinforced Door**: Remove the existing door, hinges, and strike plate. Position the new door in the frame, ensuring it is level and plumb. Secure the door with heavy-duty hinges and screws.

3. **Strike Plate and Deadbolt Installation**: Install a heavy-duty strike plate using the 3-inch screws provided, ensuring it penetrates into the wall stud for added strength. Install the deadbolt lock above the doorknob, ensuring it has at least a 1-inch throw.

4. **Measuring and Cutting Window Bars**: Measure each window carefully. Cut the bars to size, ensuring they cover the entire window without leaving gaps that could allow entry.

5. **Installing Window Bars**: Mark the drilling points on the window frame or surrounding wall. Use a drill to create pilot holes, then secure the bars with tamper-proof screws or masonry anchors. Ensure the bars are level and firmly attached.

6. **Safety Check**: Verify that all installations do not hinder the ability to exit the home in case of an emergency. For windows, consider models with quick-release mechanisms that can be opened from the inside.

Safety

- Wear safety glasses and gloves to protect against metal shards and drilling dust.
- Confirm that all modifications meet local building and fire codes, especially regarding emergency egress.
- Double-check all installations for stability and security before considering the project complete.

Cost of the Project

Approximately $1,000-$3,000, depending on the number of doors and windows secured, and whether professional installation is required.

Preparation Time

1-2 days, depending on the number of doors and windows being reinforced.

Maintenance and Care

- Regularly inspect door locks, hinges, and window bars for signs of tampering or wear.
- Lubricate door locks and hinges annually to ensure smooth operation.
- Check window bars for rust or damage, applying rust-inhibitor paint as needed.

FAQ or Common Issues

- **Q: How can I reinforce my doors without changing their appearance?**
- **A:** Use a paintable solid core door and install decorative window bars that complement your home's style.
- **Q: What if my door frames are not strong enough to support a reinforced door?**
- **A:** You may need to reinforce the frame with metal plates or replace it entirely with a more robust material.

Difficulty Rating

★★★★☆

Variations

- Smart locks can be added to reinforced doors for enhanced security features, such as remote locking and unlocking.
- In areas prone to severe weather, consider installing impact-resistant doors and windows that offer both security and protection against storms.

When installing reinforced doors and window bars for extra protection, it's essential to ensure that the installation process is executed flawlessly to maximize security. Here are some detailed troubleshooting tips to consider during and after the installation:

- **Check Door Frame Integrity**: Before installing a reinforced door, inspect the door frame for any signs of damage or weakness. If the frame is compromised, it may need to be repaired or replaced to ensure the door can withstand force

- **Alignment Issues**: After installing the door, check for proper alignment. If the door does not close smoothly or is misaligned, adjust the hinges or shims to ensure a snug fit

- **Lock Functionality**: Test the lock mechanism multiple times after installation. If the lock is sticking or not engaging properly, consider lubricating it or replacing it with a higher-quality lock

- **Window Bar Installation**: When installing window bars, ensure they are securely anchored to the wall. If the bars feel loose or wobbly, reinforce the mounting points with additional screws or brackets

- **Material Quality**: Use high-quality materials for both doors and window bars. If you notice any signs of rust or corrosion on metal components, replace them immediately to maintain security

- **Emergency Access**: Ensure that any reinforced doors or window bars do not impede emergency exits. If they do, consider installing quick-release mechanisms that allow for easy escape in case of an emergency

- **Regular Maintenance**: Schedule regular inspections of your reinforced doors and window bars. Look for any signs of wear and tear, and address issues promptly to maintain maximum protection

- **Consult a Professional**: If you encounter significant issues during installation or if you are unsure about the security of your setup, do not hesitate to consult a professional for advice or assistance

By following these troubleshooting tips, you can ensure that your reinforced doors and window bars provide the maximum level of protection for your home and family

DIY motion detector and security lighting installation - be very detailed

Project Introduction (Description - Benefits - Challenges)

Enhancing home security through the integration of motion detectors and security lighting. This project aims to deter potential intruders by illuminating dark areas and alerting homeowners to movement around their property. Benefits include increased safety, deterrence of burglars, and peace of mind. Challenges encompass selecting the right equipment, proper placement for optimal coverage, and the technical aspects of installation.

Required Materials

- Motion detectors with adjustable sensitivity and a detection range of at least 30 feet
- LED security lights, 1000-2000 lumens, with weatherproof rating (IP65 or higher)
- Outdoor-rated electrical boxes and conduit to protect wiring
- Electrical wire (14/2 or 12/2 gauge, outdoor-rated)
- Wire nuts suitable for outdoor use
- Mounting hardware including screws and wall anchors
- Silicone sealant for weatherproofing any outdoor electrical connections

Required Tools

- Drill with masonry and wood drill bits
- Screwdriver set
- Wire stripper/cutter
- Ladder
- Voltage tester
- Silicone caulk gun

- Fish tape for pulling wire through conduit

Detailed Instructions

1. **Identify Strategic Locations**: Choose areas that are dark and near potential entry points. Ensure motion detectors have a clear field of view, free from obstructions like trees or decorations.

2. **Mount Motion Detectors**: Install detectors 6-10 feet above the ground, angling them to cover the desired area. Use a drill and mounting hardware to secure them in place. Apply silicone sealant around the edges to prevent water ingress.

3. **Install Security Lights**: Position lights so they illuminate the area detected by the motion sensors. Aim lights downward to maximize visibility and minimize light pollution. Secure with screws and seal any gaps with silicone.

4. **Wire the System**: Turn off power at the breaker. Run outdoor-rated electrical wire from the power source to the motion detector, then to the security lights. Use conduit to protect wires from the elements. Connect wires in the electrical box using wire nuts, matching color to color.

5. **Connect to Power**: Attach the wiring to your home's electrical system, following local codes. Use a voltage tester to ensure connections are safe before restoring power.

6. **Test and Adjust**: Turn on the power and test the system by moving in the detector's range at night. Adjust the sensitivity and range of the motion detector as needed to avoid false alarms and ensure adequate coverage.

Safety

- Always turn off the power at the main breaker before starting electrical work.
- Use a voltage tester to double-check that wires are not live before touching them.
- Follow the manufacturer's instructions for installing and configuring motion detectors and lights.
- Ensure all outdoor electrical connections are sealed against moisture.

Cost of the Project

Approximately $150-$300, depending on the number and quality of motion detectors and lights.

Preparation Time

4-8 hours, depending on the complexity of wiring and number of lights and detectors installed.

Maintenance and Care

- Periodically clean the motion detectors and lights to ensure they remain functional.
- Check and replace any burned-out bulbs (if not using LEDs).
- Inspect the silicone sealant and reapply if necessary to maintain weatherproofing.
- Test the system regularly to ensure it activates properly.

FAQ or Common Issues

- **Q: What if the motion detector triggers too often?**
- **A:** Adjust the sensitivity settings and ensure the detector's field of view is not obstructed by moving branches or animals.
- **Q: Can I connect the lights to a switch to override the motion detector?**

- **A:** Yes, you can wire the lights through a switch for manual control. Consult an electrician if unsure how to set this up.

Difficulty Rating

★★★☆☆

Variations

- Use solar-powered lights for areas without easy access to electrical wiring.
- Integrate smart motion detectors that can send alerts to your phone for enhanced security monitoring.

Troubleshooting for DIY Motion Detector and Security Lighting Installation

1. Motion Detector Not Activating
- Check the power source to ensure the unit is receiving electricity
- Verify that the sensitivity settings are correctly adjusted
- Inspect for obstructions in the sensor's field of view
- Ensure the motion detector is installed at the recommended height and angle

2. False Alarms
- Adjust the sensitivity settings to a lower level
- Remove any potential triggers such as moving branches or animals
- Ensure the detector is not facing a heat source like air conditioning units or heaters

3. Security Light Not Turning On
- Confirm that the light bulb is functioning and properly installed
- Check the wiring connections for any loose or damaged wires
- Ensure the light is set to the correct mode (manual, auto, or test)

4. Inconsistent Lighting Activation
- Inspect the motion detector for dirt or debris that may obstruct the sensor
- Test the unit in different weather conditions to see if environmental factors affect performance
- Ensure the light is not too far from the motion detector, as distance can affect activation

5. Battery Issues (if applicable)
- Replace old batteries with fresh ones and ensure they are installed correctly
- Check for corrosion on battery terminals and clean if necessary
- If using rechargeable batteries, ensure they are fully charged

6. Interference from Other Devices
- Move the motion detector away from other electronic devices that may cause interference
- Test the system in isolation to determine if other devices are affecting performance

7. Installation Height and Angle
- Reassess the installation height; the optimal height is typically between 6 to 8 feet
- Adjust the angle of the sensor to cover the desired area without blind spots

8. Weather-Related Issues
- Ensure the motion detector is rated for outdoor use if installed outside
- Check for water damage or moisture in the unit, especially after heavy rain or snow

9. Consult the Manual
- Refer to the manufacturer's manual for specific troubleshooting steps and guidelines
- Look for any warranty information or customer support options if issues persist

By following these troubleshooting steps, you can ensure that your DIY motion detector and security lighting system operates effectively, providing maximum protection for your home and family

BOOK 4: LONG-TERM FOOD SECURITY

Creating a long-term food storage plan is essential for ensuring your household's resilience in various crisis scenarios. This plan involves selecting high-calorie, long-shelf-life items that can sustain your family's nutritional needs over extended periods. The first step in this process is to assess your family's dietary preferences, allergies, and any specific nutritional requirements to ensure the food you store will be suitable and sustainable for everyone.

For high-calorie items, focus on staples such as rice, beans, and lentils, which not only offer substantial nutritional value but also have the benefit of a long shelf life when stored properly. Incorporate whole grains like wheat berries and oats, which can be used to make bread, porridge, and other meals, providing both energy and comfort during stressful times. Canned goods, including vegetables, fruits, and meats, are also crucial as they add variety and essential nutrients to your diet. When selecting these, opt for cans without dents or rust to ensure their longevity and safety.

In addition to these staples, consider adding powdered milk, which can be reconstituted for drinking or cooking, and a variety of spices to enhance the flavor of meals, making them more palatable over long periods. Honey and salt are excellent additions as well, serving not only as flavor enhancers but also as preservatives for other foods you may harvest or procure during a crisis.

For the storage of these items, choose a cool, dry, and dark space in your home, such as a basement or a dedicated pantry. Ensure that the area is free from pests and moisture, which can spoil your food reserves. Utilize food-grade storage containers with airtight seals to protect against air, moisture, and pests. Mylar bags with oxygen absorbers can extend the shelf life of dry goods, while vacuum-sealed containers are ideal for preserving the quality of dehydrated or freeze-dried foods.

Labeling is a critical component of your food storage plan. Use permanent markers to clearly mark the purchase or packaging date on each item. Implement a rotation system where the oldest items are used first and replaced with new ones, ensuring that your stockpile remains fresh and safe to consume. This first-in, first-out (FIFO) method prevents waste and ensures that your family is accustomed to the taste and preparation of your stored food, reducing the likelihood of dietary disruptions during a crisis.

Finally, regularly review and adjust your food storage plan. As your family's needs and preferences change, so too should your stockpile. This might mean adding new items, removing others, or adjusting quantities. Additionally, stay informed about the shelf life of stored foods and incorporate new preservation techniques as they become available. By taking these steps, you can create a comprehensive and adaptable long-term food storage plan that will serve as a cornerstone of your household's crisis preparedness strategy.

CHAPTER 1: SEAL-INSPIRED FOOD STOCKPILING

When considering the nutritional content of your stockpile, it's essential to focus on macronutrients—proteins, carbohydrates, and fats. These are the primary sources of energy and are crucial for maintaining strength and health during prolonged periods of stress or crisis. For proteins, opt for canned meats such as chicken, tuna, and salmon, which offer long shelf life and are versatile for various meals. Include plant-based protein sources like quinoa and chickpeas, which are not only rich in protein but also in fiber, making them excellent for digestion and overall health. When selecting carbohydrates, prioritize whole grains such as brown rice and quinoa, which provide sustained energy and are packed with essential nutrients. Include a variety of beans, which can be stored dry or canned, offering flexibility in meal preparation and a significant source of both protein and carbohydrates.

Fats are equally important for energy and should be included in the form of oils, nuts, and seeds. Olive oil and coconut oil are excellent choices due to their long shelf life and health benefits. Nuts and seeds, such as almonds, walnuts, and flaxseeds, are not only rich in healthy fats but also provide protein and essential minerals. It's important to store these items in airtight containers to extend their shelf life and maintain freshness

Here's a complete list of recommended fats for your stockpile:

- **Olive Oil**: Rich in monounsaturated fats and antioxidants, olive oil is versatile for cooking and dressings, and it can last for up to two years when stored properly
- **Coconut Oil**: Known for its high smoke point and unique flavor, coconut oil is stable at room temperature and can last indefinitely if kept in a cool, dark place
- **Almonds**: These nuts are packed with vitamin E, magnesium, and fiber, making them a nutritious snack that can last for several months when stored in airtight containers
- **Walnuts**: High in omega-3 fatty acids, walnuts are beneficial for heart health and can be stored for about six months in a cool, dry environment
- **Flaxseeds**: A great source of omega-3s and lignans, flaxseeds can be ground for better nutrient absorption and should be kept in the refrigerator to maintain freshness for up to a year
- **Chia Seeds**: These tiny seeds are rich in fiber and protein, and they can last for several years when stored in a cool, dry place
- **Peanut Butter**: A good source of protein and healthy fats, peanut butter can last for several months unopened and can be a great addition to your food stockpile
- **Sunflower Oil**: This oil is high in vitamin E and has a relatively long shelf life, making it a good option for cooking and baking

By incorporating these fats into your food stockpile, you ensure a balanced intake of essential nutrients while also enhancing the flavor and variety of your meals.

In addition to macronutrients, vitamins and minerals are vital for maintaining health, especially under stress. Include a variety of canned fruits and vegetables to ensure a supply of essential vitamins and minerals. Consider adding powdered or freeze-dried fruits and vegetables to your stockpile as they are lightweight, space-efficient, and can be rehydrated for use in cooking. Supplements such as multivitamins can also play a crucial role in filling any nutritional gaps that may occur during a crisis.

Water is a critical component of food stockpiling and should not be overlooked. Each person requires at least one gallon of water per day for drinking and sanitation. Store a sufficient supply of water in food-grade, BPA-free containers, and consider water purification methods such as filtration systems or purification tablets as a backup. Regularly rotate your water supply to ensure freshness.

For the organization of your food stockpile, utilize shelving units designed to withstand heavy loads. Place heavier items on the lower shelves and lighter items on the upper shelves to prevent tipping. Use clear, durable containers to store dry goods, allowing for easy identification and access. Implement a labeling system with the date of purchase or packaging on each item, and adhere to the first-in, first-out principle to rotate supplies and prevent spoilage.

Regularly inspect your stockpile for signs of spoilage or pest infestation. Keep the storage area clean, cool, and dry to prevent damage to your supplies. Dedicate time to plan and prepare meals using the items in your stockpile to familiarize yourself and your family with the tastes and preparation methods. This practice not only ensures the usability of your stockpile but also helps to maintain a sense of normalcy and comfort during challenging times.

By meticulously selecting a balanced variety of foods, focusing on nutritional content, and organizing your stockpile for easy access and rotation, you can create a comprehensive and sustainable long-term food storage plan. This plan will serve as a foundation for your household's resilience, ensuring that you and your family are well-nourished and prepared for any crisis scenario.

Long-Term Food Storage Plan

When embarking on the journey of creating a long-term food storage plan, the focus should be on selecting items that not only offer high caloric content but also boast an extended shelf life. This ensures that your stockpile remains both nutritious and viable over long periods, a critical component in crisis preparedness. The initial step involves a comprehensive assessment of your storage space. Opt for a location that is cool, dry, and devoid of direct sunlight, such as a basement or a dedicated pantry area, to optimize the preservation conditions for your stored food.

For the cornerstone of your food storage, prioritize staples like rice and beans. These items are not only rich in calories but can be stored for years without losing their nutritional value. When purchasing rice, opt for white rice over brown rice, as the latter contains oils that can cause it to spoil faster. Store these staples in food-grade buckets with gamma seal lids to ensure an airtight environment, further extending their shelf life. Incorporate oxygen absorbers into each bucket before sealing to remove any residual air, which can degrade the food over time.

Beans, offering both protein and calories, are another essential. Dry beans are preferable for long-term storage due to their extended shelf life. Like rice, beans should be stored in airtight containers with oxygen absorbers. It's advisable to choose a variety of beans—such as black beans, pinto beans, and lentils—to provide dietary diversity and access to different nutrients.

Canned goods are a practical addition to any long-term food storage plan. Focus on high-calorie options like canned meats, including chicken, tuna, and beef, which can significantly boost your protein intake during a crisis. Vegetables and fruits in cans add necessary vitamins and minerals to your diet. When selecting canned goods, ensure the cans are free from dents and rust, and always check the expiration dates. Rotate these items periodically to maintain freshness, adhering to the first-in, first-out principle.

Incorporating whole grains such as wheat berries and oats is also beneficial. These can be ground into flour or used whole in various recipes, offering flexibility in meal preparation. Store whole grains in airtight containers with oxygen absorbers, similar to rice and beans, to protect against pests and extend shelf life.

Powdered milk and eggs provide a source of calcium and protein and can be easily reconstituted with water. Store these in vacuum-sealed bags or mylar bags with oxygen absorbers to maintain their quality over time. Additionally, consider adding high-calorie, nutrient-dense items like peanut butter, honey, and coconut oil to your stockpile. These foods offer not only essential fats and sugars but also serve as comfort foods, which can be psychologically beneficial in a crisis.

Spices and seasonings are crucial for making stored foods more palatable and can prevent palate fatigue. Store a variety of spices in sealed containers to keep them fresh. Salt, in particular, is not only a flavor enhancer but also a preservative for other foods you may acquire or prepare during a crisis.

For water storage, allocate at least one gallon per person per day, considering both drinking and sanitation needs. Use food-grade, BPA-free containers for water storage and include water purification options like filtration systems or purification tablets in your plan.

Regularly review and update your food storage plan. As your family's needs and preferences evolve, so too should your stockpile. This might involve adding new items, removing others, or adjusting quantities. Stay informed about the shelf life of stored foods and incorporate new preservation techniques as they become available. By meticulously selecting a balanced variety of foods, focusing on nutritional content, and organizing your stockpile for easy access and rotation, you can create a comprehensive and sustainable long-term food storage plan. This plan will serve as a foundation for your household's resilience, ensuring that you and your family are well-nourished and prepared for any crisis scenario.

Nutrient-Dense Foods for Energy and Health

When it comes to building a long-term food storage plan, selecting nutrient-dense foods is crucial for ensuring maximum energy and health for you and your family. Nutrient-dense foods are those that provide a high amount of nutrients compared to their calorie content. These foods are essential in survival situations where maintaining health and energy levels is paramount, and access to a wide variety of foods may be limited. Here's how to prioritize these foods for your stockpile:

1. **Focus on Whole Grains**: Whole grains like quinoa, brown rice, and oats are excellent sources of complex carbohydrates, fiber, vitamins, and minerals. For instance, quinoa is not only a complete protein source but also contains iron, magnesium, and manganese, making it an ideal food for energy and health. Store these grains in airtight containers in a cool, dark place to maximize their shelf life.

2. **Incorporate a Variety of Legumes**: Beans, lentils, and chickpeas are high in protein, fiber, and various nutrients while being relatively low in calories. They can be stored for years if kept in airtight containers away from light and moisture. Legumes are versatile and can be used in a variety of dishes, providing essential amino acids that are crucial when meat might be scarce.

3. **Select High-Quality Protein Sources**: Freeze-dried meats, poultry, and fish are excellent sources of high-quality protein and can be stored for extended periods. Additionally, consider plant-based protein sources like powdered or canned beans and lentils. These protein sources are vital for muscle maintenance and repair, especially in physically demanding situations.

4. **Stock Up on Dried Fruits and Vegetables**: Dried fruits and vegetables retain most of the nutrients of their fresh counterparts and are a great way to add vitamins, minerals, and fiber to your diet. Look for options like dried berries, apricots, tomatoes, and peppers. Avoid those with added sugars or preservatives to keep your food as healthy as possible.

5. **Include Nuts and Seeds**: Nuts and seeds are packed with healthy fats, proteins, vitamins, and minerals. Items like almonds, walnuts, flaxseeds, and chia seeds not only provide a quick energy boost but also contribute to heart and brain health. Store them in vacuum-sealed bags to extend their freshness.

6. **Prioritize Healthy Fats**: Healthy fats are essential for energy and cell function. Stock up on extra virgin olive oil, coconut oil, and other plant-based oils that offer a mix of essential fatty acids. Canned fish like salmon, mackerel, and sardines are also excellent sources of omega-3 fatty acids.

7. **Choose Powdered Milk or Plant-Based Alternatives**: Powdered milk can provide calcium, vitamin D, and protein, essential for bone health and muscle function. Plant-based milk powders, such as soy or almond, can offer similar benefits and may be preferable for those with dietary restrictions.

8. **Vitamin and Mineral Supplements**: While not a food, having a stock of essential vitamin and mineral supplements can help fill any nutritional gaps in your long-term food storage plan. Focus on multivitamins, vitamin D, calcium, and iron supplements to support overall health.

By carefully selecting and storing these nutrient-dense foods, you can ensure that your long-term food supply supports the health and energy needs of you and your family during extended periods of self-reliance. Remember to rotate your stockpile regularly to keep it fresh and to adjust your selections based on any changes in dietary needs or preferences.

Organizing Food Stockpiles for Easy Rotation

Organizing and labeling your food stockpiles for easy rotation is a critical step in ensuring your long-term food security. This process not only helps in maintaining the freshness of your supplies but also in minimizing waste and ensuring that you have a steady supply of nutritious food available. Here's how to effectively organize and label your food stockpiles:

1. **First, categorize your food supplies based on their type and expiration dates.** Group items such as grains, legumes, proteins, dried fruits and vegetables, nuts and seeds, fats and oils, and powdered milk or plant-based alternatives. Within these categories, further organize items by their expiration dates, placing those with the nearest dates in front for easy access.

2. **Use clear, durable labels on all storage containers.** Labels should include the name of the food item, the quantity, and the expiration date. For items you package yourself, such as bulk grains or legumes stored in airtight containers, make sure to include the date of packaging as well. Waterproof labels are recommended, especially for items stored in cooler, potentially damp areas.

3. **Implement a color-coding system for quicker identification.** Assign a specific color to each category of food. For example, use blue for grains, red for proteins, and green for vegetables. This system allows you to quickly locate items in your stockpile without having to read every label.

4. **Adopt the First-In, First-Out (FIFO) method.** This means placing newer items at the back of the storage area and moving older items to the front. This rotation ensures that you use items before they expire, reducing waste and keeping your stockpile fresh.

5. **Create an inventory list.** This list should detail what items you have, how many of them, and their expiration dates. Keep this list updated whenever you add or remove items from your stockpile. Consider using a spreadsheet for easy updating and to sort items by expiration date, category, or any other system you find useful.

6. **Designate specific storage areas for different categories of items.** For example, dedicate one shelf or cabinet for grains, another for proteins, and so on. This not only makes items easier to find but also helps in quickly assessing what you have and what you might need to restock.

7. **Utilize transparent storage containers when possible.** Being able to see the contents without opening the container or needing to read the label can save time and maintain the integrity of your stockpile. Ensure these containers are airtight to keep food fresh longer.

8. **Regularly inspect your stockpile.** At least once every three to six months, go through your stockpile to check for any signs of spoilage, pest infestation, or damaged containers. This is also an excellent time to rotate items and update your inventory list.

9. **Make adjustments based on consumption patterns.** If you notice that certain items are used more frequently than others, adjust your stockpile accordingly. This might mean increasing the quantity of these items or reorganizing your space to make them more accessible.

By meticulously organizing and labeling your food stockpiles, you ensure that your family has a reliable source of nutrition regardless of what the future holds. This methodical approach not only maximizes the shelf life of your food supplies but also contributes to the overall efficiency and effectiveness of your long-term food security strategy.

CHAPTER 2: MAINTAINING YOUR FOOD SUPPLY

Developing a cycle rotation system to keep stockpiles fresh is a critical aspect of maintaining your food supply effectively. This system ensures that no food goes to waste due to expiration and that your family always has access to fresh, nutritious food. Here's a step-by-step guide to implementing a successful cycle rotation system in your long-term food storage plan.

1. **Start by documenting the expiration dates of all food items in your stockpile.** Use a digital spreadsheet for this task as it allows for easy sorting and updating. In your spreadsheet, include columns for the item name, quantity, expiration date, and date of last rotation. This documentation will serve as the foundation of your cycle rotation system.

2. **Organize your food storage area according to the FIFO (First-In, First-Out) principle.** This means placing the oldest items in front or on top, making them more accessible for use before newer items. For instance, if you have canned vegetables with expiration dates ranging over several months or years, place those with the earliest expiration date in the most accessible location.

3. **Label shelves or storage bins with the intended use-by period.** For example, designate areas as "Use by end of the year" or "Use within six months." This visual aid will help you quickly identify which items need to be consumed first without having to check individual expiration dates constantly.

4. **Incorporate the use of transparent storage containers where possible.** This allows you to see the contents and their conditions without opening the container, thus preserving their freshness longer. Ensure these containers are airtight and made of food-grade materials to prevent contamination.

5. **Implement a regular review and rotation schedule.** Set a reminder to review your food stockpile every three months. During each review, check for any signs of spoilage or damage, update your inventory list with any new additions or subtractions, and rotate items as necessary to ensure the oldest items are used first. This is also an opportune time to donate items you may not use before their expiration to local food banks, reducing waste and helping your community.

6. **Adjust your purchasing habits based on your rotation findings.** If you notice certain items are consistently not being used before their expiration date, consider reducing the quantity of those items in future purchases. Conversely, if some items are used quickly and frequently, it may be beneficial to increase their presence in your stockpile.

7. **Engage your family in the rotation process.** Educating family members about the importance of the cycle rotation system and how it works ensures everyone is on the same page and can help maintain it. Assign tasks such as checking dates, rotating stock, and updating the inventory list to different family members based on their age and ability.

8. **Utilize cooking strategies that prioritize older stock.** Plan meals around items that need to be used soonest. This not only helps in rotating your stock but also encourages culinary creativity. For example, if you have an abundance of beans nearing their expiration, look for recipes that feature beans as a main ingredient.

9. **Store items in their optimal environment to extend shelf life.** Even within your home, different areas can have varying temperatures and humidity levels. Store grains, for example, in cool, dry places to prevent them from becoming rancid, while ensuring oils are kept in dark, cool spaces to maintain their freshness for as long as possible.

By meticulously following these steps, you can establish a robust cycle rotation system that maximizes the shelf life of your food stockpile, reduces waste, and ensures your family has a continuous supply of fresh and nutritious food. This system is not only practical but also instills discipline and organization skills that are valuable in all aspects of life, especially in maintaining long-term food security.

Cycle Rotation for Fresh Stockpiles

To develop a cycle rotation system that keeps your stockpiles fresh, it's essential to meticulously plan and execute a strategy that ensures every item in your food supply is used within its optimal freshness period, thus preventing waste and ensuring a constant supply of nutritious food for your family. The following steps provide a detailed guide to establishing an effective cycle rotation system for your long-term food storage.

1. **Inventory Assessment**: Begin by conducting a thorough inventory of your current food stockpile. Document each item, noting the quantity, expiration date, and storage location. Utilize a digital spreadsheet for this task to facilitate easy updates and sorting. This comprehensive inventory will serve as the backbone of your cycle rotation system, enabling you to track the freshness and availability of your supplies accurately.

2. **Storage Layout Optimization**: Organize your storage area to align with the FIFO (First-In, First-Out) principle. This organization method entails placing older stock in accessible areas to ensure it gets used first, while newer stock is stored further back. This might involve rearranging your pantry, shelves, or storage bins to create a system where items can be easily moved forward as they are used.

3. **Detailed Labeling**: Every item in your stockpile should be clearly labeled with its expiration date and the date it was added to your stockpile. Consider using color-coded labels to differentiate between categories of food, such as grains, proteins, and vegetables. This will not only help in identifying items quickly but also in tracking their shelf life.

4. **Establish a Rotation Schedule**: Set a regular schedule for reviewing and rotating your stockpile. This could be monthly, quarterly, or whatever frequency best suits the size of your stockpile and the shelf life of your stored items. During each rotation, move the oldest items to the front and integrate newer items into the back of the storage area. This is also an opportune time to inspect items for any signs of spoilage or damage.

5. **Incorporate Stock into Meal Planning**: Make it a habit to plan your meals around the items that need to be used first. This proactive approach ensures that you are regularly rotating through your stockpile, using items before they expire, and maintaining a fresh supply of food. It also encourages culinary creativity as you find new recipes and uses for the ingredients you have on hand.

6. **Adjust Purchasing Habits**: Use the insights gained from your rotation schedule to inform your purchasing decisions. If you find that certain items are consistently not being used before their expiration date, adjust your buying habits accordingly. This might mean purchasing smaller quantities of those items or phasing them out of your stockpile altogether.

7. **Engage Family Members**: Make the cycle rotation system a family affair by involving all household members in the process. Assign responsibilities for checking expiration dates, moving stock, and updating the inventory list. Educating your family about the importance of the rotation system not only helps in maintaining it but also instills valuable life skills.

8. **Optimize Storage Conditions**: Ensure that your storage areas provide the optimal conditions for preserving the freshness of your stockpile. This includes maintaining a cool, dry environment for most items and using airtight containers to protect against pests and moisture. Pay particular attention to items that are sensitive to temperature fluctuations or humidity, adjusting their storage conditions as needed.

9. **Regularly Update Your Inventory**: As you add new items to your stockpile or use existing items, make sure to update your inventory spreadsheet accordingly. This ongoing maintenance is crucial for keeping your cycle rotation system effective and ensuring that your stockpile remains fresh and usable.

By following these detailed steps, you can establish a robust cycle rotation system that maximizes the shelf life of your food stockpile, minimizes waste, and ensures that your family has access to fresh, nutritious food at all times. This disciplined approach to managing your food supply is a key component of long-term food security and self-reliance.

Protecting Food Reserves from Pests

Protecting your food reserves from pests and spoilage is a critical aspect of maintaining your long-term food security. Pests such as rodents, insects, and even microorganisms can quickly turn a well-stocked pantry into a wasteland if not properly managed. Similarly, spoilage can result from improper storage conditions, leading to the loss of valuable nutrition and resources. Here's a step-by-step guide to safeguarding your food reserves effectively.

1. **Choose the Right Storage Containers**: Opt for airtight containers made of food-grade materials. Glass jars with screw-on lids, heavy-duty plastic containers with snap lids, and metal containers with tight-fitting lids are excellent choices. These containers not only prevent pests from accessing your food but also reduce exposure to air, which can accelerate spoilage.

2. **Use Oxygen Absorbers**: When storing dry goods such as grains, legumes, and powdered products, include oxygen absorbers in the containers. These small packets effectively remove oxygen from the container, inhibiting the growth of aerobic bacteria and fungi, and preventing oxidation that can lead to spoilage.

3. **Maintain a Cool, Dry Environment**: Store your food reserves in a part of your home that remains cool and dry throughout the year. Basements can be ideal, provided they are not prone to flooding or high humidity. The ideal storage temperature is between 50°F and 70°F. High temperatures can accelerate spoilage, while high humidity can encourage mold growth and attract pests.

4. **Implement Pest Control Measures**: Regularly inspect your storage area for signs of pests. Use traps and baits strategically placed around the perimeter of your storage area to control rodent populations. For insects, consider using pheromone traps or ultraviolet light traps. Ensure that your storage area is sealed off from outside access points, filling any cracks or gaps where pests might enter.

5. **Regularly Inspect Your Stockpile**: At least once every three months, inspect your food reserves for any signs of pest activity or spoilage. Look for telltale signs such as gnaw marks, insect larvae, or changes in the appearance or smell of your stored food. Early detection is key to preventing widespread contamination.

6. **Practice First-In, First-Out Rotation**: Always use the oldest items in your stockpile first and replace them with newer items placed at the back. This rotation ensures that your food does not remain in storage long enough to become susceptible to spoilage or pest infestation.

7. **Keep Your Storage Area Clean**: Regularly clean your storage area to remove food particles and residues that could attract pests. Wipe down shelves and containers with a vinegar solution to deter pests and prevent mold growth. Ensure that any spills are cleaned up promptly to avoid attracting pests.

8. **Vacuum Seal Perishable Items**: For items that are particularly susceptible to spoilage, such as dried fruits, consider vacuum sealing them. This process removes air from the package, significantly extending the shelf life of the food by preventing oxidation and deterring pests.

9. **Store Grains in Freezer for Short Term**: If you have the freezer space, storing grains, flour, and legumes in the freezer for a few days upon bringing them home can kill any insect eggs that might be present. Afterward, transfer them to airtight containers for long-term storage.

10. **Use Natural Repellents**: Certain herbs and essential oils are known to repel pests. Consider placing sachets of dried lavender, mint, or bay leaves in your storage area. Cotton balls soaked in peppermint oil can also deter rodents and insects. However, ensure these natural repellents do not come into direct contact with your food.

By meticulously following these steps, you can protect your food reserves from pests and spoilage, ensuring that your stockpile remains viable and nutritious over the long term. This proactive approach to food storage not only preserves your resources but also contributes to the overall resilience and self-sufficiency of your household in times of need.

DIY Chapter: Food Security Projects

Project Title: Building Shelving Units for Efficient Food Storage

Project Introduction (Description - Benefits - Challenges): This project focuses on creating sturdy, customizable shelving units designed to maximize space and organize your long-term food storage. The benefits include improved accessibility to food items, better inventory management, and optimized storage conditions to extend the shelf life of supplies. Challenges may include accurately measuring and cutting materials, assembling the units to ensure stability, and selecting the right location for the shelving to maintain ideal storage conditions.

Required Materials:
- ¾ inch plywood sheets for shelves and sides
- 2x4 inch lumber for frame support
- Wood screws (2 ½ inches and 1 ½ inches)
- Sandpaper (medium and fine grit)
- Wood sealant or paint
- Metal shelf brackets for additional support (optional)

Required Tools:
- Circular saw or hand saw
- Drill with a variety of bits
- Screwdriver
- Tape measure
- Level
- Carpenter's square
- Paintbrush or roller (if applying sealant or paint)

Detailed Instructions:
1. **Design Your Shelving Unit:** Sketch the design based on your space and storage needs. Consider the weight of the items being stored and plan for adequate support.
2. **Cut the Plywood and Lumber:** Based on your design, cut the plywood for shelves and sides, and the 2x4 lumber for the frame. Use the carpenter's square to ensure straight cuts.
3. **Assemble the Frame:** Using the 2 ½ inch wood screws, assemble the 2x4 lumber into a frame that will support the shelving unit. Use the level to ensure the frame is even.
4. **Attach the Plywood:** Secure the plywood pieces to the frame using 1 ½ inch wood screws. Ensure each shelf is level before attaching.
5. **Sand the Unit:** Sand the entire unit with medium grit sandpaper, followed by fine grit to prepare the surface for sealing or painting.
6. **Apply Sealant or Paint:** Apply a wood sealant or paint to protect the wood and allow it to dry according to the product instructions.

7. **Install Shelf Brackets (Optional):** For additional support, especially for heavier items, install metal shelf brackets under each shelf.

8. **Position the Shelving Unit:** Choose a cool, dry place away from direct sunlight for your shelving unit to ensure the best storage conditions for your food supplies.

Safety:
- Wear safety glasses when cutting wood and sanding.
- Use gloves when handling rough materials or applying sealant.
- Ensure the work area is well-ventilated, especially when applying sealant or paint.

Cost of the Project: Approximately $100-$200, depending on the size of the shelving unit and the materials selected.

Preparation Time: 1-2 days, including drying time for paint or sealant.

Maintenance and Care:
- Regularly check the shelving unit for stability and tighten any loose screws.
- Keep the unit clean and dust-free to maintain a hygienic storage environment.
- Inspect for signs of wear or damage, especially if storing heavy items, and make repairs as needed.

FAQ or Common Issues:
- **Q: What if my shelves sag over time?**
- **A:** Reinforce sagging shelves with additional brackets or supports underneath. Consider using thicker plywood or reducing the span between supports for future projects.
- **Q: How can I protect the wood from moisture?**
- **A:** Apply a waterproof sealant and ensure your storage area has good ventilation. Use a dehumidifier in damp climates to protect both the shelving and food supplies.

Difficulty Rating: ★★★☆☆

Variations:
- Add doors to the front of the shelving unit to protect items from dust and pests.
- Install wheels on the bottom of the unit for easy mobility, especially useful in multi-use spaces or garages.
- Customize shelf heights to accommodate different sizes of storage containers, allowing for more efficient use of space.

Troubleshooting Food Security Projects

1. **Seed Germination Issues**
- Check seed viability by performing a germination test
- Ensure proper soil temperature and moisture levels
- Use a seedling heat mat if necessary to maintain warmth

2. **Pest Infestation**
- Identify the type of pest and research targeted control methods
- Implement natural deterrents like neem oil or diatomaceous earth
- Regularly inspect plants for early signs of infestation

3. **Poor Soil Quality**
- Conduct a soil test to determine pH and nutrient levels
- Amend soil with organic matter such as compost or well-rotted manure
- Rotate crops to improve soil health and reduce disease

4. **Watering Problems**
- Establish a consistent watering schedule based on plant needs

- Use mulch to retain moisture and reduce evaporation
- Install a rainwater collection system for sustainable irrigation

5. Crop Failure
- Analyze environmental factors such as weather and sunlight exposure
- Diversify crops to minimize risk of total loss
- Keep a gardening journal to track successes and failures for future reference

6. Storage Issues
- Ensure proper storage conditions to prevent spoilage
- Use airtight containers to protect against pests and moisture
- Regularly check stored food for signs of spoilage or infestation

7. Preservation Problems
- Follow tested recipes for canning to ensure safety
- Use proper techniques for drying or freezing to maintain quality
- Label and date preserved items for easy rotation and use

8. Resource Limitations
- Prioritize projects based on available space and resources
- Seek community resources or local gardening groups for support
- Consider vertical gardening or container gardening to maximize space

9. Knowledge Gaps
- Invest time in learning through books, online courses, or workshops
- Connect with experienced gardeners for mentorship
- Stay updated on best practices and new techniques in food security

10. Emergency Preparedness
- Create a plan for food security during emergencies or disasters
- Stockpile non-perishable food items and essential supplies
- Develop a network with neighbors for resource sharing during crises

Building shelving units for efficient food storage - be very detailed

Project Introduction (Description - Benefits - Challenges): Crafting shelving units tailored for efficient food storage enhances organization, accessibility, and the longevity of supplies. The project aims to optimize space, streamline inventory checks, and maintain food in ideal conditions to prevent spoilage. Challenges include precise measurement and cutting, ensuring structural integrity, and selecting an appropriate location that maintains optimal storage conditions.

Required Materials:
- Plywood sheets (¾ inch thickness) for shelves and sides
- 2x4 inch lumber for structural frames
- Wood screws (2 ½ inches for frame assembly, 1 ½ inches for attaching plywood)
- Sandpaper (medium grit for initial sanding, fine grit for finish)
- Wood sealant or paint for protection and aesthetics
- Metal shelf brackets (optional for heavy loads)

Required Tools:
- Circular saw or hand saw for cutting materials
- Power drill with various bit sizes
- Screwdriver or drill bit for screws
- Tape measure for accurate measurements
- Level to ensure shelves are even

- Carpenter's square for right angles
- Paintbrush or roller for applying sealant or paint

Detailed Instructions:
1. **Design Planning:** Measure the intended storage area. Draft a shelving unit layout that fits the space and accommodates your storage needs, considering the weight of stored items.
2. **Material Cutting:** Cut plywood sheets for shelves and sides, and 2x4 lumber for the frame, according to your design. Ensure cuts are straight using the carpenter's square.
3. **Frame Assembly:** Construct the frame by connecting 2x4s with 2 ½ inch wood screws. Use the level to verify the frame is square and even.
4. **Shelf Attachment:** Affix plywood shelves to the frame using 1 ½ inch screws. Check each shelf with a level before securing.
5. **Sanding:** Smooth all surfaces with medium grit sandpaper, followed by fine grit to prepare for finishing.
6. **Finishing:** Apply wood sealant or paint with a brush or roller. Allow to dry as per the product's instructions.
7. **Bracket Installation (Optional):** For additional support, especially on wider shelves, install metal brackets beneath each shelf.
8. **Installation:** Place the shelving unit in a cool, dry area away from direct sunlight, ideally with stable temperature and humidity levels.

Safety:
- Wear protective eyewear when cutting or sanding wood.
- Protective gloves are recommended when handling rough materials and during finishing.
- Ensure adequate ventilation when applying sealant or paint.

Cost of the Project: Estimated $100-$200, varying by the size of the unit and choice of materials.

Preparation Time: Approximately 1-2 days, factoring in drying time for finishes.

Maintenance and Care:
- Periodically inspect the unit for loose screws or signs of wear.
- Clean shelves regularly to prevent dust accumulation.
- Reapply sealant or paint as needed to maintain protective coating.

FAQ or Common Issues:
- **Q: How do I prevent the shelves from sagging under heavy weight?**
- **A:** Use thicker plywood or decrease the span between supports. Adding metal brackets can also enhance load-bearing capacity.
- **Q: Can the shelving unit be modified for different sized containers?**
- **A:** Yes, adjust shelf heights during the design phase or add adjustable shelf brackets for flexibility.

Difficulty Rating: ★★★☆☆

Variations:
- Incorporate sliding drawers or bins for small items.
- Add doors to protect contents from dust and pests.
- Modular design for easy expansion or reconfiguration.

Building shelving units for efficient food storage is essential for maximizing your space and ensuring that your supplies are organized and easily accessible Here are some troubleshooting tips to consider during the construction and use of your shelving units

- **Uneven Shelves**: If your shelves are not level, check the floor for unevenness and use shims to adjust the height of the shelving unit legs

- **Weight Distribution**: If shelves sag or bow under the weight of stored items, redistribute the weight more evenly across the shelves or consider reinforcing them with additional brackets
- **Material Selection**: If you notice that the shelves are warping or deteriorating, reassess the materials used and opt for sturdier options like plywood or metal
- **Accessibility Issues**: If items are difficult to reach, consider adjusting the height of the shelves or using pull-out bins for easier access
- **Stability Concerns**: If the shelving unit feels wobbly, ensure that it is anchored securely to the wall and that all screws and fasteners are tightened properly
- **Pest Infestation**: If you encounter pests in your food storage, ensure that all food items are stored in airtight containers and regularly inspect the shelving for signs of infestation
- **Moisture Problems**: If you notice signs of mold or mildew, check for proper ventilation in the storage area and consider using moisture absorbers to keep the environment dry
- **Overcrowding**: If shelves become overcrowded, evaluate your inventory and consider rotating items to ensure that older supplies are used first and that there is enough space for new items

By addressing these common issues, you can create a functional and efficient food storage system that meets your family's needs

Creating a DIY dehydrator for preserving food in bulk - be very detailed

Project Introduction (Description - Benefits - Challenges): Building a DIY dehydrator allows for the efficient preservation of large quantities of food, leveraging the simple yet effective method of removing moisture to extend shelf life. This project is beneficial for creating long-term, sustainable food storage without reliance on electrical dehydrators, making it ideal for off-grid living or emergency preparedness. Challenges include ensuring even airflow, maintaining optimal temperature, and constructing a durable frame.

Required Materials:
- 1x2 inch cedar wood boards for the frame (cedar is naturally resistant to rot and insects)
- Stainless steel mesh for trays (non-toxic and easy to clean)
- Aluminum foil or reflective material for the interior (to enhance heat retention)
- Hinges and latch for the door
- Clear polycarbonate or glass for the door (allows sunlight in while retaining heat)
- High-temperature black paint (for the exterior to absorb more heat)
- Weather stripping for door seal (to minimize heat loss)

Required Tools:
- Saw (hand saw or power saw)
- Drill with screwdriver bits
- Staple gun (for attaching mesh)
- Paintbrush
- Tape measure
- Level
- Scissors (for cutting mesh)

Detailed Instructions:
1. **Construct the Frame:** Cut the cedar boards to create a box frame. The size can vary, but a standard size is 24 inches wide, 36 inches tall, and 18 inches deep. Assemble the frame using screws for a sturdy build.
2. **Add Interior Shelving Supports:** Inside the frame, install horizontal supports where the stainless steel mesh trays will slide in. Space these supports evenly, about 2 inches apart, to allow for adequate airflow between trays.
3. **Prepare and Install the Mesh Trays:** Cut the stainless steel mesh to fit the interior dimensions of the frame, allowing for a half-inch overlap on each side. Staple the mesh onto smaller cedar wood frames that fit snugly into the shelving supports.

4. **Paint the Exterior:** Apply high-temperature black paint to the exterior surfaces of the dehydrator. This enhances heat absorption. Allow the paint to dry completely according to the manufacturer's instructions.

5. **Install the Door:** Attach the clear polycarbonate or glass door to the front of the dehydrator using hinges. Install a latch to keep the door closed. Seal the door edges with weather stripping to retain heat.

6. **Line the Interior with Reflective Material:** Cover the interior surfaces with aluminum foil or another reflective material to improve heat retention and distribution.

7. **Position the Dehydrator:** Choose an area with maximum direct sunlight exposure, ideally south-facing, with minimal shading from trees or structures during the day.

Safety:
- Wear protective gloves when handling and cutting the stainless steel mesh to avoid cuts.
- Use safety glasses when sawing wood or drilling to protect your eyes from debris.
- Ensure the dehydrator is placed on a stable, level surface to prevent tipping.

Cost of the Project: Approximately $100-$200, depending on the size of the dehydrator and the materials sourced.

Preparation Time: 1-2 days, including drying time for paint and assembly.

Maintenance and Care:
- Regularly check and clean the mesh trays to prevent food residue buildup.
- Inspect the dehydrator for any signs of wear, especially the door seal and mesh integrity.
- Cover or store the dehydrator in a protected area during adverse weather to prolong its lifespan.

FAQ or Common Issues:
- **Q: How can I increase the temperature inside the dehydrator if it's not hot enough?**
- **A:** Enhance heat absorption by ensuring the dehydrator is properly oriented towards the sun and consider adding more reflective surfaces inside.
- **Q: What if the food is drying unevenly?**
- **A:** Rotate the trays periodically to promote even drying. Ensure that food slices are uniform in thickness.

Difficulty Rating: ★★★☆☆

Variations:
- Add a solar-powered fan to improve air circulation for more efficient drying.
- Construct a dual-chamber dehydrator with one section painted black for heat absorption and another clear for enhanced sunlight penetration, improving temperature regulation.

To create a DIY dehydrator for preserving food in bulk, it's essential to understand the common issues that may arise during the process. Here's a troubleshooting guide to help you address potential problems effectively

Troubleshooting Guide:

1. **Dehydrator Not Heating Up**
- Check the power source to ensure it's plugged in and functioning
- Inspect the heating element for any visible damage or wear
- Ensure that the thermostat is set to the correct temperature

2. **Uneven Drying**
- Rotate trays periodically to promote even airflow
- Avoid overcrowding trays; leave space between food items
- Ensure that food is cut into uniform sizes for consistent drying

3. **Food is Not Drying Properly**

- Increase the temperature setting if food is still moist after the recommended drying time
- Check humidity levels in the room; high humidity can affect drying efficiency
- Ensure that the dehydrator is well-ventilated to allow moisture to escape

4. Food is Over-Dried or Burnt
- Reduce the temperature setting to prevent excessive heat exposure
- Monitor the drying process closely, especially for delicate items like herbs or fruits
- Use a timer to keep track of drying times and avoid leaving food unattended

5. Unpleasant Odors During Drying
- Clean the dehydrator thoroughly before use to remove any residual odors
- Ensure that food is fresh and free from spoilage before dehydrating
- Consider using a fan to improve air circulation and reduce odors

6. Dehydrated Food is Sticking to Trays
- Use parchment paper or silicone mats to line trays for easy removal
- Lightly oil the trays before placing food on them to prevent sticking
- Allow food to cool slightly before attempting to remove it from the trays

By following these troubleshooting tips, you can enhance your DIY dehydrator experience and ensure that your food preservation efforts are successful

BOOK 5: WATER SECURITY & MANAGEMENT

Establishing a water reserve is a critical step in ensuring your family's safety and self-sufficiency during emergencies or long-term crises. A well-planned water reserve provides a reliable source of water for drinking, cooking, and basic hygiene, which is essential for maintaining health and well-being when regular water sources become compromised. The first step in creating a robust water security plan involves identifying suitable water sources that can be stored for long-term use. This includes municipal water, which should be stored properly to prevent contamination, and natural water sources such as rainwater, which can be collected and purified for storage. When selecting water containers, it's crucial to choose options that are made from food-grade materials and are designed to prevent the growth of harmful bacteria. Polyethylene-based plastics, which are BPA-free, are a popular choice due to their durability and safety for storing drinking water. These containers come in various sizes, from portable 5-gallon jugs to large 55-gallon barrels, allowing for flexibility in storage capacity based on your family's needs and available space.

For optimal storage, water containers should be placed in a cool, dark area of your home, such as a basement or a dedicated storage room, to minimize exposure to light and heat which can degrade water quality over time. It's also important to ensure that your storage area is accessible in case of an emergency but secure enough to prevent contamination or tampering. To maintain the purity of the water, it's advisable to rotate your stockpile every six months, using the older supplies first and replenishing them with fresh water. This rotation not only ensures the water remains fresh but also provides an opportunity to inspect the containers for any signs of damage or leaks, which could compromise the safety of the water.

In addition to storing municipal or tap water, collecting rainwater is an effective way to supplement your water reserve. Setting up a rainwater harvesting system can be as simple as placing a clean barrel or a specially designed rainwater collection tank under a downspout of your home's gutter system. However, it's essential to use a first-flush diverter, which ensures the initial runoff, which may contain contaminants from the roof, is not collected, and only clean water enters your storage container. The collected rainwater should then be filtered and purified before being used for drinking or cooking to ensure it's free from pathogens and pollutants.

The purification of collected water, whether it's from rainwater or another source, can be achieved through various methods. Boiling is the most straightforward method, where water is heated to a rolling boil for at least one minute to kill any bacteria or viruses. Chemical purification, using household bleach or water purification tablets, is another effective method, especially for treating large quantities of water. However, it's crucial to follow the recommended dosages to ensure the water is safe for consumption. For a more long-term solution, investing in a high-quality water filter system, capable of removing bacteria, viruses, and other contaminants, can provide a reliable source of clean water for your family.

By taking these initial steps to identify, collect, and store water, you're laying the foundation for a comprehensive water security plan that will ensure your family has access to this vital resource in times of need.

To further enhance your water security plan, consider the implementation of a greywater recycling system for non-potable uses. Greywater, which is wastewater from sinks, showers, and washing machines, can be treated and reused for irrigation, flushing toilets, and cleaning, significantly reducing the demand on your primary water reserve. Setting up a basic greywater system involves redirecting the drainage from these sources to a filtration system, which can be as simple as a series of tanks or barrels equipped with filters to remove solids and impurities. The filtered water should then be stored separately from your potable water supply and clearly labeled to avoid any cross-contamination. It's important to use biodegradable soaps and detergents to ensure the greywater does not harm your garden plants or soil quality.

Creating contingency plans for water shortages and emergencies is another critical aspect of water security. This includes mapping out alternative water sources in your area, such as streams, lakes, or public wells, and understanding how to safely extract and purify water from these sources. Portable water filters, purification tablets, and collapsible containers should be included in your emergency kit, allowing you to collect and treat water on the go. Additionally, educating your family on water conservation techniques, such as capturing rainwater for garden use, fixing leaks promptly, and reducing water usage during drought conditions, can help extend your water reserve during prolonged emergencies.

For those looking to take their water security to the next level, building a rainwater harvesting system for home use can provide a substantial supplement to your water supply. This system involves the installation of larger collection tanks, more sophisticated filtration and purification systems, and possibly a pump to distribute the water throughout your home for non-potable uses. The design of your system should take into account the average rainfall in your area, the roof catchment area, and your family's water usage to determine the necessary storage capacity. Materials for a more advanced rainwater harvesting system might include PVC piping for gutters and downspouts, first-flush diverters, mesh filters to keep out debris, large storage tanks or cisterns, and UV or reverse osmosis filters for purification. Regular maintenance of your rainwater harvesting system, including cleaning gutters, inspecting tanks for leaks, and replacing filters, will ensure it remains an effective component of your water security strategy.

In addition to these practical measures, staying informed about local water issues, such as contamination risks, drought conditions, and water restrictions, can help you adapt your water security plan as needed. Joining community-based water conservation programs or workshops can also provide valuable insights and resources for enhancing your home's water resilience.

By integrating these strategies into your overall water security and management plan, you can ensure that your family remains prepared and self-sufficient in the face of water-related challenges. Whether it's through efficient storage, conservation practices, or the development of alternative water sources, taking proactive steps now will safeguard your access to this essential resource, regardless of what the future holds.

CHAPTER 1: ESTABLISHING A WATER RESERVE

When embarking on the journey of establishing a water reserve for your home, the first and most critical step is to accurately calculate the amount of water your family will need in an emergency situation. This calculation should not only account for drinking water but also for cooking, personal hygiene, and other essential uses. A general guideline is to allocate at least one gallon of water per person per day. However, considering the unpredictability of emergencies, it's prudent to aim for a supply that can sustain your household for a minimum of two weeks.

To begin, list each family member and calculate daily water needs individually, then multiply this by the number of days you're planning for. Don't forget to include pets in your calculations, as they too will need a clean water supply. For instance, a family of four with a medium-sized dog would require at least five gallons of water per day, equating to seventy gallons for a two-week period.

Once you have determined the total volume of water needed, the next step is selecting the appropriate storage containers. Opt for food-grade, BPA-free containers that are specifically designed for water storage. These containers come in various sizes, from portable 5-gallon jugs to larger 55-gallon barrels. When choosing containers, consider the space available in your home for storage. It's essential to store water in a cool, dark place to prevent bacterial growth and to preserve the quality of the water. Spaces such as a basement, a garage, or a dedicated storage closet are ideal, provided they remain consistently cool and are not exposed to direct sunlight.

In addition to the primary large containers, having a number of smaller, portable containers is advisable. These can be invaluable in situations where you may need to relocate or if access to your main water supply is compromised. Portable containers should also be made of durable, food-grade material and equipped with secure, leak-proof lids.

Filling your containers properly is just as important as selecting them. If you're using tap water that's been treated by a municipal water system, it's generally safe to store without additional treatment. Fill the containers to the top to minimize the air space, as oxygen can promote bacterial growth over time. After filling, tightly seal the containers and label each with the date of storage. This practice will help you keep track of your water supply and ensure rotation if necessary.

For those relying on well water or natural water sources, purification before storage is crucial. Water from these sources should be filtered and disinfected to remove any pathogens, chemicals, or sediments. Boiling is the most reliable method of disinfection; however, chemical treatments with specific proportions of household bleach or water purification tablets can also be effective. Follow the recommended guidelines for purification to ensure the safety of your stored water.

Remember, establishing a water reserve is an ongoing process that requires regular maintenance. Every six months, inspect your water supply for any signs of container damage or water contamination. If using municipal water, you can rotate your supply by using the stored water for gardening or other non-drinking purposes and then replenishing your storage with fresh water. This rotation ensures your emergency water supply remains fresh and safe for consumption.

By following these detailed steps, you are not only securing a vital resource for your family's survival in emergencies but also instilling a sense of preparedness and resilience.

To further enhance the reliability of your water reserve, consider incorporating water treatment solutions that can be used on an as-needed basis. This includes having a stockpile of water purification tablets, a high-quality water filter, and even a small, portable distillation unit. These items can be critical in situations where your stored water might become compromised or if you need to purify water from alternative sources. For instance, a water filter designed to remove bacteria, protozoa, and viruses can make nearly any water source safe for drinking. Look for filters that meet or exceed EPA standards for water purification.

Additionally, understanding the proper use and maintenance of these purification devices is essential. Regularly review the manufacturer's instructions and practice using these devices to ensure you're prepared to operate them under stress or in less-than-ideal conditions. For water purification tablets, familiarize yourself with the correct dosage and contact time required for effective treatment. This knowledge will be invaluable during emergencies when access to clean water might be limited.

Another critical aspect of managing your water reserve is to develop a comprehensive plan for water rationing in the event of a prolonged crisis. While it's important to have a generous supply, circumstances may arise that limit your access to water for an extended period. In such cases, knowing how to prioritize water usage for drinking, cooking, and hygiene can conserve your supply until it can be replenished. Establish guidelines for minimal water usage and educate all family members on these practices. For example, limiting showers, reusing cooking water for cleaning, and minimizing the use of water for cleaning tasks can significantly extend your water reserve.

In addition to personal use, consider the needs of any homegrown food sources or critical plant life. While human hydration and hygiene are the priorities, having a plan for drip irrigation or minimal water use for essential gardening can help sustain a food source without depleting your primary water reserve. This might include collecting and using greywater for irrigation or setting up a rain barrel system to capture water specifically for this purpose.

Lastly, staying informed about the status of local water sources and community water management plans is crucial. In the event of a natural disaster or other emergency, local authorities may provide guidance or resources for accessing clean water. Being connected with your community through local emergency networks or social media groups can provide timely information that might impact your water usage and replenishment plans.

By taking these comprehensive steps to establish, maintain, and manage your water reserve, you're not only preparing your household for short-term emergencies but also ensuring your long-term resilience in various crisis situations. Regularly reviewing and updating your water security plan, based on changing needs or advancements in water purification technology, will keep your strategy effective and your family safe. Remember, water is a fundamental resource that requires careful planning and management to ensure its availability and safety in times of need.

Identifying and Storing Water Sources

Identifying and storing water sources for long-term crises involves a strategic approach to ensure you have a reliable supply of water in emergency situations. The first step in this process is to assess potential water sources that are accessible to you. This could include municipal water supplies, natural water bodies such as rivers, lakes, and streams, rainwater collection, and even dew collection methods. Each source has its unique considerations for purification and storage to ensure safety and longevity.

For municipal water, it's advisable to store this water in food-grade, BPA-free containers. These containers should be thoroughly cleaned and sanitized before filling them. Fill the containers to the brim to minimize the presence of oxygen, which can promote bacterial growth. It's crucial to label each container with the date of storage and to store them in a cool, dark place, ideally at temperatures between 50°F and 70°F to maintain water quality over time. Regular rotation of this water every six months ensures freshness and usability.

Natural water sources require more rigorous treatment before storage. First, identify nearby rivers, lakes, or streams that could serve as potential water sources. Before considering storage, water from these sources must be purified to remove pathogens and contaminants. Filtration systems designed to remove bacteria, protozoa, and viruses are essential, followed by chemical treatment with water purification tablets or household bleach in the correct proportions to ensure safety. Once treated, this water can be stored similarly to municipal water, in clean, sanitized, food-grade containers, away from direct sunlight and at stable, cool temperatures.

Rainwater collection presents a sustainable option for long-term water storage. Setting up a rainwater harvesting system involves collecting runoff from your roof into barrels or tanks. It's important to use a first-flush diverter to ensure the initial, potentially contaminated water is not collected. The collected rainwater should then be filtered to remove debris and treated to eliminate pathogens before being stored. Large, dark-colored barrels made of food-grade material are ideal for storing rainwater, as they prevent light penetration, reducing the risk of algae growth. Ensure these barrels are covered and fitted with a screen to prevent the entry of insects and debris.

Dew collection, though less common, can supplement your water supply. This involves laying out clean, absorbent cloths or sheets overnight in areas where dew formation is likely, such as grassy fields or metal surfaces. In the morning, wring out the collected water into a container and purify it before storage.

For all these water sources, the key to long-term storage is ensuring the water is free from contaminants before sealing it in containers. Use of oxygen absorbers in sealed containers can further extend the shelf life of stored water by preventing oxidation. Additionally, inspecting your stored water supply regularly for signs of contamination or leaks and maintaining cleanliness around storage areas are critical steps in ensuring your water reserve remains safe and reliable over time.

In summary, identifying and storing water sources for long-term crises requires careful planning, preparation, and maintenance. By assessing available water sources, treating and purifying water according to specific source requirements, and adhering to best practices for storage, you can secure a vital water supply to support your household in emergency situations.

Water Containers and Storage Methods

Selecting the right water containers and employing effective storage methods are critical steps in establishing a resilient water reserve for your home. The choice of containers and how you store them can significantly impact the longevity and safety of your water supply. Here's a detailed guide to help you make informed decisions in this regard.

Firstly, focus on the material of the water containers. Food-grade plastic, specifically those labeled as HDPE (High-Density Polyethylene) or #2 plastic, is highly recommended due to its durability and safety for storing drinking water. These containers are designed to not leach harmful chemicals into the water, ensuring it remains safe for consumption over time. Stainless steel containers are another excellent option, especially for those looking for a more robust and rodent-proof solution. However, ensure the steel is not treated with any interior lining that might interact with the water, as this can introduce contaminants.

When selecting the size of the containers, consider both portability and storage capacity. For individual use, containers ranging from 5 to 7 gallons are manageable to transport if evacuation becomes necessary. For stationary, long-term storage, larger containers such as 55-gallon drums or IBC (Intermediate Bulk Container) totes, which can hold up to 275 gallons, are more suitable. These larger containers offer a substantial volume of water but require a dedicated space and should be placed on a solid, level surface to prevent any risk of tipping or cracking.

The location of water storage is another critical factor. Choose a cool, dark place to store your water containers, as sunlight and heat can promote algae and bacteria growth, even in sealed containers. A basement or a dedicated storage room that doesn't experience extreme temperature fluctuations is ideal. If outdoor storage is your only option, ensure containers are well-protected from direct sunlight, perhaps by storing them in a sturdy shed or under a tarp that blocks UV rays.

To maintain the quality of the stored water, consider adding a small amount of unscented bleach (approximately 8 drops per gallon) before sealing the containers. This will help in preventing microbial growth. It's also essential to rotate your water supply every six months to a year, replacing it with fresh water and sanitizing the containers to ensure the water remains safe for consumption.

For those living in areas prone to freezing temperatures, it's crucial to leave some space in each container to allow for expansion as the water freezes, preventing the container from cracking. Conversely, in very hot climates, ensure that your storage location is ventilated to avoid excessive pressure build-up inside the containers that could lead to leaks or bursts.

Lastly, always label your water containers with the date of storage and the date for next rotation. This practice will help you keep track of your water supply's freshness and ensure that you're always prepared with a safe and reliable water source.

By following these detailed recommendations for selecting and managing your water containers, you can establish a secure and sustainable water reserve that adheres to the principles of Navy SEAL preparedness, ensuring your family's safety and resilience in any situation.

Locating Natural Water Sources

In the quest for establishing a resilient water reserve, identifying natural water sources in both wilderness and urban settings is a critical skill. This endeavor requires a keen understanding of the environment and the ability to apply practical techniques for locating water that can sustain you and your family during a crisis. Here's how to approach this task with precision and safety in mind.

Wilderness Water Sources:

1. **Follow Animal Tracks:** Animals instinctively head towards water sources. Observing the direction of animal tracks, especially in the early morning or late afternoon, can lead you to natural water sources. Look for paths beaten down by wildlife, as these often lead to streams or ponds.

2. **Look for Vegetation:** Lush, green vegetation in an otherwise dry area often indicates the presence of water nearby. Trees such as willows, cottonwoods, and cattails grow near water. In desert landscapes, birds circling overhead can also indicate the presence of water.

3. **Utilize Topography:** Valleys and low-lying areas collect rainwater and may host streams or springs. If you're in a mountainous area, head downhill, as water flows down due to gravity. Rocky crevices at lower elevations are potential sites for springs.

4. **Morning Dew:** Collecting morning dew can be a labor-intensive but effective method to gather water. Use a clean cloth to absorb dew from grass and plants, then wring the water into a container. This method is more about supplementing your water supply rather than fulfilling all your needs.

Urban Water Sources:

1. **Rainwater Harvesting:** Set up systems to collect rainwater from rooftops. Use food-grade barrels or large containers to catch water from downspouts. Ensure the roof materials are non-toxic and the water is filtered and purified before use.

2. **Air Conditioning Units:** Air conditioners condense moisture from the air, producing water that's often drained away. Collect this water in clean containers. Although generally safe, it's advisable to purify this water before drinking.

3. **Water Heaters and Toilet Tanks:** In an emergency, water heaters can provide gallons of potable water. The water in the upper tank of a toilet (not the bowl) is also typically clean, though it should be purified as a precaution.

4. **Public Fountains and Water Features:** Many urban areas have decorative fountains, water features, or even emergency water stations in public parks. While these should not be your first choice due to potential contamination, they can be considered in dire situations if the water is treated before consumption.

Safety and Purification:

Regardless of the source, always purify water before use. Boiling is the most effective method, ensuring water reaches a rolling boil for at least one minute to kill pathogens. Chemical purification with unscented household bleach (8 drops per gallon) or iodine, and filtration using a portable filter with a pore size of 0.2 microns or smaller, are also reliable methods.

Mapping and Documentation:

Keep a detailed map or document of all identified water sources in your area, including the following elements to enhance your preparedness and ensure you have reliable access to water in emergencies

1. **Source Type**: Identify whether the water source is a river, lake, pond, spring, or well, as different sources may have varying levels of accessibility and reliability

2. **Location Coordinates**: Record the GPS coordinates or a clear description of the location to facilitate easy navigation, especially in low visibility conditions

3. **Seasonal Reliability**: Note the reliability of each source throughout the year, indicating any seasonal variations that may affect water availability, such as droughts or heavy rainfall

4. **Water Quality Assessment**: Include observations on the water quality, such as clarity, color, and odor, which can help you determine if the water is safe to use without purification

5. **Purification Steps**: Document any necessary purification steps required for each source, such as boiling, filtration, or chemical treatment, to ensure the water is safe for consumption

6. **Access Routes**: Map out the best routes to reach each water source, considering factors like terrain, obstacles, and potential hazards that may impede access

7. **Legal Considerations**: Be aware of any legal restrictions regarding water collection in your area, as some locations may have regulations that you need to follow

8. **Backup Sources**: Identify alternative water sources in case your primary options become unavailable, ensuring you have multiple strategies for securing water

This resource will prove invaluable in emergency situations, providing you with multiple options to secure water.

By applying these strategies with diligence and care, you can effectively locate and utilize natural water sources, ensuring a vital component of your survival strategy is well in hand.

CHAPTER 2: WATER PURIFICATION AND FILTRATION

Ensuring the safety and purity of your water supply is paramount in any survival situation. Waterborne pathogens, including bacteria, viruses, and protozoa, can pose serious health risks. To mitigate these risks, it's essential to understand and apply effective water purification and filtration techniques. This section delves into various methods, focusing on practicality and accessibility for individuals with varying levels of knowledge and resources.

Boiling Water

Boiling is the most straightforward and effective method to purify water. It doesn't require any specialized equipment beyond a heat source and a pot. Here's how to properly boil water for purification:

1. Fill a pot with water, leaving some space at the top to prevent boiling over.
2. Place the pot on a heat source and bring the water to a rolling boil.
3. Keep the water boiling for at least one minute. At altitudes above 5,000 feet, extend the boiling time to three minutes to account for the lower boiling point of water.
4. Let the water cool before drinking or storing it. To improve the taste, pour the water back and forth between two clean containers to aerate it.

Chemical Purification

Chemical purification involves adding substances like iodine or chlorine bleach to kill microorganisms. This method is useful when boiling is not an option.

1. Iodine: Add five drops of 2% tincture of iodine to each quart (liter) of clear water. For cloudy water, use ten drops. Stir and let it stand for at least 30 minutes before use.
2. Chlorine bleach: Use unscented household bleach that contains 5.25% to 6% sodium hypochlorite. Add eight drops to one gallon (about 3.8 liters) of water. Double the dosage for cloudy or colored water. Stir and let it stand for 30 minutes.

Solar Disinfection (SODIS)

Solar disinfection uses sunlight to kill pathogens in water. This method requires clear plastic PET bottles and sunlight.

1. Fill clear PET bottles with water, leaving some space at the top.
2. Shake the bottles to oxygenate the water, enhancing the effectiveness of the process.
3. Place the bottles on a reflective surface, such as a metal roof or aluminum foil, and expose them to full sunlight.
4. Leave the bottles in the sun for at least six hours on a sunny day or two consecutive days if it's overcast.

Filtration Systems

Portable water filters are a practical option for removing pathogens. When selecting a filter, consider the pore size—0.2 microns or smaller is effective against most bacteria and protozoa.

1. Before using, prime the filter as directed by the manufacturer.
2. Fill the source container with water, attach the filter, and pump or squeeze the water through to a clean container.

3. Clean and dry the filter after each use according to the manufacturer's instructions to maintain its effectiveness.

Homemade Water Filter

Creating a simple water filter can reduce particulates and improve the taste, although it should be used in conjunction with boiling or chemical treatment to ensure safety.

1. Cut the bottom off a large plastic bottle and invert it.
2. Layer clean sand, activated charcoal, gravel, and more sand inside the bottle.
3. Pour water through the filter into a clean container. Repeat if necessary to improve clarity.

Ultraviolet (UV) Light Purification

Handheld UV light purifiers are effective against a wide range of pathogens. They're particularly useful for travelers and those with limited access to other purification methods.

1. Fill a container with water and stir it to disperse any particles.
2. Insert the UV light purifier and turn it on, stirring the water gently to expose all areas to the light.
3. Follow the manufacturer's recommended exposure time, usually about one minute per liter.

Each of these methods has its advantages and limitations. Boiling and chemical treatments are highly effective but can alter the taste of water. Solar disinfection and filtration offer more convenience but may require specific conditions or equipment. Understanding these methods allows you to choose the most appropriate technique based on your situation, ensuring you always have access to safe drinking water.

Designing and installing a rainwater collection system

Project Introduction (Description - Benefits - Challenges)

Creating a rainwater collection system is an efficient way to harness natural resources to supplement your water supply. This project involves designing and installing a system that captures, stores, and makes rainwater available for non-potable uses such as irrigation, washing cars, or flushing toilets. Benefits include reducing dependence on municipal water systems, lowering water bills, and promoting sustainable water use. Challenges include navigating local regulations on rainwater harvesting, ensuring the system is properly filtered to prevent debris accumulation, and maintaining water quality.

Required Materials

- Gutters and downspouts (preferably PVC or aluminum for durability)
- First flush diverter (to discard the initial rainwater which may contain contaminants)
- Mesh screen or leaf guards (to keep debris and insects out)
- Rainwater storage tank (food-grade polyethylene tank, capacity depending on need and space)
- Stand or platform for the tank (to elevate the tank for gravity-fed pressure)
- PVC pipes and fittings (for connecting components)
- Water filtration system (for basic filtering of collected water)
- Overflow valve (to redirect excess water away from the foundation)
- Hose bib or spigot (for easy access to the stored water)

Required Tools

- Drill with various bits
- Saw (for cutting PVC pipes and modifying gutters if necessary)
- Tape measure
- Level

- PVC cement
- Silicone sealant
- Safety glasses
- Gloves

Detailed Instructions

1. **Assess Roof and Gutter System**: Ensure your roof and gutters are in good condition, capable of channeling rainwater efficiently. Install or repair gutters and downspouts as needed.

2. **Install Leaf Guards and Mesh Screen**: Attach leaf guards to gutters and a mesh screen at the top of the downspout to filter out debris and insects.

3. **Set Up First Flush Diverter**: Install a first flush diverter on the downspout. This device captures the initial flow of rainwater, which may contain contaminants from the roof, and diverts it away from the storage tank.

4. **Position Rainwater Storage Tank**: Place the tank on a solid, level stand or platform to ensure stability and to utilize gravity for water pressure. Ensure it's close enough to the downspout for easy connection.

5. **Connect Downspout to Tank**: Use PVC pipes to channel water from the downspout to the tank. Include an overflow valve in the system to handle excess water during heavy rainfall.

6. **Install Filtration System**: Set up a basic filtration system between the downspout and the storage tank to remove smaller particles. This can be as simple as a mesh filter.

7. **Secure Tank with Overflow Valve**: Ensure the tank has an overflow valve that redirects water away from your home's foundation when the tank is full.

8. **Install Hose Bib or Spigot**: Attach a hose bib or spigot at the bottom of the tank for easy access to the water.

Safety

- Wear safety glasses and gloves when cutting PVC pipes and handling tools.
- Ensure the platform or stand for the tank is securely built to handle the weight of a full tank.
- Follow local regulations and guidelines for rainwater harvesting to ensure safe and legal installation.

Cost of the Project

Approximately $200-$500, varying by the size of the system and the capacity of the storage tank.

Preparation Time

1-2 days, depending on the complexity of the system and site-specific requirements.

Maintenance and Care

- Regularly check and clean gutters, downspouts, and mesh filters to ensure efficient water collection.
- Inspect the tank and connections periodically for leaks or damage.
- Clean the first flush diverter and filtration system as recommended by the manufacturer to maintain water quality.

FAQ or Common Issues

- **Q: Can collected rainwater be used for drinking?**
- **A:** While technically possible with proper filtration and purification, this guide focuses on non-potable uses. For potable uses, additional treatment and testing would be required to ensure safety.
- **Q: What if my tank overflows during heavy rain?**
- **A:** An overflow valve is crucial to direct excess water away from the foundation of your home. Consider installing additional storage or a rain garden to utilize overflow.

Difficulty Rating

★★★☆☆

Variations

- Incorporate a solar-powered pump for areas requiring water distribution uphill or over long distances.
- Add a rain garden or infiltration basin as an overflow solution to enhance groundwater recharge and landscape irrigation.
- For colder climates, consider a winter bypass system to prevent freezing and damage to the collection system.

When designing and installing a rainwater collection system, it's essential to anticipate potential issues that may arise during operation. Here's a troubleshooting list to help you address common problems:

- **Clogged Gutters and Downspouts**: Regularly inspect and clean your gutters and downspouts to ensure water flows freely into your collection system
- **Overflowing Storage Tanks**: Install an overflow pipe to redirect excess water away from your foundation and ensure your tank has a proper drainage system
- **Contaminated Water**: Use first-flush diverters to prevent debris and contaminants from entering your storage tank, and consider adding a filtration system for additional safety
- **Leaks in the System**: Check all connections and seals for leaks, and use appropriate sealants or replace damaged components as needed
- **Insufficient Water Collection**: Evaluate the size of your catchment area and storage tank; consider expanding your system if you consistently run low on water
- **Algae Growth**: Keep your storage tank covered to block sunlight and reduce algae growth, and clean the tank periodically to maintain water quality
- **Pest Infestation**: Ensure that all openings are screened to prevent insects and animals from accessing your water supply

By addressing these common issues proactively, you can ensure that your rainwater collection system operates efficiently and provides a reliable source of water for your home and family

SEAL-Endorsed Water Purification Methods

In any survival scenario, ensuring access to safe drinking water is paramount. Navy SEALs, trained to survive in diverse environments, rely on proven water purification methods adaptable to any situation. These methods, endorsed by SEALs, are designed for efficiency, effectiveness, and practicality, ensuring you can secure safe drinking water whether in a remote wilderness or an urban setting. Here we delve into these SEAL-endorsed techniques, providing detailed guidance on implementing them in various scenarios.

Distillation

Distillation is a process that mimics the natural water cycle, involving evaporation and condensation to remove impurities, including salts, heavy metals, and bacteria. To set up a basic distillation system:

1. Fill a pot halfway with water from your source.

2. Place a smaller pot or collection container inside the larger pot. Ensure the smaller pot is floating and not touching the bottom.

3. Invert the lid of the larger pot so that it creates a concave shape. This will allow evaporated water to condense and drip into the smaller container.

4. Bring the water to a gentle boil. As it evaporates, it will condense on the lid and drip into the smaller container, leaving impurities behind.

5. To enhance condensation, place ice or cold water on the inverted lid. This temperature difference accelerates the condensation process.

6. Collect the distilled water from the smaller pot, which is now safe for drinking.

Reverse Osmosis (RO)

Reverse osmosis is a filtration method that uses a semipermeable membrane to remove ions, unwanted molecules, and larger particles from drinking water. For a DIY approach in a survival scenario:

1. Obtain a RO filtration unit designed for portable use. These units are compact and can be operated manually.

2. Connect the feed water line to your water source. Ensure the source water is pre-filtered to remove large particulates that could clog the RO membrane.

3. Apply pressure to the system, typically through a hand pump mechanism, forcing water through the RO membrane.

4. Collect the purified water from the output line. The process is slow but yields high-purity water.

5. Regularly clean and maintain the RO membrane according to the manufacturer's instructions to ensure its longevity and effectiveness.

Chlorination

Chlorination is a chemical process that eliminates microorganisms in water. While not the primary choice due to its taste and potential health effects with long-term use, it's effective in emergency situations:

1. Use household liquid bleach containing 5.25% to 6% sodium hypochlorite. Avoid using scented or color-safe bleaches.

2. Add 2 drops of bleach per quart (liter) of clear water. For cloudy water, double the amount.

3. Stir the water and let it stand for at least 30 minutes. The water should have a slight chlorine odor. If not, repeat the dose and let it stand for another 15 minutes.

Ultraviolet (UV) Light Sterilization

UV light sterilization is a method that uses ultraviolet light to kill or inactivate microorganisms by disrupting their DNA, rendering them harmless:

1. Portable UV sterilizers are available and can be powered by batteries or solar chargers, making them suitable for field use.

2. Fill a clear water container and stir to disperse any particulates.

3. Insert the UV light into the water and turn it on. Stir the water gently to ensure all parts are exposed to the UV light.

4. Expose the water to UV light for the manufacturer-recommended time, typically around one minute per liter.

5. The water is now safe to drink. Ensure the UV device is kept clean and the bulb is replaced as per the manufacturer's guidelines to maintain effectiveness.

CHAPTER 3: MAINTAINING WATER SECURITY

Ensuring the security of your water supply involves vigilant monitoring and regular maintenance to prevent contamination and ensure availability during emergencies. One critical aspect of maintaining water security is the implementation of a greywater recycling system for non-potable uses. This system allows you to reuse water from sinks, showers, and laundry, reducing the demand on your primary water reserve. Here's how to set up a basic greywater recycling system using readily available materials and straightforward techniques.

First, identify the sources of greywater in your home, which typically include bathroom sinks, showers, and washing machines. Kitchen sinks are generally not recommended due to the higher risk of contamination from food residues. Once you've identified suitable greywater sources, you'll need to divert this water from the sewage line. This can be achieved by installing a three-way valve in the plumbing beneath each source, which allows you to switch between directing water to the sewage system or to your greywater recycling system.

For the collection and storage of greywater, use a food-grade 55-gallon drum or a similar container. Place this container at a lower elevation than your greywater sources to facilitate gravity-fed flow, minimizing the need for additional pumps. If gravity feed is not feasible due to your home's layout, a small sump pump can be installed to transport water from the source to the storage container. Ensure the container is covered to prevent debris entry and reduce evaporation, and consider adding a mesh filter at the entry point to catch hair and other solids.

Before using greywater for irrigation or other non-potable purposes, it's essential to filter it to remove particulates and reduce odors. A simple filtration system can be constructed using layers of gravel, sand, and activated charcoal in a large bucket or barrel with holes drilled at the bottom for drainage. Pass greywater through this filter to improve its quality before use. Remember, even filtered greywater should not be used on edible plants unless it is further treated to remove pathogens.

To distribute greywater for irrigation, connect a hose or PVC piping from the storage container to the areas you intend to water. Use a drip irrigation system or soaker hoses to apply water directly to the soil, avoiding contact with plant leaves to minimize the risk of spreading pathogens. It's also advisable to rotate the areas you irrigate with greywater to prevent soil saturation and the buildup of salts or potential contaminants.

Regular maintenance of your greywater recycling system is crucial for its efficiency and safety. Clean the filters monthly, inspect the storage container and plumbing for leaks, and flush the system with clean water every few months to prevent clogging and the accumulation of unwanted residues. Additionally, monitor the plants and soil in the areas irrigated with greywater for any signs of distress, which may indicate the need for adjustments in your system.

By following these detailed steps to implement and maintain a greywater recycling system, you can significantly enhance your home's water security. This system not only conserves precious freshwater resources but also provides a sustainable solution for managing household water, aligning with the Navy SEAL principle of resourcefulness and resilience in the face of challenges.

Safe Water Storage Practices

Ensuring your water remains uncontaminated over time is paramount for maintaining a healthy, safe environment for you and your family. Contamination can occur through various means, including the introduction of bacteria, viruses, or chemical pollutants into your water supply. To mitigate these risks, it's essential to adopt rigorous storage practices that align with the Navy SEALs' emphasis on preparedness and resilience. Here, we delve into the initial steps and considerations for safeguarding your water against contamination, focusing on container selection, preparation, and the initial phase of storage.

Selecting the appropriate containers for water storage is your first line of defense against contamination. Containers made of food-grade plastic or stainless steel are ideal choices. Food-grade plastic containers, marked with a recycling symbol #2, HDPE (High-Density Polyethylene), are designed to be safe for long-term water storage, as they do not leach harmful chemicals into the water. Stainless steel containers offer durability and resistance against physical damage, but it's crucial to ensure they are not lined with any material that could interact with water. Regardless of the material, all containers should be new or thoroughly cleaned and sanitized before use to remove any residues or contaminants that could affect the water quality.

Preparing your containers for water storage involves a meticulous cleaning process. Begin by washing the containers with hot, soapy water to remove any dirt, residues, or manufacturing chemicals. Rinse them thoroughly with clean water to ensure no soap remains. Next, sanitize the containers by rinsing them with a solution made from one teaspoon of unscented household bleach per quart of water. Allow the containers to air dry completely before filling them with water. This sanitization step is crucial for eliminating any bacteria or viruses that might be present on the container surfaces, ensuring that your stored water remains safe for consumption.

When filling your containers with water, it's advisable to use a potable water source that has already been treated, such as tap water from a municipal system. If you're using water from a well or natural source, it should be purified before storage to remove any pathogens or contaminants. Fill the containers to the top to minimize the amount of air between the water and the lid, as oxygen can promote the growth of certain bacteria. However, if you're in an area with freezing temperatures, leave some space to allow for the expansion of water as it freezes, preventing the container from cracking or bursting.

After filling, tightly seal the containers with their original lids to prevent the entry of contaminants. If using screw-top lids, ensure they are secured firmly to create an airtight seal. For added protection, you can apply food-grade silicone sealant around the threads of screw-top lids to prevent air and contaminants from entering. Label each container with the date of storage using a waterproof marker. This practice is essential for tracking the age of your water supply and managing rotation schedules to ensure freshness.

Store your filled water containers in a cool, dark place away from direct sunlight and heat sources. Ultraviolet light and heat can degrade plastic containers over time and promote the growth of algae and bacteria in the water. A basement or a dedicated storage closet are ideal locations, as they typically maintain a consistent temperature and are less likely to be exposed to sunlight. Ensure the storage area is clean and free from chemicals or toxic substances that could contaminate the water through the container.

To further protect your water supply from contamination, it's crucial to implement a regular inspection routine. Every few months, visually inspect the containers for any signs of damage, such as cracks, leaks, or bulging, which could compromise the water's safety. Containers showing signs of wear or damage should be replaced immediately. Additionally, check the storage area for any potential risks, such as new sources of contamination or changes in temperature that could affect the water quality.

Rotating your water supply is another key practice in maintaining its safety and freshness. Even properly stored water should be used and replaced on a regular basis, ideally every six months to one year. This rotation ensures that your water supply remains fresh and reduces the risk of chemical degradation or bacterial growth over time. When rotating your water, use the oldest containers first, following the "first in, first out" principle. Before using the stored water, inspect it for any changes in color, odor, or taste, which could indicate contamination. If any of these changes are detected, the water should be purified before use or discarded.

Purification of stored water before use is a prudent step, even if the water was initially treated and the containers were properly prepared. Boiling is the most reliable method for purifying water, ensuring that any pathogens are killed. For every quart of water, bring it to a rolling boil for at least one minute, or three minutes at elevations above 6,500 feet, where water boils at a lower temperature. Alternatively, chemical purification using unscented household bleach or water purification tablets can be effective, following the manufacturer's instructions for the correct dosage and contact time.

In addition to these individual practices, fostering a community approach to water storage and safety can enhance resilience. Sharing knowledge and resources, such as bulk purchasing of water purification supplies or organizing community water storage facilities, can provide an added layer of security. Engaging in community workshops or training sessions on water purification and storage practices can also spread valuable skills and foster a culture of preparedness.

Lastly, staying informed about potential threats to your water supply, such as natural disasters, industrial accidents, or infrastructure failures, is essential for timely response and adaptation of your water storage practices. Monitoring local news and maintaining communication with local water authorities can provide early warnings that enable you to take additional protective measures if needed.

By integrating these practices into your routine, you can ensure that your stored water remains safe, clean, and ready for use in any situation. This comprehensive approach to water storage, combining meticulous preparation, regular maintenance, and community engagement, embodies the Navy SEALs' principles of preparedness and resilience, providing you and your family with a reliable foundation for water security.

Greywater Recycling System Setup

To establish a greywater recycling system for non-potable uses in your home, it's imperative to follow a step-by-step process that ensures the system is both efficient and safe. Greywater, which is wastewater from non-toilet sources such as showers, sinks, and washing machines, can be a valuable resource for irrigation and other non-potable applications, reducing the overall demand on your freshwater supply. Here's a detailed guide to setting up a basic yet effective greywater recycling system:

1. **Identify Greywater Sources**: Determine which fixtures in your home will contribute to your greywater system. Common sources include bathroom sinks, showers, bathtubs, and laundry machines. Avoid including kitchen sink water due to its high levels of organic waste, which can complicate treatment and increase the risk of contamination.

2. **Install Diverter Valves**: For each identified greywater source, install a three-way diverter valve into the existing plumbing. This valve allows you to direct greywater either to the sewer/septic system or to your greywater recycling system as needed. Ensure that these valves are easily accessible for hassle-free operation.

3. **Set Up a Collection System**: Position a large collection tank or barrel, preferably with a capacity of 55 gallons or more, to collect the diverted greywater. The tank should be made of a durable, food-grade material and covered to prevent debris, insects, and small animals from entering. If your sources are at a higher elevation than the tank, gravity will do the work of moving the water. Otherwise, you may need to install a pump to transport the greywater from its source to the collection tank.

4. **Implement a Filtration System**: Before using the collected greywater, pass it through a filtration system to remove particulates such as hair, lint, and other solids. A simple yet effective filtration setup can include a series of buckets or barrels filled with layers of coarse gravel, sand, and activated charcoal. Each layer serves to progressively remove smaller particles from the water, with the charcoal helping to reduce odors.

5. **Plan for Greywater Distribution**: For irrigation purposes, connect a distribution network from the collection tank to your garden or landscaping. Utilize drip irrigation hoses or soaker hoses laid out on the ground to distribute the water evenly. This method ensures that greywater is applied directly to the soil, avoiding contact with edible plant parts and reducing the risk of pathogen transmission.

6. **Implement a Surge Tank**: To deal with fluctuations in greywater production, incorporate a surge tank between your filtration system and the distribution network. This tank acts as a buffer, accommodating excess water during high output periods and providing a steady supply during low output times. It also allows for any residual particulates to settle before the water is distributed, further reducing the risk of clogging your irrigation system.

7. **Conduct Regular Maintenance**: Maintenance is crucial for the longevity and efficiency of your greywater recycling system. Clean the filters regularly to prevent clogging and inspect the system for leaks or malfunctions. Additionally, monitor the garden or landscape areas receiving greywater to ensure that the soil is not becoming oversaturated or showing signs of salt buildup, which can be harmful to plants.

8. **Adhere to Local Regulations**: Before implementing a greywater recycling system, check with local health and building departments to ensure compliance with regulations. Some areas may have specific requirements for greywater systems, including permits, design standards, and usage restrictions.

By meticulously following these steps, you can successfully set up a greywater recycling system in your home, contributing to water conservation efforts and reducing your reliance on municipal water supplies for non-potable uses. This system not only aligns with the principles of sustainability and resourcefulness but also provides a practical solution for managing household water in a more environmentally friendly manner.

Contingency Plans for Water Shortages

In the face of water shortages and emergencies, having a well-thought-out contingency plan is not just advisable; it's essential for ensuring the safety and resilience of your household. The first step in crafting this plan involves a thorough assessment of your current water usage, identifying non-essential uses that can be minimized or eliminated during a crisis. This might include reducing the frequency of laundry, taking shorter showers, or repurposing greywater for non-potable uses such as flushing toilets or watering plants. By understanding and adjusting your daily water consumption habits, you can significantly extend the lifespan of your stored water supplies during periods of scarcity.

Next, it's crucial to calculate your household's minimum daily water needs. The average person requires at least half a gallon of drinking water per day, but this figure can vary based on age, health, climate, and physical activity levels. In addition to drinking, water is also needed for cooking, personal hygiene, and medical care. A detailed calculation should therefore account for these necessities, aiming for a minimum of one gallon per person per day as a baseline for planning purposes. Remember, in a crisis, the goal is to ensure survival, not comfort, so prioritizing water usage becomes a critical skill.

Once you've established your daily water needs, the next step is to develop a comprehensive inventory of your available water sources. This inventory should include not only your primary water supply but also alternative sources that can be accessed in an emergency. Rainwater collection systems, nearby streams or lakes, and even the water in your hot water tank can serve as vital reserves when your main supply is compromised. For each source, document its location, the quantity of water it can provide, and any treatment required to make the water safe for consumption. It's also wise to invest in portable water filters or purification tablets to ensure you can treat water from alternative sources if necessary.

Creating a water rationing schedule is another key component of your contingency plan. This schedule should outline how water will be allocated for drinking, cooking, and hygiene, ensuring that the most critical needs are met first. In times of severe shortage, you may need to allocate water strictly for drinking and minimal cooking, with hygiene practices adjusted accordingly. For instance, using sanitizing wipes for personal hygiene or collecting rainwater for flushing toilets can help conserve your potable water supply.

Additionally, establishing a routine for monitoring water levels in your storage containers will help you track consumption and manage your reserves more effectively. Regular checks will alert you to any leaks or contamination issues early on, allowing you to address them before they become critical problems. This routine should include a method for rotating your water supply, using the oldest stored water first to ensure freshness and reduce the risk of contamination over time.

In preparing for water shortages, it's also important to engage with your local community. Sharing plans and resources can provide mutual support and additional options in a crisis. For example, neighbors might agree to share water from a communal well or pool resources to invest in a larger, more efficient water purification system. Building these relationships before an emergency arises can significantly enhance your collective ability to withstand water scarcity challenges.

By taking these initial steps to assess your water needs, identify and inventory sources, and plan for rationing and monitoring, you're laying the groundwork for a robust contingency plan that will help you navigate water shortages and emergencies with confidence. This preparation, grounded in the principles of efficiency, conservation, and community cooperation, is your first line of defense in ensuring your household's resilience in the face of water-related challenges.

To further solidify your water security during shortages or emergencies, training and drills play a crucial role. Just as emergency drills for fires or earthquakes prepare individuals for those specific scenarios, water shortage drills can help your household understand and practice the rationing schedule and emergency water use protocols. Set aside days where you live off your stored water supply or limit your water usage to the bare minimum based on your rationing plan. This not only tests your preparedness but also highlights areas for improvement in your plan or identifies additional resources you may need.

Investing in water-saving technologies and fixtures can also enhance your ability to manage through water shortages. Low-flow toilets, showerheads, and faucet aerators reduce the amount of water used in daily activities without sacrificing functionality. Additionally, consider installing a rainwater catchment system if you haven't already. Even a simple setup can capture rainwater from your roof, providing an additional water source for non-potable uses or, with proper treatment, as an emergency potable water supply. Ensure that your system includes a first-flush diverter to prevent the initial, most contaminated runoff from entering your storage tanks.

Understanding the signs of water contamination and knowing how to test your water are essential skills in managing water security. Purchase water testing kits to regularly check the safety of your stored water and any water from alternative sources. Look for changes in color, odor, or taste that could indicate contamination. If contamination is suspected, know how to properly disinfect your water, whether through boiling, chemical purification, or filtration. Keeping a supply of the necessary materials on hand, such as unscented household bleach or purification tablets, ensures you're always prepared to make your water safe for consumption.

Collaboration with local water management authorities can provide additional insights and resources for dealing with water shortages. These organizations often offer workshops or materials on water conservation techniques, emergency water supply locations, and updates on the local water situation. They can also be a valuable resource for understanding the broader community's plans for water management during crises, allowing you to align your personal contingency plan with community efforts.

Lastly, maintaining a mindset of adaptability and resilience is key. Water shortages and emergencies can evolve rapidly, presenting unforeseen challenges that require quick thinking and flexibility. By staying informed about local water conditions, continuously updating your contingency plan based on new information or changes in your household's needs, and practicing your emergency protocols, you'll enhance your ability to navigate these challenges successfully. Remember, the goal is not just to survive a water shortage but to manage it in a way that preserves your health, safety, and well-being until normal conditions are restored.

Through meticulous planning, practical training, and a commitment to conservation and community cooperation, you can build a comprehensive strategy for water security that stands up to the challenges of shortages and emergencies.

DIY WATER PROJECTS

Building a rainwater harvesting system for home use is a practical and efficient way to secure a sustainable water supply. This project involves collecting rainwater from your roof, storing it, and making it safe for use. The process is straightforward but requires attention to detail to ensure the system is efficient, safe, and durable.

First, assess your roof to determine its suitability for rainwater collection. Ideal roofing materials are metal, slate, or asphalt shingles. Avoid roofs made of toxic materials or those that may leach chemicals into the water. Calculate the catchment area of your roof in square feet by measuring the length and width of your home and multiplying these numbers together. This calculation is crucial as it helps estimate the volume of water you can collect. For every inch of rainfall, you can collect approximately 0.62 gallons of water per square foot of roof area.

Next, choose high-quality gutters and downspouts to channel water from your roof to your storage container. Ensure they are made of durable materials such as PVC or aluminum to withstand weather conditions and the weight of moving water. Install gutter guards to prevent leaves and debris from entering your system, which can lead to blockages and contamination.

For the storage container, select a dark, food-grade polyethylene tank to inhibit algae growth and ensure water safety. The size of the tank will depend on your roof's catchment area and your water usage needs. Place the tank on a stable, level foundation made of concrete or packed gravel. This foundation prevents the tank from sinking or tilting, which could cause structural issues.

Install a first-flush diverter between the downspout and the storage tank. This device ensures the initial rain, which may contain contaminants from the roof, is diverted away from the tank, allowing only clean water to enter. The diverter should be cleaned regularly to maintain its effectiveness.

Connect the downspout to the tank using PVC pipes or flexible hoses. Include an overflow valve at the top of the tank to redirect excess water away from the foundation of your home. This valve is critical during heavy rainfall to prevent water from backing up and damaging the system.

Before using the collected rainwater, it's essential to filter and purify it, especially if it will be used for drinking or cooking. Simple filtration can be achieved with a sediment filter installed before the water enters the storage tank. For purification, consider options like UV light purifiers or chlorine tablets, depending on your specific needs and the intended use of the water.

Regular maintenance of your rainwater harvesting system is vital to ensure its longevity and the safety of the water. This includes cleaning the roof, gutters, and first-flush diverter, inspecting the tank for leaks or damage, and testing the water quality periodically.

By following these detailed steps, you can build a reliable rainwater harvesting system that provides a sustainable source of water for your home. This project not only contributes to water conservation efforts but also ensures you have an emergency water supply in times of need.

Moving on to the creation of a DIY water filtration and purification unit, this project is essential for ensuring the safety and potability of your harvested rainwater, especially if it's intended for drinking, cooking, or personal hygiene. The process involves setting up a multi-barrier system that includes sediment filtration, activated carbon treatment, and a final disinfection stage. Each step is designed to remove different contaminants, from large debris to microscopic pathogens.

Begin by assembling your filtration unit with a sediment filter. This can be a commercially available unit or a homemade version using fine mesh and sand. The purpose of this layer is to remove larger particles such as leaves, dirt, and other visible contaminants from the water. Place this filter at the point where water enters your storage tank to ensure that it is the first line of defense in your purification process.

Next, incorporate an activated carbon filter. Activated carbon is effective at removing chemicals such as chlorine, pesticides, and many organic compounds that can affect water taste and odor. It also reduces some heavy metals and can assist in improving the clarity of your water. You can create a simple activated carbon filter by filling a PVC pipe or a suitable container with activated carbon granules. Water should pass through this filter after it has been cleared by the sediment filter but before it reaches the final disinfection stage.

For the final disinfection stage, UV light purification offers a chemical-free method to kill bacteria, viruses, and other microorganisms. This requires a UV light purifier, which can be installed in-line with your water system, ensuring that all water passing through is exposed to UV light for a sufficient duration to be disinfected. Alternatively, for a more budget-friendly option, chlorine tablets can be used. However, it's important to follow the recommended dosages to avoid over-chlorination, and water should be allowed to stand after treatment to let the chlorine dissipate before use.

To assemble your DIY water filtration and purification unit, start by connecting the sediment filter to the outlet of your storage tank. Ensure all connections are secure to prevent leaks. From the sediment filter, lead the water through the activated carbon filter. Finally, install the UV purifier or add chlorine tablets to the water in a designated treatment tank following the carbon filter. It's crucial to test your system with a water quality test kit to ensure all contaminants are effectively removed before using the water for consumption.

Regular maintenance of your filtration and purification system is crucial. Replace or clean the sediment filter and activated carbon as per the manufacturer's recommendations or as needed based on your water quality tests. The UV purifier bulb also needs to be replaced periodically, typically once a year, to maintain its effectiveness. Keep a log of maintenance activities to track the performance of your system and address any issues promptly.

By meticulously following these steps, you can establish a comprehensive water filtration and purification system that ensures your harvested rainwater is safe for use. This DIY project not only enhances your self-sufficiency in managing water resources but also contributes to the health and well-being of your household by providing clean, potable water.

Building a rainwater harvesting system for home use - be very detailed

Project Introduction (Description - Benefits - Challenges)

Harnessing rainwater for home use through a well-designed harvesting system can significantly reduce reliance on municipal water supplies, lower utility bills, and provide an eco-friendly source of water for gardening, flushing toilets, and other non-potable uses. The project involves collecting rainwater from your roof, filtering it, and storing it securely. Benefits include sustainability, cost savings, and emergency water supply resilience. Challenges encompass dealing with zoning and building codes, ensuring water quality, and maintaining the system.

Required Materials

- **PVC or aluminum gutters and downspouts**: Select gutters with a minimum width of 5 inches to accommodate heavy rainfall, ensuring they are sloped at a 1/4 inch per 10 feet for optimal drainage. Downspouts should be at least 3 inches in diameter to prevent clogging and should be fitted with elbows to direct water into the storage system

- **First flush diverter**: Install a first flush diverter that can hold at least 10% of the roof's surface area in gallons, ensuring it effectively discards the initial runoff that contains contaminants. This device should be easily accessible for maintenance and should have a valve to allow for manual flushing

- **Mesh screens or leaf guards**: Use mesh screens with a maximum opening of 1/16 inch to effectively filter out debris and insects while allowing water to flow freely. Leaf guards should be installed at the top of the gutters to prevent leaves and larger debris from entering the system

- **Food-grade polyethylene rainwater storage tank**: Choose a tank made from UV-resistant, food-grade polyethylene with a capacity ranging from 500 to 5,000 gallons, depending on your household needs and available space. Ensure the tank has a wide opening for easy cleaning and maintenance

- **Concrete blocks or a sturdy stand**: Elevate the storage tank using concrete blocks or a custom-built stand that raises the tank at least 2 feet off the ground. This elevation allows for gravity-fed water distribution and helps prevent contamination from ground-level debris

- **PVC pipes (¾ inch or 1 inch) and fittings**: Use schedule 40 PVC pipes for durability, with ¾ inch pipes suitable for smaller systems and 1 inch for larger flows. Ensure all fittings are solvent-welded to create a watertight seal and prevent leaks

- **Water filtration system**: Incorporate a multi-stage filtration system that includes a sediment filter (5 microns) followed by a carbon filter to remove chlorine, taste, and odor. Consider adding a UV filter for additional purification, especially if the water will be used for drinking

- **Overflow valve**: Install an overflow valve at the top of the tank to manage excess water during heavy rainfall. This valve should direct overflow water away from the foundation of your home and into a designated drainage area

- **Hose bib or spigot**: Install a hose bib or spigot at the bottom of the tank, ensuring it is at least 12 inches above ground level for easy access. Use a ball valve for reliable operation and consider adding a quick-connect fitting for garden hoses or irrigation systems

Required Tools

- Power drill with drill and screwdriver bits
- Hacksaw or PVC cutter, for cutting pipes to length
- Tape measure
- Spirit level
- PVC glue and primer
- Silicone sealant
- Safety glasses and gloves

Detailed Instructions

1. **Evaluate and Prepare the Roof and Gutters**: Ensure your roof is in good condition and that existing gutters and downspouts are clean and unobstructed. Install gutters if absent, ensuring a slight slope towards downspouts for efficient water flow.

2. **Install Leaf Guards and Mesh Screens**: Fit leaf guards onto the gutters and attach mesh screens at the top of downspouts to prevent debris and insects from entering the system.

3. **Set Up the First Flush Diverter**: Install the first flush diverter on the downspout closest to the storage tank. This device ensures the initial, most contaminated rainwater is diverted away, enhancing water quality.

4. **Position and Secure the Storage Tank**: Place the storage tank on a solid, level base of concrete blocks or a stand to ensure stability and facilitate gravity-fed water flow. Position it as close to the downspout as possible to simplify plumbing.

5. **Plumb the System**: Connect the downspout to the tank using PVC pipes. Incorporate an overflow valve into the design to direct excess water away from the foundation of your house.

6. **Install Filtration**: Between the downspout and the tank, install a filtration system to remove smaller particles. This can be a commercially available unit or a homemade filter with replaceable elements.

7. **Install the Hose Bib or Spigot**: Fit a hose bib or spigot at the bottom of the tank for easy access. Ensure it's high enough to fit a watering can or bucket underneath.

Safety

- Always wear safety glasses and gloves when cutting PVC or working with tools to prevent injury.
- Ensure the tank's base is stable and strong enough to support the weight of a full water tank to prevent collapse.
- Follow local regulations regarding rainwater harvesting to ensure compliance and safety.

Cost of the Project

Estimated at $200-$600, depending on tank size, materials chosen, and whether existing gutters can be utilized.

Preparation Time

1-2 days, allowing for setup and drying times for adhesives and sealants.

Maintenance and Care

- Inspect and clean gutters and mesh screens regularly to ensure unimpeded water flow.
- Check the first flush diverter and clean it out after heavy rainfalls to keep the system functioning correctly.
- Periodically inspect the tank and plumbing for leaks or damage, especially after extreme weather events.

FAQ or Common Issues

- **Q: Can I use rainwater for drinking?**
- **A:** While technically possible with proper treatment and filtration, this guide focuses on non-potable uses. For drinking, additional purification and regular water quality testing would be necessary.
- **Q: What should I do if my tank overflows?**
- **A:** An overflow valve is essential for directing excess water away safely. Consider connecting the overflow to a drainage system or a rain garden to manage surplus water sustainably.

Difficulty Rating

★★★☆☆

Variations

- For larger properties, consider linking multiple tanks for increased storage capacity.
- Install a solar-powered water pump to distribute water for irrigation or into the home for toilets and washing machines.
- In colder climates, add insulation around the pipes and tank to prevent freezing, or design the system so it can be easily drained and disconnected during winter months.

Troubleshooting:

- **Low Water Flow:** Check for clogs in the gutters or downspouts, ensure the first flush diverter is functioning properly, and inspect the filter for debris
- **Overflow Issues:** Verify that the overflow pipe is correctly positioned and not blocked, and consider adding additional overflow outlets if necessary
- **Water Quality Concerns:** Regularly clean the collection surface and storage tank, use appropriate filters, and consider adding a UV light treatment system for purification
- **System Leaks:** Inspect all connections and joints for signs of wear or damage, and replace any faulty components immediately
- **Pump Malfunctions:** Ensure the pump is properly connected to power, check for any blockages in the intake, and consult the manufacturer's manual for troubleshooting steps
- **Freezing Conditions:** Insulate exposed pipes and consider using heat tape in colder climates to prevent freezing and bursting
- **Inadequate Storage Capacity:** Assess your water needs and consider expanding your storage system with additional tanks or cisterns if necessary

Creating a DIY water filtration and purification unit - be very detailed

Project Introduction (Description - Benefits - Challenges): This project guides you through creating a DIY water filtration and purification unit, leveraging simple, effective techniques to ensure access to clean drinking water. The benefits include cost savings, self-reliance, and the peace of mind that comes with knowing your water is safe. Challenges involve sourcing materials, assembling the unit correctly, and ensuring the water is purified to a safe drinking standard.

Required Materials:
- 2 food-grade 5-gallon buckets with lids
- Ceramic water filter with a spigot
- Drill with 1/2 inch and 1/4 inch drill bits
- Two rubber O-rings
- One rubber washer
- One wingnut that fits the ceramic filter's threaded end
- Activated charcoal granules
- Clean sand (preferably silica sand)
- Gravel or small pebbles
- Coffee filters or cheesecloth

Required Tools:
- Drill
- Measuring tape or ruler
- Marker

Detailed Instructions:
1. **Prepare the Buckets:** Drill a 1/2 inch hole in the bottom of one bucket and in the lid of the other bucket. These holes should align when the buckets are stacked.
2. **Assemble the Filtration System:** Insert the ceramic filter's threaded end through the hole in the bottom of the top bucket. Secure it with the rubber washer on the inside and the wingnut outside the bucket. Ensure a tight fit to prevent leaks.
3. **Create the Pre-Filter Layer:** Place a coffee filter or cheesecloth at the bottom of the top bucket, over the ceramic filter's base. This will catch larger particles before they reach the ceramic element.
4. **Add the Charcoal Layer:** Fill the bottom third of the top bucket with activated charcoal granules. This layer will help remove chemicals and odors from the water.
5. **Add the Sand Layer:** Over the charcoal, add a layer of clean sand to the halfway mark of the bucket. The sand acts as a finer filter, catching smaller particles.

6. **Add the Gravel Layer:** Fill the remaining space in the top bucket with gravel or small pebbles. This layer helps distribute the water evenly across the finer filters below and catches the largest particles.

7. **Stack and Seal the Buckets:** Place the top bucket (the one with the filter and layers of media) into the lid of the bottom bucket. Ensure the ceramic filter extends into the bottom bucket.

8. **Prepare for Use:** Pour water into the top bucket and allow it to filter through to the bottom bucket. The first few gallons should be discarded to flush out any dust or loose material from the charcoal, sand, and gravel.

Safety:
- Wear gloves when handling activated charcoal to avoid staining your hands.
- Ensure all drilled holes are smooth to prevent injury during assembly and use.
- Use only food-grade materials to avoid contaminants leaching into your water.

Cost of the Project: Approximately $50-$100, depending on the cost of the ceramic filter and availability of other materials.

Preparation Time: 2-3 hours, including time to source materials and assemble the unit.

Maintenance and Care:
- Replace the ceramic filter according to the manufacturer's recommendations, usually after filtering 1,000 gallons of water.
- Regularly clean the buckets, sand, and gravel layers every 6 months, or more frequently if the water flow rate decreases significantly.
- Replace the activated charcoal annually to ensure effective chemical filtration.

FAQ or Common Issues:
- **Q: What if water flows too slowly through the filter?**
- **A:** Check for blockages in the ceramic filter or the pre-filter layer. Increasing the size of the hole in the bottom bucket may also improve flow rate.
- **Q: Can I purify rainwater with this system?**
- **A:** Yes, this system can purify rainwater, but it's essential to pre-filter it to remove large debris before running it through the DIY unit.

Difficulty Rating: ★★★☆☆

Variations:
- For larger volumes of water, use bigger containers or multiple units in parallel.
- Add a UV light purification stage by incorporating a UV water purifier between the ceramic filter and the spigot for an additional layer of microbial safety.
- Incorporate a second ceramic filter to increase the flow rate and volume of purified water available.

Creating a DIY water filtration and purification unit is essential for ensuring access to clean water in emergency situations. Here are some troubleshooting tips to help you address common issues that may arise during the construction or use of your filtration system

Troubleshooting:

- **Clogged Filters**: If you notice a decrease in water flow, your filter may be clogged. Clean or replace the filter media as needed. Regular maintenance is crucial to keep the system functioning effectively

- **Unpleasant Odors**: If the water has an unusual smell, it may indicate contamination. Check the source water and ensure that all components of the filtration system are clean and free from mold or bacteria

- **Cloudy Water**: If the water appears cloudy after filtration, it may be due to insufficient filtration media or a need for additional layers. Consider adding more layers of sand or activated charcoal to improve clarity

- **Inconsistent Water Quality**: If the water quality varies, ensure that the filtration system is properly sealed and that there are no leaks. Regularly test the water for contaminants to ensure it meets safety standards

- **System Failure**: If the entire system fails to produce water, check for blockages in the intake or output lines. Ensure that all connections are secure and that the water source is accessible

- **Bacterial Growth**: If you notice any signs of bacterial growth, such as slime or discoloration, disinfect the system using a diluted bleach solution and rinse thoroughly before use

By following these troubleshooting tips, you can maintain an effective DIY water filtration and purification unit, ensuring that you and your family have access to safe drinking water when it matters most

BOOK 6: OFF-GRID ENERGY SOLUTIONS

Embarking on the journey to establish off-grid energy solutions for your home begins with setting up a solar power system, a cornerstone of sustainable living. Solar power harnesses the sun's energy, converting it into electricity to run your household appliances, lighting, and even heating systems without reliance on the main power grid. This section will guide you through the initial steps of selecting and installing a basic solar panel array, ensuring you have a reliable and renewable energy source.

The first step in this process is to evaluate your energy needs. Start by calculating the total wattage of the appliances and devices you intend to power. This calculation is crucial as it determines the size of the solar panel array and battery storage you'll need. For instance, if your daily energy usage amounts to 3 kilowatt-hours (kWh), you'll require a solar system that can produce this amount of power during your area's average sunlight hours.

Next, selecting the right location for your solar panels is paramount. Opt for a spot that receives maximum direct sunlight exposure throughout the day. A south-facing roof is ideal in the Northern Hemisphere, as it ensures your panels absorb the most sunlight. If roof mounting is not feasible, consider ground-mounted panels in a clear, unshaded area. It's essential to avoid locations where shadows from trees, buildings, or other structures could fall on the panels, especially during peak sunlight hours.

When choosing solar panels, look for high-efficiency models that offer the best output per square foot. Monocrystalline panels, though more expensive, are typically more efficient and space-saving compared to polycrystalline panels. Assess the wattage rating of each panel to ensure it aligns with your energy needs and available space for installation.

The installation of solar panels requires careful planning and adherence to safety standards. Begin by securing mounting brackets to your roof or chosen structure, ensuring they are anchored properly to withstand weather conditions. Attach the solar panels to these brackets using the manufacturer-provided hardware. It's crucial to maintain a slight tilt angle, optimizing the panels' exposure to the sun based on your geographical location.

Wiring the solar panels is a critical step that should comply with local electrical codes. Connect each panel's positive and negative terminals in a series or parallel configuration, depending on your system's voltage requirements. Use weatherproof wiring and connectors to safeguard against environmental damage. A charge controller should be installed between the solar panels and the battery bank to regulate the charging process and prevent battery damage.

Choosing the right battery storage system is essential for ensuring a continuous power supply, especially during nighttime or cloudy days. Deep-cycle batteries are recommended for solar systems due to their ability to withstand repeated charge and discharge cycles. The capacity of your battery bank should be sufficient to store the energy produced by your solar panels, allowing for at least a few days of autonomy based on your calculated energy needs.

Finally, an inverter is necessary to convert the direct current (DC) electricity generated by your solar panels into alternating current (AC), the form of electricity used by most household appliances. Select an inverter with a wattage rating that matches or exceeds your total energy consumption. Ensure the inverter is connected correctly to both the battery bank and your home's electrical panel to seamlessly integrate solar power into your household's energy system.

By meticulously following these steps, you can successfully set up a basic solar panel array that not only reduces your dependency on the main power grid but also contributes to environmental conservation. This project, while requiring an upfront investment, offers long-term savings on electricity bills and provides a sustainable energy solution for your home.

To ensure the longevity and efficiency of your solar power system, regular maintenance is crucial. Solar panels typically require minimal upkeep, but keeping them clean from dust, debris, and snow will maximize their energy production. A soft brush or cloth, along with soapy water, can be used for cleaning; avoid abrasive materials that could scratch the panels. Additionally, inspect your panels periodically for any signs of damage or wear and tear, such as cracks or discoloration, which could affect their performance.

Monitoring your system's performance is also essential to ensure it operates at optimal efficiency. Many modern solar systems come equipped with monitoring software that allows you to track energy production and consumption in real-time. This technology can alert you to any issues or inefficiencies in the system, such as a sudden drop in energy output, which could indicate a problem with one or more of the panels or connections.

The charge controller, a critical component of your solar system, requires attention to ensure it functions correctly. It regulates the flow of electricity from the panels to the battery bank, preventing overcharging and damage to the batteries. Periodically check the charge controller's indicators to confirm it's operating as expected. If your system is equipped with a Maximum Power Point Tracking (MPPT) charge controller, it will automatically adjust the charging rate depending on the panels' output, maximizing the energy stored in the battery bank.

Battery maintenance is another key aspect of your solar power system's upkeep. Deep-cycle batteries, while durable, have a finite lifespan and their capacity diminishes over time. Regularly check the battery terminals for corrosion and clean them as necessary. If you're using lead-acid batteries, ensure the electrolyte levels are maintained and top them up with distilled water if they're low. For lithium-ion batteries, although maintenance is minimal, it's important to monitor their state of charge and avoid depleting them completely, as this can reduce their lifespan.

The inverter, which converts DC electricity from your solar panels and batteries into AC electricity for your home, should be checked regularly for any error messages or indicators of malfunction. Ensure it's kept in a well-ventilated area to prevent overheating, which can lead to efficiency losses or damage. If your inverter has a fan, listen for any unusual noises that could indicate a problem.

Finally, it's wise to have a professional inspection of your solar power system conducted annually. A certified technician can perform a thorough check of all components, including the mounting system, to ensure everything is secure and operating efficiently. They can also test the system's electrical safety features and make any necessary repairs or adjustments.

By dedicating time to the regular maintenance and monitoring of your solar power system, you can enjoy the benefits of renewable energy for many years. This proactive approach not only safeguards your investment but also supports your commitment to sustainable living. With the right care, your solar power system will continue to provide a reliable, clean energy source, reducing your environmental footprint and contributing to a healthier planet.

CHAPTER 1: BUILDING ENERGY INDEPENDENCE

Installing a wind turbine for supplemental power generation is an effective way to complement your solar power system, ensuring a more consistent and diversified source of off-grid energy. Wind turbines convert the kinetic energy from wind into electrical power that can be used directly by appliances or stored in batteries for later use. This section will guide you through the process of selecting, siting, and installing a small-scale wind turbine for residential use.

First, assess the wind resource in your area. Wind speed is the most critical factor in determining a wind turbine's electricity production. An ideal location for a wind turbine is where the average annual wind speed is at least 12 miles per hour (mph). Utilize online resources such as the U.S. Department of Energy's Wind Exchange map or consult with local meteorological data to evaluate wind speeds in your region. Keep in mind that wind speed increases with height above ground, so a turbine mounted on a taller tower will generally produce more power than one on a shorter tower in the same location.

Next, choose the type of wind turbine that best suits your needs. There are two main types of wind turbines: horizontal-axis turbines, which are the most common and resemble traditional windmills, and vertical-axis turbines, which are better suited for turbulent or less consistent wind conditions. For most residential applications, a horizontal-axis turbine with a rated capacity of 5 to 15 kilowatts (kW) is sufficient, depending on your energy needs.

Selecting the right location for your wind turbine is crucial. The turbine should be installed in an open area, free from obstructions such as trees, buildings, and hills that could block or divert wind flow. The general rule is that a wind turbine should be mounted at least 30 feet above any obstacle within a 300-foot radius. This might mean installing the turbine on a tower that is 60 to 100 feet tall to maximize wind exposure. Ensure the chosen location is accessible for maintenance and is in compliance with local zoning regulations, which may dictate maximum tower height and minimum distance from property lines.

When it comes to installation, the foundation for your wind turbine tower is a critical component that ensures stability and safety. The type of foundation required—whether it be a concrete pad, deep-set anchors, or a combination thereof—will depend on the soil type, turbine size, and tower height. Follow the manufacturer's recommendations for foundation specifications to ensure proper support.

The electrical system of a wind turbine includes the turbine itself, a charge controller, a battery bank (for storage), and an inverter (to convert DC to AC power). Connect the turbine's output to the charge controller, which regulates the charging of the battery bank to prevent overcharging. The battery bank should be sized according to your energy storage needs, capable of storing enough power to cover periods of low wind. Finally, the inverter converts the stored DC power into AC power that can be used by your home's electrical system.

Safety and maintenance are paramount for the longevity and efficiency of your wind turbine. Regular inspections should be conducted to check for wear and tear on moving parts, ensure electrical connections are secure, and verify that the tower remains upright and stable. Lubrication of moving parts, as per the manufacturer's instructions, is necessary to reduce friction and prevent premature wear.

By carefully selecting and installing a wind turbine, you can significantly enhance your home's energy independence. Wind power, especially when used in conjunction with solar panels, provides a more reliable and sustainable off-grid energy solution, reducing reliance on fossil fuels and lowering your environmental impact. Remember, the success of your wind energy system hinges on thorough planning, adherence to local regulations, and regular maintenance to ensure optimal performance and safety.

Solar Power for Off-Grid Energy

To set up a solar power system for off-grid energy, begin by calculating your energy needs to determine the size of the solar panel array and battery storage required. For example, if your daily energy consumption is 3 kilowatt-hours (kWh), you need a system that can generate this amount during peak sunlight hours. Start by listing all electrical appliances you plan to use, noting their wattage and the number of hours they'll be in operation each day. Add up these figures to get your total daily energy requirement.

Select a location for your solar panels that receives maximum sunlight exposure throughout the day. A south-facing roof in the Northern Hemisphere is ideal, but if roof mounting isn't an option, a ground-mounted system in an unobstructed area works as well. Ensure there are no shadows cast on the panels, especially during peak sunlight hours, as this significantly reduces their efficiency.

When choosing solar panels, opt for high-efficiency monocrystalline panels. Although they come at a higher initial cost compared to polycrystalline panels, their superior efficiency and smaller space requirement make them a better choice for off-grid setups. Check the wattage rating of each panel to ensure it meets your energy needs and fits the available installation space.

For mounting the solar panels, use durable brackets securely anchored to the roof or ground mount system. The panels should be installed at an angle that maximizes sun exposure, which varies based on your geographical location. Use a solar angle calculator to determine the optimal tilt angle for your panels.

Wiring the panels requires connecting their positive and negative terminals in a series or parallel configuration to match your system's voltage requirements. Use outdoor-rated, UV-resistant wiring and waterproof connectors to ensure longevity and safety. A charge controller is essential to regulate the charging of the battery bank, preventing overcharging and damage. Select a charge controller that matches the voltage and current specifications of your solar panels and battery bank.

For battery storage, deep-cycle batteries are recommended due to their ability to withstand repeated discharge and recharge cycles. The capacity of your battery bank should be sufficient to store the energy produced by your solar panels, allowing for autonomy during nights or cloudy days. Calculate your storage needs based on your daily energy consumption and the autonomy required, typically a few days' worth of energy usage.

An inverter is necessary to convert the DC electricity generated by the solar panels and stored in the batteries into AC electricity, which is used by most household appliances. Choose an inverter with a wattage rating that exceeds your total energy consumption to ensure it can handle the load of all connected appliances simultaneously.

Connect the solar panel array to the charge controller using the appropriate gauge of wire to handle the expected current flow. From the charge controller, connect to the battery bank, ensuring proper polarity is maintained to prevent damage. The inverter is then connected to the battery bank, converting DC to AC power for household use. Ensure all connections are tight and secure to minimize resistance and potential energy loss.

Regular maintenance of your solar power system includes cleaning the solar panels periodically to remove dust, debris, and snow, which can reduce their efficiency. Inspect the system components regularly for signs of wear or damage, such as frayed wiring or loose connections. The battery terminals should be checked for corrosion and cleaned as necessary, and the electrolyte levels in lead-acid batteries should be maintained.

By following these detailed steps, you can set up a reliable and efficient solar power system for off-grid energy, providing a sustainable and self-sufficient energy source for your home. This setup not only reduces reliance on the main power grid but also decreases environmental impact by utilizing renewable energy.

Wind Turbine Installation for Power

When embarking on the installation of a wind turbine for supplemental power generation, the first step is to conduct a detailed assessment of your local wind resource. This involves utilizing an anemometer to measure wind speed at the proposed installation site over a period, ideally a year, but shorter periods can be used with historical wind data to supplement findings. The anemometer should be placed at the same height as the proposed turbine's hub height to ensure accurate measurements. Data collected will help in determining if your site meets the minimum average wind speed requirement of 12 miles per hour, which is considered viable for residential wind power generation.

After confirming the suitability of your site based on wind speed, the next step is selecting the appropriate wind turbine size and type. For residential use, turbines ranging from 5 to 15 kilowatts are commonly used, depending on household energy needs and wind resource availability. Horizontal-axis wind turbines (HAWTs) are preferred for their efficiency in consistent wind conditions. It's crucial to choose a turbine with a high-quality generator, durable blades, and a reliable inverter that matches your home's energy requirements. The turbine should be certified by a recognized authority such as the Small Wind Certification Council, ensuring it meets safety and performance standards.

The turbine's tower height is a critical factor in capturing optimal wind speeds. The general guideline is to install the turbine at least 30 feet above anything within a 300-foot radius. This might necessitate a tower that is 60 to 100 feet tall. Towers can be self-supporting, guyed, or monopole, with the choice depending on site-specific factors such as wind speed profile, zoning restrictions, and budget. Guyed towers are less expensive and easier to install but require a larger footprint, while monopole towers are sleeker but more costly.

For the foundation, a concrete pad is commonly used, with the size and depth dependent on the soil type and the turbine's size. The foundation must be engineered to withstand not only the weight of the tower and turbine but also dynamic loads from wind forces. In some cases, anchor points for guyed towers may also need to be cemented into the ground to ensure stability.

Electrical wiring from the turbine to your home's power system requires careful planning to comply with local electrical codes. Use outdoor-rated, UV-resistant cables for all external wiring. The turbine's output is connected to a charge controller, which regulates the flow of electricity to the battery bank or directly to the home's electrical panel. If a battery bank is used, it should be sized to store sufficient power for times when wind speeds are low. The inverter, which converts the turbine's DC output to AC compatible with household appliances, should be matched to the system's total wattage output.

Safety systems are an integral part of the installation, including an automatic brake or a manual disconnect to stop the turbine in high winds or for maintenance. Lightning protection and grounding are also essential to protect the system and your home from electrical surges.

Regular maintenance is crucial to ensure the longevity and efficiency of your wind turbine system. This includes periodic checks for bolt tightness, lubrication of moving parts, inspection of electrical connections, and blade condition. Most turbines require at least an annual inspection, with more frequent checks necessary after severe weather events.

By meticulously planning and executing each step of the installation process, from site assessment to selecting the right turbine and ensuring proper maintenance, you can significantly enhance your home's energy independence with wind power. This not only reduces reliance on the grid but also contributes to a more sustainable and environmentally friendly energy solution for your household.

Backup Generators and Battery Storage

Selecting the right backup generator and battery storage system is a critical step in ensuring your home remains powered during outages or off-grid living scenarios. The process involves understanding your energy needs, evaluating generator types, and choosing a battery storage solution that complements your energy setup. This section will guide you through each step with detailed precision, ensuring you make informed decisions for your home's energy independence.

First, calculate your home's energy requirements by listing all essential appliances and devices you need to power during an outage. Include items like refrigerators, lighting, water pumps, and medical equipment. For each device, note its wattage and multiply by the number of hours it's used daily to calculate daily energy consumption in watt-hours (Wh). Summing these figures will give you a baseline for selecting a generator and battery capacity.

When choosing a backup generator, consider fuel types available in your area, such as gasoline, diesel, propane, or natural gas. Gasoline generators are common but require frequent refueling, while propane and natural gas generators offer longer run times with less maintenance. Diesel generators are known for their durability and efficiency in larger models. Evaluate the generator's power output, measured in watts, to ensure it meets or exceeds your calculated energy needs. Look for models with automatic start features and safety shut-offs to protect against overloads.

For battery storage, deep-cycle batteries are preferred for their ability to discharge and recharge repeatedly. Lead-acid batteries are cost-effective and widely available, but require regular maintenance to check water levels and clean terminals. Lithium-ion batteries, though more expensive upfront, offer a longer lifespan, higher energy density, and virtually no maintenance. Calculate the battery bank size by dividing your daily energy requirement in watt-hours by the battery's voltage, typically 12V, 24V, or 48V, to get the amp-hours (Ah) needed. Then, consider adding 20-30% more capacity to account for inefficiencies and days with higher energy usage.

Connecting your generator to a transfer switch allows for safe switching between grid power and generator power, preventing backfeeding which can be dangerous to utility workers and damage your electrical system. Ensure the transfer switch is installed by a licensed electrician and matches your generator's capacity.

For integrating battery storage, use a charge controller between the generator (or solar panels if applicable) and the battery bank to regulate charging and prevent overcharging. Select a charge controller with a maximum input voltage and current rating that exceeds your system's maximum output to ensure safety and longevity.

Maintenance of your backup generator involves regular oil changes, filter replacements, and fuel system checks, especially if stored without use for extended periods. Run the generator monthly for at least 30 minutes to charge the battery, lubricate engine parts, and prevent fuel stagnation. For battery storage, inspect connections for corrosion, ensure proper ventilation to prevent gas buildup, and keep the storage area clean and dry. For lead-acid batteries, check water levels monthly and refill with distilled water as needed. Lithium-ion batteries require minimal maintenance but monitoring the state of charge and avoiding complete discharges will prolong their lifespan.

By following these detailed steps for selecting and maintaining a backup generator and battery storage system, you can ensure a reliable power source for your home during outages or off-grid living. This setup not only provides peace of mind but also supports your journey towards energy independence, aligning with the principles of resilience and preparedness emphasized throughout this guide.

CHAPTER 2: ENERGY EFFICIENCY IN CRISIS

In times of crisis, energy efficiency becomes not just a matter of environmental concern but a vital aspect of survival. The ability to maximize the utility of every watt of power generated by your off-grid energy solutions can make the difference between comfort and hardship. This section delves into strategies and modifications to ensure that your home remains a bastion of safety and efficiency, even when external power sources are compromised.

Firstly, focus on insulation and weatherproofing as foundational elements of energy efficiency. Proper insulation in walls, attics, and floors minimizes the loss of heat during winter and keeps your home cooler in the summer, reducing the need for heating and cooling. Use spray foam, rigid foam boards, and batt insulation, ensuring they are properly installed to cover gaps and leaks. For windows, double-glazing with Low-E coating and argon gas filling offers excellent thermal performance. Additionally, weather stripping around doors and windows can prevent air leaks, further conserving energy.

Next, consider the heating and cooling systems. In a crisis, traditional HVAC systems can be energy hogs. Switch to a ductless mini-split heat pump system for more efficient heating and cooling. These systems allow for zoned temperature control, meaning you can heat or cool only the areas in use, significantly reducing energy consumption. For hot water, a solar water heating system can be integrated with your existing water heater, preheating the water using the sun's energy and thus requiring less electricity or gas to bring the water to temperature.

Lighting is another area where efficiency can be significantly improved. Replace all incandescent bulbs with LED bulbs. LEDs use at least 75% less energy and last 25 times longer than incandescent lighting. Focus on task lighting rather than whole-room lighting wherever possible, and make use of natural light during the day to reduce the need for artificial lighting.

Appliances and electronics should be carefully managed to avoid unnecessary power drain. Opt for energy-efficient appliances with the ENERGY STAR label, indicating they meet energy efficiency guidelines set by the U.S. Environmental Protection Agency. Unplug appliances and electronics when not in use, as many continue to draw power even when turned off, a phenomenon known as phantom load. Utilize power strips to easily cut power to multiple devices at once.

In managing your off-grid energy system, whether solar, wind, or hybrid, monitoring and maintenance are key to ensuring efficiency. Regularly clean solar panels and check wind turbine blades for damage to ensure optimal operation. Use a system monitor to track energy production and consumption in real time, allowing you to adjust usage and identify any issues promptly. Battery health is crucial in off-grid systems; ensure they are kept at the recommended charge level and stored in a temperature-controlled environment to maximize lifespan and performance.

Water usage can also impact energy consumption, particularly if you are pumping water from a well or using a water purification system. Implement low-flow fixtures in showers, faucets, and toilets to reduce water use. If using a well, consider a solar-powered pump to reduce energy consumption. For water purification, a gravity-fed system can be more energy-efficient than one requiring electric pumps.

Finally, cultivate energy-conscious habits among all household members. Simple actions like turning off lights when leaving a room, taking shorter showers, and only running the dishwasher or washing machine with full loads can collectively make a significant impact on reducing energy consumption.

By implementing these strategies, your home can remain a resilient, energy-efficient haven, capable of withstanding the challenges of a crisis situation. Each step not only contributes to immediate energy savings but also bolsters your long-term sustainability and independence from the grid.

Energy Reduction in Survival Scenarios

Reducing energy consumption in survival scenarios is crucial for extending the life of your off-grid energy solutions and ensuring you have enough power to meet essential needs. One effective method to achieve this is by implementing a layered approach to lighting and appliance use, prioritizing energy efficiency in every aspect of your daily routine. Start by evaluating each room in your home to identify where energy savings can be made, focusing on lighting, appliances, and heating or cooling systems.

For lighting, replace all existing incandescent or halogen bulbs with high-efficiency LED bulbs. LEDs not only consume up to 75% less energy but also have a longer lifespan, reducing the need for replacements. When selecting LEDs, opt for those with a luminous efficacy of 100 lumens per watt or higher to maximize brightness per unit of energy consumed. Additionally, incorporate motion sensors in less-frequented areas such as hallways or bathrooms to ensure lights are only on when needed, further conserving energy.

In terms of appliances, conduct an audit to identify older, less efficient models that could be consuming excessive amounts of power. Replace these with ENERGY STAR-rated appliances, which are certified to use less energy without sacrificing performance. For example, an ENERGY STAR-certified refrigerator can use 50% less energy than models made before 1993. When using appliances, be strategic; run dishwashers and washing machines only with full loads, and switch to cold water cycles to reduce energy used for heating.

Heating and cooling systems are often the largest consumers of energy in homes. To reduce consumption, install a programmable thermostat that adjusts the temperature based on time of day and occupancy. Setting the thermostat to lower temperatures in winter and higher in summer, even by a few degrees, can result in significant energy savings. For instance, setting the thermostat to 68°F during the day and 60°F at night during winter months can save up to 10% on heating bills. Ensure your home is well-insulated and sealed against drafts around windows and doors to prevent heat loss, which can be achieved by using weather stripping and caulking.

Water heating is another area where energy can be conserved. Install low-flow showerheads and faucet aerators to reduce hot water use. If possible, upgrade to a tankless water heater, which heats water on demand and eliminates the energy wasted by maintaining the temperature of stored water in a tank. A tankless water heater can be 24%–34% more energy-efficient for homes that use less than 41 gallons of hot water daily.

For your off-grid energy system, regularly clean and maintain solar panels and wind turbines to ensure they are operating at peak efficiency. Dust, debris, and snow can reduce solar panel efficiency by up to 25%. For wind turbines, check that blades are free of damage and obstructions that could reduce their effectiveness. Use a system monitor to track energy production and consumption, allowing you to adjust your usage patterns and identify areas where further savings can be made.

Finally, educate all household members on the importance of energy conservation and establish guidelines for minimizing waste. Simple habits like turning off lights when leaving a room, unplugging chargers when not in use, and avoiding opening the refrigerator or freezer unnecessarily can collectively make a significant difference in your home's energy consumption.

By implementing these detailed techniques, you can significantly reduce energy consumption in survival scenarios, ensuring your off-grid energy solutions provide reliable power for longer periods. Each step not only contributes to immediate energy savings but also supports the sustainability and resilience of your home in the face of crisis situations.

SEAL Energy Conservation for Long-Term Outages

In the face of long-term outages, adopting Navy SEAL energy conservation strategies can be a game-changer for maintaining essential functions and comfort in your home. These strategies are not just about having the right equipment but also about adopting a mindset of efficiency and preparedness. Here's how you can implement these strategies effectively:

1. **Prioritize Energy Usage**: Start by identifying critical needs that require power, such as refrigeration for food, lighting for safety, and heating or cooling for extreme weather conditions. Once identified, allocate your energy resources to these priorities to ensure that your most crucial needs are met first.

2. **Insulate and Seal Your Home**: Minimize energy loss by thoroughly insulating your home. Focus on sealing windows, doors, and any other areas where air can escape. Use weather stripping and caulk to seal these leaks. Proper insulation of walls, attics, and basements can significantly reduce the need for heating and cooling, conserving energy in the process.

3. **Solar Cookers and Passive Solar Heating**: Utilize solar energy for cooking and heating without the need for electrical power. A solar cooker can be made with simple materials like cardboard boxes, aluminum foil, and a glass cover. Positioning your home to take advantage of passive solar heating through large, south-facing windows can also reduce reliance on heating systems.

4. **LED Lighting**: Replace all lighting with LED bulbs, which use a fraction of the energy of traditional bulbs. This simple switch can extend the life of your power reserves significantly. For maximum efficiency, use task lighting over general room lighting, focusing light where it is needed most.

5. **Manual Tools Over Electric**: In situations where power is scarce, opt for manual tools instead of their electric counterparts. For example, use a manual can opener, a hand-cranked washing machine, or a solar-powered calculator. These tools do not require electricity and can perform the task equally well.

6. **Solar Chargers for Devices**: Invest in portable solar chargers for essential devices such as phones, radios, and flashlights. These chargers can keep your devices powered without tapping into your home's energy reserves. Ensure these chargers are placed in an area receiving maximum sunlight for optimal charging.

7. **Energy-Efficient Appliances**: If possible, invest in energy-efficient appliances that have a low standby power consumption and use less energy when in operation. Look for appliances with the ENERGY STAR label, indicating they meet energy efficiency guidelines set by the U.S. Environmental Protection Agency.

8. **Use Thermal Mass for Temperature Regulation**: Incorporate materials with high thermal mass like stone, brick, or concrete in your home design. These materials can absorb heat during the day and release it at night, helping to maintain a stable indoor temperature without the need for powered heating or cooling.

9. **Water Conservation**: Reducing water usage indirectly conserves energy by decreasing the demand on water heating systems and water pumps. Fix leaks, install low-flow fixtures, and collect rainwater for garden use. Remember, every drop of water saved is energy saved.

10. **Routine Maintenance and Efficiency Audits**: Regularly check and maintain your energy systems, including solar panels, wind turbines, and generators, to ensure they are operating at peak efficiency. Conduct energy audits to identify areas where energy use can be reduced or where efficiency can be improved.

By implementing these Navy SEAL-inspired energy conservation strategies, you can significantly reduce your energy consumption during long-term outages, ensuring that your limited resources are used efficiently and sustainably. Remember, the key to effective energy conservation lies not only in the measures you implement but also in the mindset of preparedness and adaptability.

Optimizing Solar and Wind Energy Systems

To ensure your solar and wind energy systems operate efficiently for continuous use, especially during long-term crises, it's crucial to optimize their performance and reliability. This involves a series of steps and considerations that go beyond mere installation, focusing on maximizing output, ensuring durability, and maintaining these systems to provide a steady and reliable energy source.

1. **Maximizing Solar Panel Efficiency**: Position your solar panels in a location that receives maximum direct sunlight exposure throughout the day. An ideal setup is a south-facing area, free from shading by trees, buildings, or other structures. The angle of your panels should be adjusted according to your geographical location to capture the optimal amount of sunlight. For most locations in the United States, setting the panels at a tilt angle equal to your latitude will yield the best results. Use a solar tracking system if possible, which adjusts the panels' angle to follow the sun's path across the sky, significantly increasing energy capture compared to fixed panels.

2. **Wind Turbine Placement**: When installing a wind turbine, conduct a thorough assessment of your property to identify the site with the highest wind speed and least turbulent flow. This often means placing the turbine on a tower that is tall enough to clear obstructions such as trees and buildings which can cause wind shadow and turbulence. The higher the turbine is placed, the more consistent and powerful the wind it can capture. Ensure that the turbine is positioned at least 30 feet above anything within a 500-foot radius to maximize wind capture.

3. **System Monitoring and Maintenance**: Regularly monitor the performance of your solar panels and wind turbine. This includes checking the energy output through an energy monitor and inspecting the physical condition of the equipment. For solar panels, clean the surface with a soft cloth and mild detergent to remove dust, bird droppings, and other debris that can block sunlight. For wind turbines, check the blades for wear and tear and ensure all bolts and connections are tight. Lubricate moving parts annually or according to the manufacturer's instructions to prevent rust and ensure smooth operation.

4. **Battery Storage Optimization**: Use deep-cycle batteries designed for energy storage to ensure that the power generated by your solar panels and wind turbine can be stored efficiently. Batteries should be kept in a clean, dry, and temperature-controlled environment to maximize their lifespan and efficiency. Regularly check the battery terminals for corrosion and clean them with a solution of baking soda and water when necessary. Ensure the battery bank is sized appropriately for your energy needs, providing enough storage to cover your power requirements during periods of low sunlight or wind.

5. **Inverter Efficiency**: Choose an inverter that matches the output of your solar and wind energy systems. The inverter converts the DC electricity generated by your panels and turbine into AC power that can be used by household appliances. An inverter with a high efficiency rating will minimize energy loss during this conversion process. Consider inverters with features such as Maximum Power Point Tracking (MPPT) for solar panels, which optimize the match between the solar array and the battery bank or grid.

6. **Load Management**: Strategically manage your energy consumption by prioritizing essential loads and using high-consumption appliances during peak production times. Implement energy-efficient appliances and LED lighting throughout your home to reduce the overall energy demand. Use timers or smart systems to run heavy appliances like washing machines and dishwashers during the day when solar production is at its peak.

7. **Hybrid Systems**: For the most reliable energy supply, consider a hybrid system that combines solar panels, wind turbines, and possibly a backup generator. This setup ensures that you have multiple sources of power to compensate for the variability in solar and wind energy production. A well-designed hybrid system

can provide a nearly uninterrupted power supply, significantly enhancing your home's resilience during crises.

By meticulously following these steps, you can optimize your solar and wind energy systems for continuous use, ensuring that your home remains powered and protected during extended periods of crisis. Regular attention to system maintenance, combined with strategic energy management, will maximize the efficiency and reliability of your off-grid energy solutions.

ENERGY PROJECTS

To ensure your off-grid energy solutions are both efficient and reliable, it's crucial to focus on the optimization and maintenance of your systems. This involves a detailed approach to selecting, installing, and caring for the components of your solar and wind power setups. Here, we'll delve into the specifics of optimizing these systems for long-term, continuous use, providing you with the knowledge to make informed decisions and the skills to keep your energy solutions running smoothly.

When selecting a solar panel, consider monocrystalline panels for their efficiency and durability, especially in limited space scenarios. For larger installations where space is less of a concern, polycrystalline panels offer a cost-effective solution. Ensure the panels you choose are rated for high wind and hail impact resistance, bearing in mind the specific weather conditions of your area. When installing solar panels, use mounting brackets designed for your roof type, whether it's shingle, metal, or tile, to prevent water leakage and ensure stability. The mounting system should allow for adjusting the angle of the panels to optimize sun exposure throughout the year. Use stainless steel hardware for its resistance to rust and corrosion.

For the wiring of solar panels, opt for UV-resistant outdoor-rated cables to connect the panels to the charge controller and battery bank. These should be sized according to the system's amperage to minimize voltage drop over the distance they cover. Employ a charge controller with Maximum Power Point Tracking (MPPT) technology to maximize the efficiency of power transfer from the panels to the battery bank. This technology adjusts the electrical operating point of the modules or array to deliver the maximum power available.

When choosing a battery storage system, deep-cycle lead-acid batteries are a common, cost-effective choice for off-grid systems, but lithium-ion batteries, while more expensive upfront, offer a longer lifespan and higher efficiency, making them a worthwhile investment for systems where reliability and maintenance are paramount. Batteries should be housed in a well-ventilated area to prevent the buildup of hazardous gases and to maintain temperature stability, which is crucial for battery longevity. Implement a battery management system (BMS) for lithium-ion setups to monitor cell health and balance charge across the battery bank, ensuring optimal performance and preventing overcharging or deep discharge.

The inverter is the heart of your power conversion process, transforming DC electricity from your panels and batteries into AC power for household use. Select an inverter with a capacity that matches or exceeds your peak power demand while ensuring it has a high efficiency rating to minimize energy loss during conversion. For systems that will be expanded over time, consider an inverter that allows for modular expansion.

Regular maintenance of your solar power system includes cleaning the panels bi-annually or more frequently if in a dusty area, checking all electrical connections for corrosion or wear, and verifying the integrity of the mounting system. For wind turbines, maintenance tasks include inspecting the blades for damage, ensuring bolts are tight and secure, and lubricating moving parts annually. The electrical system of the turbine, including the generator and connections to the home and battery bank, should be checked for signs of wear or corrosion and repaired as necessary.

By adhering to these detailed recommendations for selecting, installing, and maintaining your solar and wind energy systems, you can ensure that your off-grid energy solution is optimized for efficiency, reliability, and longevity. This proactive approach to energy management will not only provide you with a sustainable power source but also offer peace of mind knowing that your system is built and maintained to the highest standards.

Installing a basic solar panel array for home use

Project Introduction (Description - Benefits - Challenges): This project focuses on installing a basic solar panel array to provide renewable energy for home use. Benefits include reducing electricity bills, decreasing carbon footprint, and increasing energy independence. Challenges encompass understanding the technical aspects of solar installation, navigating local regulations and permits, and ensuring optimal placement for maximum sunlight exposure.

Required Materials:
- Solar panels (100-watt panels are a common choice for small-scale installations)
- Mounting brackets and hardware (specific to roof type or ground mount)
- Charge controller (to regulate the voltage and current from the panels to the battery)
- Deep cycle batteries (for energy storage)
- Inverter (to convert DC electricity from the panels/batteries to AC electricity for home use)
- Wiring and connectors (suitable for outdoor use and rated for the system's voltage)
- Grounding equipment (grounding rod and wire to protect the system from lightning strikes)

Required Tools:
- Drill with various bits (for mounting brackets)
- Wrench set (for tightening bolts and nuts)
- Wire cutters and strippers (for preparing electrical connections)
- Multimeter (for testing voltage and current)
- Safety equipment (gloves, safety glasses, and possibly a hard hat if working at heights)

Detailed Instructions:
1. **Site Assessment:** Choose an area with maximum direct sunlight exposure, ideally south-facing, with minimal shading from trees or structures during the day.
2. **Mounting System Installation:** Install the mounting brackets on the roof or a suitable ground mount structure. Ensure the mounting surface is stable and can support the weight of the panels.
3. **Panel Installation:** Attach the solar panels to the mounting brackets, securing them tightly. Panels should be angled to capture the most sunlight, which varies by location.
4. **Wiring:** Connect the solar panels to the charge controller using the appropriate gauge of wire. Ensure positive and negative terminals are correctly matched. Use waterproof connectors or a sealed junction box for outdoor use.
5. **Battery Connection:** Connect the charge controller to the deep cycle batteries. Include a fuse or circuit breaker in line with the positive cable for safety.
6. **Inverter Connection:** Connect the battery bank to the inverter, converting DC power to AC power for home use. Ensure the inverter is placed in a ventilated area to prevent overheating.
7. **Grounding:** Install a grounding rod near the solar array and connect it to the system's grounding point to protect against lightning and electrical surges.
8. **System Testing:** Use a multimeter to test the voltage and current at various points in the system to ensure everything is functioning correctly.

Safety:
- Always follow local electrical codes and standards for solar installations.
- Use personal protective equipment when working with electrical components or at heights.
- Ensure all electrical connections are tight and secure to prevent arcing or fires.

Cost of the Project: Approximately $1000-$3000, depending on the scale of the system and the quality of components used.

Preparation Time: 2-3 days, including planning, installation, and testing.

Maintenance and Care:
- Regularly clean the solar panels to remove dust, leaves, or snow that could block sunlight.
- Check all electrical connections annually for signs of corrosion or wear.
- Monitor the system's performance to detect any issues early.

FAQ or Common Issues:
- **Q: What if my solar panels aren't generating enough power?**

- **A:** Check for shading, dirt, or obstructions on the panels. Ensure the system components are correctly sized and the panels are properly angled.
- **Q: Can I expand my solar panel system later?**
- **A:** Yes, systems can be designed for expansion. Consider future needs when selecting a charge controller and inverter to facilitate easy upgrades.

Difficulty Rating: ★★★☆

Variations:
- Incorporate a solar tracking system to adjust the angle of the panels throughout the day for increased efficiency.
- Add a wind turbine to the system for additional renewable energy generation, especially useful in areas with less consistent sunlight.
- Implement a hybrid system with grid-tied capabilities, allowing for excess energy to be sold back to the utility company.

Troubleshooting:

- Check all connections to ensure they are secure and free of corrosion
- Verify that the solar panels are clean and free from debris that could block sunlight
- Inspect the inverter for any error codes or warning lights indicating a malfunction
- Ensure that the batteries are charged and functioning properly, testing with a multimeter if necessary
- Confirm that the solar charge controller is set to the correct voltage for your battery system
- Look for any shading on the panels during peak sunlight hours that could reduce efficiency
- Test the output voltage of the solar panels to ensure they are producing the expected amount of power
- Review the installation manual for any specific troubleshooting steps related to your system
- If the system is not functioning, consider resetting the inverter or charge controller as per the manufacturer's instructions
- Consult with a professional if issues persist after performing these checks

Building a DIY wind turbine for supplemental energy

Project Introduction (Description - Benefits - Challenges): Harnessing wind energy through a DIY wind turbine can significantly reduce electricity costs, promote sustainability, and provide a reliable power source in off-grid situations. The project involves constructing a turbine that converts wind energy into electrical power. Benefits include renewable energy generation, independence from the grid, and environmental conservation. Challenges encompass understanding aerodynamics, electrical systems, and securing the turbine against strong winds.

Required Materials:
- PVC pipes or lightweight aluminum for blades (3-5 blades, 2-4 feet in length)
- Permanent magnet alternator (PMA) or motor to generate electricity
- Tower or pole for mounting the turbine (10-20 feet high, depending on location)
- Deep cycle battery for storing electricity
- Charge controller to regulate the battery charging
- Inverter to convert DC power from the battery to AC power for home use
- Electrical cables and wiring for connections
- Guy wires and ground anchors for stabilizing the tower

Required Tools:
- Saw (for cutting blades if using PVC)
- Drill with various bits (for assembling components)
- Wrench set (for securing bolts and nuts)
- Wire cutters and strippers (for electrical connections)
- Multimeter (for testing electrical output)

- Safety equipment (gloves, safety glasses)

Detailed Instructions:
1. **Design and Construct Blades:** Cut the PVC pipes or aluminum to the desired length for blades. Shape them to optimize wind capture. If using PVC, a simple airfoil shape can be achieved by cutting and heating the pipes.
2. **Assemble the Turbine Head:** Attach the blades to the hub of the PMA or motor. Ensure they are evenly spaced and securely fastened.
3. **Mount the PMA or Motor:** Secure the PMA or motor to the nacelle (the housing that will be attached to the top of the tower). Make sure it can rotate to face the wind direction.
4. **Prepare the Tower:** Install the tower or pole at a location with maximum wind exposure, away from obstructions. Use guy wires and ground anchors to stabilize the tower.
5. **Install the Turbine:** Lift and secure the turbine head to the top of the tower. Ensure it is well-balanced and can rotate freely.
6. **Wire the System:** Connect the output of the PMA or motor to the charge controller, then to the battery, and finally to the inverter. Use appropriate gauge cables and ensure all connections are tight and waterproof.
7. **Ground the System:** Install a grounding rod near the base of the tower and connect it to the turbine structure to protect against lightning strikes.
8. **Test and Adjust:** Monitor the turbine's output with a multimeter. Adjust the blade angles or position of the turbine for optimal performance.

Safety:
- Always wear safety glasses and gloves when working with tools and electrical components.
- Securely fasten all components to prevent accidents in high winds.
- Work with a partner when lifting and installing the turbine on the tower.

Cost of the Project: Approximately $500-$2000, varying with the size of the turbine and quality of materials.

Preparation Time: 2-4 days, depending on skill level and assistance.

Maintenance and Care:
- Regularly check and tighten bolts and electrical connections.
- Inspect blades for damage and replace if necessary.
- Monitor battery health and replace when its capacity diminishes.
- Lubricate moving parts annually to ensure smooth operation.

FAQ or Common Issues:
- **Q: What if the turbine doesn't produce enough power?**
- **A:** Check for obstructions blocking the wind, adjust blade angles, or consider a higher mounting position.
- **Q: How do I protect the system from strong winds or storms?**
- **A:** Ensure the turbine can yaw (rotate) to align with wind direction, and use a tilt-down tower or a brake system to protect it during extreme weather.

Difficulty Rating: ★★★★☆

Variations:
- Implement a vertical axis wind turbine design for urban environments with turbulent winds.
- Add a solar panel array to create a hybrid system for more consistent power generation.
- Use a larger alternator and battery bank for increased power output to support more significant energy needs.

Troubleshooting:

- If the wind turbine is not spinning, check for obstructions in the blades or ensure that the wind direction is favorable
- If the turbine spins but does not generate power, verify the connections to the battery or inverter for any loose or damaged wires
- If the output voltage is lower than expected, inspect the generator for wear and tear or consider recalibrating the system
- If the turbine makes unusual noises, examine the bearings and ensure they are properly lubricated and free of debris
- If the system shuts down unexpectedly, check the battery for overcharging or overheating issues and ensure proper ventilation
- If the turbine is producing inconsistent power, assess the wind speed and consider adjusting the blade pitch for optimal performance

BOOK 7: TACTICAL GEAR AND TOOLS

When assembling a DIY emergency tool kit, the selection of each item should be made with careful consideration of its utility, durability, and versatility in a variety of survival situations. The goal is to compile a set of tools that can aid in immediate repair needs, facilitate survival strategies, and ensure personal safety during crises. Here's a detailed guide to creating an efficient, reliable emergency tool kit tailored to these needs.

1. **Multi-Tool**: Choose a high-quality multi-tool that includes pliers, wire cutters, a knife, a saw, and screwdrivers. Look for one made from stainless steel for durability and rust resistance. The multi-tool serves as the cornerstone of your kit, providing versatility without taking up much space.

2. **Fixed-Blade Knife**: Select a full-tang, fixed-blade knife for tasks that require more strength than a multi-tool can provide. The blade should be at least 4 inches long, made of high-carbon steel for sharpness retention and ease of sharpening. Ensure the handle is ergonomically designed for a secure grip, even in wet conditions.

3. **Flashlight**: Include a durable, waterproof flashlight with LED bulbs. LEDs consume less power, providing longer battery life while offering bright illumination. Choose a model with multiple brightness settings, including a strobe feature for signaling. Opt for rechargeable batteries and include a solar charger in your kit.

4. **Fire Starter Kit**: Your kit should have multiple fire-starting tools: waterproof matches, a magnesium fire starter, and a ferrocerium rod. Each offers a reliable method for starting fires in various conditions. Store them in waterproof containers to ensure they remain dry.

5. **Paracord**: Add at least 50 feet of 550 paracord. Its strength and versatility make it invaluable for building shelters, repairing gear, or even fishing. Paracord bracelets are a compact way to carry this essential item.

6. **Duct Tape**: A roll of heavy-duty duct tape can repair gear, seal leaks, and even serve as a makeshift bandage in a pinch. Look for a thick, waterproof variant for maximum utility.

7. **Compact Folding Saw**: A lightweight, high-tensile blade folding saw is crucial for cutting wood for fires or shelter construction. Choose one with a locking mechanism to ensure safety during use.

8. **Water Purification Tablets**: In situations where water safety is compromised, having a quick method for purification is vital. Include a bottle of water purification tablets that can treat several gallons of water.

9. **Signal Mirror**: A durable, high-visibility signal mirror can be a lifesaver for signaling rescuers. Select a compact model with a sighting hole for accuracy.

10. **Whistle**: A loud, pealess whistle is essential for signaling help. It should be durable, waterproof, and capable of producing a high-decibel sound that can be heard from a distance.

11. **Compass**: Include a high-quality compass for navigation. Look for a model with a luminous, easy-to-read dial and a sturdy, waterproof construction. Learning basic navigation skills to use in conjunction with your compass is also advisable.

12. **First Aid Kit**: Assemble a compact first aid kit containing adhesive bandages of various sizes, antiseptic wipes, antibiotic ointment, gauze pads, medical tape, pain relievers, and any personal medications. Consider taking a basic first aid course to familiarize yourself with the use of these items.

13. **Sewing Kit**: A small sewing kit with needles, thread, safety pins, and buttons can repair clothing and gear. Opt for strong, all-purpose thread and include a few heavy-duty needles capable of piercing tough materials.

14. **Gloves**: Durable work gloves protect your hands during tasks like gathering wood or clearing debris. Choose gloves that offer a balance between protection and dexterity.

15. **Storage**: All these items should be stored in a sturdy, waterproof bag or container that's easy to carry. Organize the contents in a way that allows quick access to frequently used items. Consider a bag with multiple compartments or use zippered pouches for organization.

By meticulously selecting and organizing these tools, you create a comprehensive emergency tool kit that's prepared to handle a wide range of survival scenarios. Regularly review and maintain the contents of your kit, replacing or sharpening tools as necessary to ensure readiness when needed.

CHAPTER 1: ESSENTIAL SEAL GEAR FOR SURVIVAL

In the realm of survival, the gear you carry can mean the difference between overcoming an obstacle and facing a potentially dire situation. This section delves into the essential gear that mirrors the Navy SEALs' standard for survival, focusing on the specifics of each item to ensure you're fully prepared for any scenario. The selection of gear is not just about having tools; it's about being equipped with versatile, durable, and reliable items that have been tested in the most challenging conditions.

1. **Tactical Flashlight**: Opt for a tactical flashlight with a minimum output of 600 lumens, capable of strobe mode for disorienting potential threats. The flashlight should be constructed from aircraft-grade aluminum for durability and be waterproof to at least IPX8 standard. The power source should be a rechargeable 18650 lithium-ion battery, offering a balance between runtime and brightness. For ease of use, ensure it has a tail switch for one-handed operation.

2. **Survival Watch**: A rugged, all-weather survival watch with GPS functionality is indispensable. Look for features such as a barometer, compass, altimeter, and sunrise/sunset times. The casing should be shock-resistant and water-resistant to at least 100 meters. Solar charging capabilities are a plus, reducing the need to carry spare batteries.

3. **Tactical Pen**: A tactical pen, made from high-grade aluminum or titanium, serves as a writing instrument and a self-defense tool. It should feature a glass breaker tip and be designed to fit comfortably in your hand. Ensure the ink cartridge is pressurized, allowing you to write in extreme conditions, including wet surfaces and upside down.

4. **Survival Knife**: A fixed-blade survival knife with a full tang design ensures maximum strength. The blade, approximately 4 to 6 inches in length, should be made from high-carbon stainless steel for corrosion resistance and ease of sharpening. The handle must offer a firm grip, even in wet conditions, and include a lanyard hole. A sheath with multiple carry options enhances portability and accessibility.

5. **Tactical Backpack**: Choose a backpack with a minimum capacity of 40 liters, made from high-denier, water-resistant nylon fabric. It should feature MOLLE (Modular Lightweight Load-carrying Equipment) webbing for attaching additional pouches and gear. Look for a pack with adjustable shoulder, chest, and waist straps to distribute weight evenly. A hydration bladder compartment is essential for maintaining fluid intake without having to stop and unpack.

6. **Water Purification System**: A portable water filter capable of removing bacteria, protozoa, and viruses without the use of chemicals is crucial. Select a filter with a pore size of 0.2 microns or smaller. The system should be lightweight, with the ability to purify up to 1000 liters of water before needing a filter replacement. Additionally, carry water purification tablets as a backup, containing either chlorine dioxide or iodine, capable of treating up to one liter of water per tablet.

7. **First Aid Kit**: Assemble a comprehensive first aid kit that includes adhesive bandages of various sizes, gauze, medical tape, antibiotic ointment, antiseptic wipes, a tourniquet, emergency blanket, nitrile gloves, and tweezers. Personal medications and a compact guide on first aid procedures are also essential. The kit should be packed in a waterproof, durable case for easy access.

8. **Fire Starter**: Carry a magnesium fire starter rod and a waterproof container of matches. The magnesium rod should be capable of thousands of strikes, producing sparks at temperatures high enough to ignite tinder in any weather condition. Additionally, include a windproof lighter as a more convenient ignition source for when quick fire creation is necessary.

9. **Paracord**: At least 50 feet of 550 paracord is indispensable for its strength and versatility. It can be used for securing gear, erecting shelters, or emergency rappelling. Ensure the paracord is genuine mil-spec, featuring a seven-strand core that can be used for fishing line or sewing thread in a pinch.

10. **Emergency Shelter**: A compact, lightweight emergency bivvy or tent made from heat-reflective polyethylene can significantly increase your chances of survival in harsh conditions. It should be windproof, waterproof, and capable of reflecting up to 90% of your body heat back to you. Look for a shelter that packs down small and can be quickly deployed.

Each piece of gear selected for inclusion in your survival kit should be evaluated not only for its primary function but also for its ability to serve multiple purposes, thereby reducing the overall weight and bulk of your gear. Regularly review and maintain your equipment to ensure it remains in optimal condition, ready for use when needed. Remember, the right gear, when used effectively, can provide more than just survival; it can offer a tactical advantage in the face of adversity.

Key Tactical Gear Used by SEALs

In the demanding world of Navy SEALs, the tactical gear they rely on is not just about carrying equipment; it's about ensuring survival, operational success, and the ability to adapt to rapidly changing environments. Each piece of gear is chosen for its reliability, functionality, and the tactical advantage it provides in the field. This section delves into the critical components of SEAL gear, emphasizing the importance of each item in survival and combat situations.

Tactical Flashlights are indispensable in the gear lineup, providing not just illumination but also serving as a tool for signaling and disorientation in confrontations. SEALs opt for flashlights that offer high lumens, durability, and water resistance, such as those made from aircraft-grade aluminum. These flashlights often feature multiple modes, including strobe effects, and are powered by rechargeable batteries, ensuring they are always mission-ready.

Survival Watches go beyond merely telling time; they are compact computers on the wrist. Chosen for their ruggedness, these watches come equipped with GPS, barometric pressure readings, compass bearings, and altimeter data. They are essential for navigation, timing operations, and monitoring environmental conditions. The preferred watches are solar-powered, eliminating the need for battery replacement, and are water-resistant to withstand extreme conditions.

Tactical Pens, while seemingly mundane, serve multiple purposes in a SEAL's kit. Constructed from heavy-duty materials like aluminum or titanium, these pens function as writing instruments, glass breakers, and last-resort self-defense tools. The design is sleek yet robust, with features that allow them to be used in all weather conditions, making them an understated yet vital piece of gear.

Survival Knives are perhaps the most iconic piece of SEAL gear. A high-quality, fixed-blade knife with a full tang provides a level of reliability and versatility unmatched by other tools. These knives are used for everything from combat to survival tasks such as building shelters or preparing food. The blades are typically made from high-carbon stainless steel for durability and ease of maintenance, with handles designed for a secure grip in all conditions.

Tactical Backpacks are the backbone of carrying gear, designed for durability, flexibility, and accessibility. These packs are made from high-denier, water-resistant materials and feature modular webbing for attaching additional pouches or equipment. The capacity and compartmentalization are carefully considered to allow for efficient packing and quick access to essential items. Hydration systems are integrated into these backpacks, ensuring water is always within reach.

Water Purification Systems are critical for survival, allowing SEALs to secure safe drinking water from virtually any source. Portable filters that can eliminate pathogens and purify water without the need for boiling or chemical treatments are a must-have. These systems are lightweight, with filters that have a long lifespan before needing replacement, and are complemented by purification tablets for redundancy.

First Aid Kits in the field are compact but comprehensive, containing not just basic bandages and antiseptics but also specialized items like tourniquets, emergency blankets, and surgical tools. These kits are tailored to address both common injuries and life-threatening situations, packed in a way that allows for rapid access in an emergency.

Fire Starters such as magnesium rods and waterproof matches are essential for warmth, cooking, and signaling. The ability to start a fire in any weather condition is a fundamental survival skill, and SEALs carry multiple redundant systems to ensure they can always produce a flame when necessary.

Paracord, with its incredible strength and versatility, is invaluable for tasks ranging from securing equipment to emergency rappelling. Genuine mil-spec paracord is preferred for its reliability and the multitude of uses it offers in survival situations.

Emergency Shelters, made from lightweight, reflective materials, provide immediate protection from the elements. These shelters are designed for quick setup, offering a temporary refuge that can significantly improve survival chances in adverse conditions.

Each item in a SEAL's tactical gear is chosen with the utmost consideration for its utility, durability, and contribution to mission success. This gear represents a balance between preparedness for any situation and the need to remain agile and responsive in the field. The selection process is rigorous, ensuring that every piece of equipment can withstand the extreme demands of SEAL operations and the unpredictable nature of survival scenarios.

Tools for Defense and Survival

When selecting tools for defense, utility, and survival, it's crucial to focus on versatility, durability, and effectiveness. These tools must serve multiple purposes, from ensuring personal safety to facilitating basic survival tasks. Here's a detailed guide to making informed choices about the essential tools for your survival kit.

1. **Tactical Knife**: A tactical knife is indispensable for both defense and utility. Opt for a knife with a fixed blade, as it offers more stability and strength than a folding knife. The blade should be made of high-carbon stainless steel, which ensures both durability and ease of sharpening. A blade length of 4 to 6 inches is ideal, balancing portability with functionality. The handle should provide a secure grip, even in wet conditions, and include a pommel at the end that can be used as a hammer. For added versatility, select a knife with a serrated edge along part of the blade, useful for sawing through ropes or branches.

2. **Multi-Tool**: A high-quality multi-tool complements the tactical knife, providing a range of tools in one compact package. Look for a multi-tool that includes pliers, wire cutters, a saw, a can opener, screwdrivers, and a file. Stainless steel construction is preferred for its resistance to rust and corrosion. Ensure the multi-tool has a locking mechanism for each tool, enhancing safety and effectiveness during use.

3. **Tactical Flashlight**: Choose a tactical flashlight with a minimum output of 600 lumens and multiple light modes, including a strobe function for disorienting potential attackers. The flashlight should be durable, with an aircraft-grade aluminum body and waterproofing to at least IPX8 standard. A rechargeable battery system, preferably with a USB charging port, offers convenience and reliability. The flashlight's design should include a bezel edge for self-defense purposes and a clip or lanyard for secure carry.

4. **Paracord**: Paracord, specifically Type III 550 paracord, is a lightweight nylon rope known for its high tensile strength and versatility. Carry at least 50 feet of paracord, which can be used for building shelters, securing gear, or even as a makeshift tourniquet. Ensure the paracord is genuine mil-spec, featuring a seven-strand core that can be unraveled for use as fishing line or thread.

5. **Portable Water Filter**: A portable water filter is essential for accessing clean drinking water. Select a filter capable of removing bacteria, protozoa, and microplastics, with a pore size of 0.2 microns or smaller. The filter should be lightweight and have a high flow rate for easy use. Look for models that can filter up to 1000 liters of water before needing a replacement cartridge. Additionally, carry water purification tablets as a backup.

6. **Fire Starter**: For starting fires under any conditions, include a magnesium fire starter and waterproof matches in your kit. The magnesium fire starter should be capable of thousands of strikes, producing hot sparks that can ignite tinder. Waterproof matches should be stored in a waterproof container as an additional fire-starting method.

7. **Compact Folding Saw**: A compact folding saw with a durable, high-tensile blade is invaluable for cutting wood for fires or shelter construction. Choose a saw with a locking mechanism to ensure safety and efficiency. The saw should be lightweight and foldable for easy storage and transport.

8. **Emergency Whistle**: An emergency whistle made from durable, weather-resistant material can signal for help in crisis situations. Look for a whistle that produces a loud, piercing sound that can be heard over long distances. A pealess design prevents the whistle from jamming or freezing in cold weather.

9. **Compass**: A reliable compass is essential for navigation in unfamiliar environments. Select a compass with a luminous, easy-to-read dial, and a durable, waterproof construction. A sighting mirror on the compass can aid in accuracy when taking bearings.

10. **First Aid Kit**: Assemble a compact first aid kit tailored to your specific needs, including adhesive bandages, gauze, medical tape, antiseptic wipes, antibiotic ointment, a tourniquet, and any personal medications. The kit should be packed in a waterproof, durable case for protection against the elements.

By carefully selecting these tools for defense, utility, and survival, you equip yourself with the means to handle a wide range of situations, from everyday tasks to unexpected emergencies. Each tool has been chosen for its proven reliability and multifunctionality, ensuring you're prepared for whatever challenges you may face. Regularly review and maintain your tools to keep them in optimal condition, ready for use when the need arises.

Organizing Gear for Emergency Access

Organizing your gear for rapid access during emergencies is a critical skill that can significantly impact your ability to respond effectively to unforeseen situations. The key is to ensure that every piece of equipment is placed thoughtfully, allowing for both quick retrieval and optimal functionality under stress. Here's a step-by-step guide to achieving an organized, efficient setup that mirrors the precision and readiness of Navy SEALs.

1. **Categorize Your Gear**: Begin by categorizing your gear based on its purpose and frequency of use. Essential categories might include medical supplies, navigation tools, communication devices, water purification systems, and personal defense items. This categorization process helps in identifying what needs to be most accessible.

2. **Use Color-Coded Bags or Pouches**: Assign a color to each category of gear. For instance, medical supplies could be stored in a red pouch, navigation tools in blue, and communication devices in black. This color-coding system allows for quick visual identification, reducing the time spent searching for specific items.

3. **Prioritize Placement Based on Urgency and Frequency**: Items that are likely to be needed urgently, such as a first aid kit or a tactical flashlight, should be placed in the most accessible compartments of your backpack or tactical vest. Less frequently used items can be stored in less accessible spots. Always

keep the most critical gear within easy reach, preferably in side pockets or compartments that can be opened without removing the pack.

4. **Utilize Modular Storage Systems**: Opt for backpacks and vests with modular storage systems, such as MOLLE (Modular Lightweight Load-carrying Equipment) webbing. This system allows you to attach and arrange pouches and gear in a highly customizable layout. It enables gear to be organized in a way that maximizes space and accessibility, allowing for quick adjustments based on the mission or situation.

5. **Implement a Standard Packing Order**: Always pack your gear in the same order. Consistency in packing ensures that, even in complete darkness or under extreme stress, you know exactly where each item is located. Muscle memory can be a lifesaver when time is of the essence.

6. **Regularly Review and Adjust Your Setup**: Conditions and needs can change, so it's important to regularly review your gear organization. After each training session or emergency situation, reassess the placement of your gear. Ask yourself what worked well and what could be improved. This continuous improvement process ensures your setup remains optimized for rapid access.

7. **Practice Retrieval Under Various Conditions**: Regularly practice accessing your gear under different conditions, including at night, in confined spaces, and when wearing gloves. This practice helps to identify any practical issues with your organization system and ensures you're comfortable and proficient with your gear layout.

8. **Label Everything**: For gear that isn't immediately identifiable by touch or color, consider using durable, waterproof labels. Labels are particularly useful for items stored in similar-looking pouches or for gear that is used less frequently and thus less familiar.

9. **Use Gear Tethers for Critical Items**: For items that are essential and small enough to be easily misplaced, such as a compass, flashlight, or multi-tool, use retractable gear tethers. These tethers allow you to use the item while ensuring it remains attached to your pack or vest, preventing loss.

10. **Optimize Gear for Quick Deployment**: For items like emergency shelters or tourniquets, pre-stage them for quick deployment. This might mean partially unfolding a shelter or pre-looping a tourniquet. The goal is to minimize the steps required to use the item, speeding up its deployment.

By meticulously organizing your gear for rapid access, you ensure that, in any emergency, you can respond with the efficiency and effectiveness of a Navy SEAL. This level of preparedness not only enhances your ability to protect yourself and others but also instills a deep sense of confidence that, no matter what challenges arise, you are ready to face them head-on.

CHAPTER 2: CHOOSING SURVIVAL EQUIPMENT

When selecting the right survival equipment, it's crucial to focus on versatility, durability, and utility. The gear you choose should serve multiple purposes, withstand harsh conditions, and be compact enough to carry without weighing you down. Let's dive into the specifics of choosing the essential tools for your survival kit, ensuring you're prepared for any scenario.

Firstly, when choosing a multi-tool, opt for one made from high-grade stainless steel, featuring a variety of tools including pliers, a knife, a saw, a screwdriver, and a can opener. The Leatherman Wave Plus is a prime example, offering 18 tools in one compact design, making it indispensable for repairs, food preparation, and emergency situations.

For a fixed-blade knife, select a full tang blade for maximum strength. The blade should be at least 4 inches long, made from carbon steel or high-quality stainless steel for ease of sharpening and rust resistance. The KA-BAR Becker BK2 Campanion Fixed Blade Knife is highly recommended for its robust construction and versatility in outdoor and survival tasks.

A flashlight is another essential piece of equipment. Choose a model with multiple brightness settings and a strobe mode for signaling. LED technology offers longer battery life and durability. The Fenix PD35 TAC 1000 Lumen CREE XP-L LED Tactical Flashlight is an excellent choice, providing powerful illumination and a durable, waterproof design.

For fire starting, a magnesium fire starter is reliable in wet conditions and offers thousands of strikes. The Light My Fire Swedish FireSteel 2.0 Army Magnesium Firestarter produces a 3,000-degree Celsius spark, making it effective even in damp environments.

Paracord, with a minimum breaking strength of 550 pounds, is essential for building shelters, repairing gear, and countless other survival tasks. Opt for Type III paracord, ensuring it's genuine mil-spec for maximum durability and reliability.

Duct tape, known for its versatility, should be included for making repairs, creating makeshift tools, or medical bandaging in a pinch. Gorilla Tape offers a strong, weather-resistant option that sticks to rough and uneven surfaces.

A compact folding saw, such as the Silky GOMBOY Curve Professional Folding Saw, can be invaluable for cutting wood for shelters, fires, or signaling. Its ability to fold makes it safe and easy to transport.

Water purification tablets, like the Potable Aqua Water Purification Tablets, are a must-have for ensuring safe drinking water from any source. They're lightweight, easy to use, and effective against pathogens.

For navigation, a high-quality compass that is reliable and accurate is essential. The Suunto MC-2G Global Navigator Compass, with its global needle, is designed for precise navigation anywhere in the world.

A comprehensive first aid kit should include various bandages, antiseptics, pain relievers, and specific medications based on personal needs. The Adventure Medical Kits Mountain Series Backpacker Medical Kit is designed for groups of up to four people and offers supplies tailored for outdoor adventures.

A sewing kit, while often overlooked, is crucial for repairing gear and clothing. Include needles, thread, safety pins, and buttons. A simple, compact sewing kit can be a lifesaver when dealing with tears or missing buttons.

Lastly, gloves protect your hands during tasks like gathering wood, handling tools, or moving through rough terrain. Choose durable, all-purpose gloves with a good grip, such as Mechanix Wear - MultiCam FastFit Tactical Gloves, which offer protection without sacrificing dexterity.

By focusing on these specific recommendations for materials, tools, and techniques, you'll ensure your survival kit is well-equipped for any situation, combining Navy SEAL resilience with practical preparedness.

Selecting Multi-Tools and Knives

When it comes to equipping yourself for survival scenarios, the selection of multi-tools and knives cannot be overstated in terms of importance. These tools are not just accessories but lifelines in various situations you may encounter. The key to choosing the right multi-tool and knife lies in understanding their features, materials, and the specific uses they are designed for.

Starting with multi-tools, the ideal choice should offer a balance between functionality and portability. Look for a multi-tool that includes the most essential functions without being overly bulky. A good multi-tool should have at least a pair of pliers, a wire cutter, a knife blade, a saw, a couple of screwdrivers (flathead and Phillips), and a bottle/can opener. The material of the tool is crucial; stainless steel is preferred for its corrosion resistance and strength. The Gerber Suspension Multi-Plier is an exemplary model, featuring a butterfly opening design for easy access to tools and a sturdy stainless steel construction. Its locking mechanism ensures safety while the tools are in use, and its lightweight design does not compromise on the range of tools it offers.

For knives, the selection process should focus on blade quality, handle ergonomics, and the knife's overall durability. A fixed-blade knife is recommended for its strength and reliability. The blade should be made of high-carbon stainless steel, which combines the rust resistance of stainless steel with the edge-holding capabilities of high-carbon steel. The handle should provide a comfortable, non-slip grip and be durable enough to withstand harsh conditions. The Morakniv Companion Heavy Duty Knife is a standout choice, featuring a 4.1-inch high-carbon stainless steel blade that is exceptionally tough and capable of performing a wide range of tasks. Its rubber handle offers a secure grip even in wet conditions, and the knife comes with a durable plastic sheath that makes it easy to carry.

When selecting a knife, consider the length and thickness of the blade. A blade length of 4 to 6 inches is versatile enough for most survival tasks, from preparing food to cutting through materials. The thickness should be around 0.125 to 0.25 inches, providing a good balance between strength and precision. The edge of the blade should be a full flat grind or a Scandinavian grind, both of which are excellent for wood carving, food preparation, and other survival tasks. The blade's tip should be strong and capable of piercing, making a drop point or a clip point design ideal for survival knives.

In addition to the primary tools, consider the inclusion of a multi-tool or knife that incorporates a fire starter. The ability to start a fire is critical in survival situations for warmth, cooking, and signaling for help. Some multi-tools and knives come with a ferrocerium rod that can spark to ignite tinder. For instance, the Bear Grylls Survival Series by Gerber includes a knife with an integrated fire starter, offering both a reliable blade and a means to make fire.

Finally, when assembling your survival kit, remember that the best tools are the ones you know how to use effectively. Familiarize yourself with the features and functions of your multi-tool and knife. Practice using them in various tasks to ensure you can rely on them confidently when needed. By selecting tools that offer the right combination of features, durability, and ease of use, you equip yourself with the means to handle many challenges that may come your way in survival scenarios.

Fire-Starting Kits and Emergency Lighting

Fire-starting kits and emergency lighting are indispensable components of any survival gear, ensuring you can generate warmth, cook food, and signal for help under any conditions. The key to an effective fire-starting kit lies in its reliability and versatility, while emergency lighting must offer durability and sufficient brightness when you need it most. Here's how to assemble and utilize these critical tools with precision.

For your fire-starting kit, prioritize items that are waterproof or can be easily waterproofed. A magnesium fire starter rod paired with waterproof matches and a butane lighter provides a good foundation. The magnesium rod, capable of producing sparks even when wet, should be your primary tool. Look for a rod that is at least 3 inches long for ease of use and longevity. The UST BlastMatch Fire Starter is a recommended choice for its one-handed operation and ability to produce a shower of sparks in any weather. Complement this with UCO Stormproof Matches, which can burn for up to 15 seconds even after being submerged in water, and a windproof butane lighter like the Zippo Windproof Lighter, which offers reliability in windy or wet conditions.

In addition to these primary tools, include tinder that can catch fire quickly. Commercially prepared tinder, such as QuickFire Instant Fire Starters, is designed to ignite easily and burn for several minutes, giving you ample time to add kindling. For a DIY option, cotton balls soaked in petroleum jelly are lightweight, compact, and ignite easily with a spark. Store these in a waterproof container or zip-lock bag to keep them dry.

Emergency lighting should consist of at least one high-lumen LED flashlight and a headlamp, allowing for hands-free operation. The Fenix PD35 TAC 1000 Lumen CREE XP-L LED Tactical Flashlight stands out for its high output and durability. It features multiple brightness settings, including a strobe mode for signaling. Pair this with the Black Diamond Spot 325 Headlamp, which offers a balance of brightness and battery life, along with a waterproof rating that ensures functionality in adverse weather conditions.

For redundancy, include glow sticks and a solar-powered lantern. Glow sticks, such as Cyalume SnapLight Green Glow Sticks, provide up to 12 hours of light without the need for batteries, making them ideal for signaling or short-term illumination. The MPOWERD Luci Outdoor 2.0 Solar Inflatable Light is a compact, solar-rechargeable lantern that can provide up to 24 hours of light on a single charge, perfect for extended periods without access to power.

Remember, the effectiveness of your fire-starting kit and emergency lighting hinges not just on the quality of the tools, but also on your ability to use them proficiently. Regularly practice with your fire-starting tools in various conditions and familiarize yourself with the operation of your flashlights and headlamps, including changing batteries and adjusting settings in the dark. This hands-on experience ensures that when the need arises, you can confidently and efficiently use these tools to secure warmth, cook food, and signal for help, embodying the resilience and preparedness of a Navy SEAL.

DIY Chapter: Tactical Gear Projects

Project Introduction (Description - Benefits - Challenges)

Building a tactical gear organizer allows for quick access and efficient storage of essential survival tools and equipment. The benefits include improved readiness, organization, and ease of access in emergency situations. Challenges include designing a system that accommodates various gear sizes and ensuring durability under heavy use.

Required Materials

- Heavy-duty nylon fabric (1000D recommended) for the main structure
- Velcro strips (both hook and loop sides) for adjustable compartments
- Heavy-duty sewing thread and needles
- Buckles and straps for securing the organizer
- Metal D-rings for hanging additional gear
- Foam padding for protecting delicate items
- Waterproof fabric liner for moisture protection

Required Tools

- Sewing machine capable of handling heavy-duty fabrics
- Fabric scissors
- Measuring tape
- Marker or fabric chalk
- Heavy-duty hole punch or grommet tool

Detailed Instructions

1. **Measure and Cut Fabric**: Based on the gear you plan to organize, measure and cut the nylon fabric to create a back panel and individual pouches or loops.
2. **Sew Velcro Strips**: Attach Velcro strips to the back panel and corresponding pieces on the pouches or loops. This allows for customizable placement and secure attachment of gear.
3. **Assemble Pouches and Loops**: Sew the sides of the pouches and loops, reinforcing the stitches to handle the weight of the gear. Attach buckles and straps as needed for closure.
4. **Attach D-rings**: Securely sew metal D-rings to the top or sides of the back panel for additional hanging options.
5. **Add Foam Padding**: Insert foam padding into pouches designed for delicate items, providing extra protection.
6. **Install Waterproof Liner**: Line the back panel and inside of pouches with waterproof fabric to protect gear from moisture.
7. **Final Assembly**: Sew all components onto the back panel, ensuring even spacing and secure attachment. Reinforce stitches at stress points.

Safety

- Use gloves when handling heavy-duty fabrics and sharp tools to prevent cuts.
- Ensure the sewing machine is properly set up for heavy fabrics to avoid needle breakage.

Cost of the Project

Approximately $50-$100, depending on the size of the organizer and the quality of materials chosen.

Preparation Time

8-10 hours, including measuring, cutting, and sewing.

Maintenance and Care

- Regularly check for loose stitches or wear and repair as necessary.
- Clean with a damp cloth and mild soap; avoid harsh chemicals that could degrade the fabric.
- Store in a dry, cool place to prevent moisture buildup and mildew.

FAQ or Common Issues

- **Q: What if my sewing machine can't handle the heavy-duty fabric?**
- **A:** Consider hand-sewing critical areas or using a professional service for the toughest parts.
- **Q: How can I ensure the organizer holds up under heavy use?**
- **A:** Focus on reinforcing stitches, especially at stress points, and choose high-quality, durable materials.

Difficulty Rating

★★★☆☆

Variations

- Add a fold-out panel for additional storage space that can be hidden when not in use.
- Incorporate clear plastic windows on pouches for easy identification of contents.
- Design the organizer to be modular, with detachable sections for specific missions or needs.

Troubleshooting:

- If your tactical gear is not fitting properly, check the adjustment straps and ensure they are tightened to your body shape
- If you experience discomfort while wearing your gear, consider adding padding or adjusting the placement of heavy items to distribute weight more evenly
- If your gear is not providing adequate protection, reassess the materials used and consider upgrading to more durable options
- If you notice wear and tear on your gear, inspect for any damaged components and replace them immediately to maintain functionality
- If your gear is difficult to access in an emergency, practice quick-release techniques and reorganize your setup for better accessibility
- If your gear is too bulky, evaluate the necessity of each item and remove non-essential components to streamline your load
- If your gear is not weather-resistant, apply appropriate treatments or invest in waterproof covers to protect against the elements
- If you find your gear is not blending well with your environment, consider using camouflage patterns or colors that match your surroundings

Building a tactical gear organizer for quick access

Project Introduction (Description - Benefits - Challenges)

Creating a tactical gear organizer ensures quick and efficient access to essential equipment and tools. The organizer will be designed to accommodate a variety of gear sizes, from small gadgets to larger equipment, making it versatile for different survival scenarios. Benefits include enhanced organization, faster retrieval of gear in urgent situations, and protection of equipment from damage. Challenges involve selecting durable materials that can withstand heavy use and designing a system that is both flexible and robust.

Required Materials

- Heavy-duty nylon fabric (1000D recommended) for durability and resistance to wear and tear
- Velcro strips (both hook and loop sides) for creating adjustable and customizable compartments
- High-strength sewing thread designed for outdoor use
- Buckles and adjustable straps for securing the organizer and its contents
- Metal D-rings for attaching additional gear externally
- Foam padding to provide cushioning for delicate items
- Waterproof fabric liner to protect gear from moisture

Required Tools

- Heavy-duty sewing machine capable of stitching through thick fabric layers
- Sharp fabric scissors for precise cutting of materials
- Measuring tape for accurate sizing of components
- Fabric marker or chalk for marking cut lines and assembly points
- Grommet tool for reinforcing holes and adding attachment points

Detailed Instructions

1. **Design Planning**: Sketch the layout of the organizer, including back panel dimensions and the size and placement of pouches or compartments. Consider the types of gear to be stored and allow for flexibility in arrangement.

2. **Cutting Materials**: Using the fabric scissors, cut the nylon fabric according to the planned dimensions for the back panel and pouches. Cut Velcro strips to match the widths of pouch openings.

3. **Sewing Velcro and Pouches**: Attach Velcro strips to the pouches and the back panel, ensuring the hook side is on the pouches and the loop side on the panel. Sew the sides of the pouches, reinforcing the stitches for durability.

4. **Assembling the Organizer**: Arrange and sew the pouches onto the back panel based on the initial design. Incorporate buckles and straps for securing larger items and attach D-rings at strategic points for additional gear.

5. **Padding and Lining**: Insert foam padding into select pouches for fragile items. Line the back panel and the interior of pouches with waterproof fabric to safeguard against moisture.

6. **Final Assembly**: Double-check the arrangement of all components and make any necessary adjustments. Reinforce all stitches, especially at stress points where gear weight will be concentrated.

Safety

- Wear protective gloves when cutting materials and handling sharp tools to prevent injuries.
- Ensure the sewing area is well-lit and free of obstructions to safely operate the sewing machine.

Cost of the Project

Estimated cost is $50-$100, varying with the choice of materials and the size of the organizer.

Preparation Time

Approximately 8-10 hours, depending on sewing proficiency and complexity of the design.

Maintenance and Care

- Regularly inspect the organizer for any signs of wear or loose stitches and repair as needed.
- Clean with a damp cloth to remove dirt and grime. Avoid using harsh chemicals that could damage the fabric.
- Store in a dry, ventilated area to prevent mold and mildew buildup.

FAQ or Common Issues

- **Q: What if I don't have a heavy-duty sewing machine?**
- **A:** Consider hand-sewing with a durable needle and thread for small sections, or seek a local tailor or upholstery shop that can handle heavy-duty sewing tasks.

- **Q: How can I ensure the organizer fits all my gear?**
- **A:** Measure your gear before designing the organizer. Plan for adjustable and multi-sized compartments using Velcro and straps to accommodate various items.

Difficulty Rating

★★★☆☆

Variations

- For larger gear, add a foldable extension panel that can be rolled out or zipped onto the main organizer.
- Integrate a removable pouch system using heavy-duty zippers, allowing for customization based on the mission or outing.
- Consider adding a detachable shoulder strap or MOLLE (Modular Lightweight Load-carrying Equipment) webbing for compatibility with tactical backpacks and vests.

Troubleshooting:

- If your gear organizer is unstable, check that all screws and fasteners are tightened properly
- If items are difficult to access, consider rearranging the layout for better visibility and reach
- If the organizer is too small, evaluate your gear inventory and consider expanding the size or adding additional organizers
- If the materials are not holding up, assess the quality of the materials used and replace them with more durable options
- If the organizer is not fitting in the designated space, measure the area again and adjust the dimensions of the organizer accordingly
- If you find that your gear is getting damaged, ensure that the compartments are adequately padded or lined to protect your equipment
- If you experience difficulty in locating specific items, implement a labeling system to enhance organization and retrieval speed

Assembling a DIY emergency tool kit

Project Introduction (Description - Benefits - Challenges): Assembling a DIY emergency tool kit equips you with the necessary tools for a wide range of survival situations, from minor repairs to emergency scenarios. The benefits of creating your own kit include customization to fit your specific needs, cost savings compared to pre-assembled kits, and the assurance of quality in selecting each item. Challenges may include deciding on the essential tools to include and organizing them in a compact, portable manner.

Required Materials:
- Durable, waterproof carrying case or backpack with a minimum capacity of 30 liters, made from high-denier nylon or similar material to withstand harsh conditions and prevent water ingress
- Multi-tool with pliers, knife (preferably 3-inch stainless steel blade), screwdriver (flat and Phillips), and can opener, featuring a locking mechanism for safety during use
- Adjustable wrench with a jaw capacity of at least 1.5 inches, made from chrome vanadium steel for durability and corrosion resistance
- Compact flashlight with a minimum output of 300 lumens, featuring a beam distance of at least 100 meters, and extra batteries or a solar-powered option with a built-in USB charging port
- Fire starter kit including waterproof matches (at least 20), a reliable lighter, and tinder (such as cotton balls soaked in petroleum jelly) for easy ignition in wet conditions
- Paracord (50 feet) with a minimum breaking strength of 550 pounds, suitable for various applications such as securing items, building shelters, or creating traps
- Duct tape (small roll) with a width of 1.88 inches and a length of at least 10 yards, known for its strong adhesive properties and versatility in repairs
- Safety whistle with a sound output of at least 100 decibels, made from durable plastic or metal, to signal for help in emergencies
- Compact first aid kit containing adhesive bandages, antiseptic wipes, gauze pads, medical tape, scissors, tweezers, and a CPR face shield, all organized in a waterproof pouch

- Water purification tablets (such as those containing sodium dichloroisocyanurate) capable of treating at least 10 liters of water, effective against bacteria and viruses
- Emergency blanket made from mylar material, capable of retaining up to 90% of body heat, lightweight and compact for easy storage
- Hand-cranked or battery-operated radio with NOAA weather band capability, featuring a USB charging port and a built-in flashlight for added functionality
- Notepad and pencil made from waterproof materials, allowing for note-taking in wet conditions, with at least 50 pages for ample writing space
- Sewing kit with at least 10 needles of various sizes, a selection of thread (including heavy-duty and waterproof options), and a small pair of scissors for repairs
- Spare cash in small denominations (preferably $1, $5, and $10 bills) and copies of important documents (such as IDs, insurance papers, and medical records) stored in a waterproof bag to ensure accessibility during emergencies

Required Tools:
- Label maker or permanent marker for item identification
- Scissors for cutting paracord and duct tape

Detailed Instructions:
1. **Select a Carrying Case:** Choose a durable, waterproof case or backpack that is lightweight and has multiple compartments for organization.
2. **Organize Tools and Supplies:** Use the compartments to separate tools based on their use. For example, keep all fire-starting materials together and first aid items in another section.
3. **Label Everything:** Use a label maker or permanent marker to label each item or compartment. This makes it easy to find what you need quickly in an emergency.
4. **Pack the Multi-Tool:** Ensure the multi-tool is easily accessible, preferably in an outer pocket or top compartment.
5. **Store the Flashlight:** Place the flashlight in an easily accessible spot. If it's battery-operated, reverse the batteries to prevent accidental drainage and store extra batteries nearby.
6. **Prepare the Fire Starter Kit:** Pack waterproof matches, a lighter, and tinder in a waterproof bag. Consider adding a magnesium fire starter for redundancy.
7. **Include Navigation Tools:** If space allows, include a compact, waterproof map of your area and a compass.
8. **Add an Emergency Blanket and First Aid Kit:** These are critical for managing shock and injuries. Check the first aid kit to ensure it's fully stocked.
9. **Water Purification:** Include water purification tablets and a small, collapsible water container.
10. **Communication Tools:** A hand-cranked radio can provide updates during disasters, and a safety whistle can signal for help.
11. **Personal Items:** Add a notepad and pencil for notes or messages, and a sewing kit for repairs. Store spare cash and copies of important documents in a waterproof bag.
12. **Final Check:** Go through the kit to ensure all items are packed and labeled. Test the flashlight and radio to confirm they're working.

Safety:
- Check tools for sharp edges and cover or wrap them to prevent injury.
- Ensure batteries are installed correctly and spare batteries are stored safely.
- Familiarize yourself with the use of each item, especially the multi-tool and fire starter, to avoid accidents.

Cost of the Project: Approximately $100-$200, depending on the quality and brand of tools selected.

Preparation Time: 2-3 hours, including shopping for supplies and assembling the kit.

Maintenance and Care:
- Regularly check the kit for expired items, especially first aid supplies and water purification tablets, and replace as necessary.
- Test the flashlight and radio periodically to ensure they're in working order, replacing batteries if needed.
- Keep the kit in a cool, dry place and review its contents every six months to make any necessary updates.

FAQ or Common Issues:
- **Q: What if I can't find a waterproof case?**
- **A:** Use a regular backpack and store items in zip-lock bags or waterproof pouches to protect them from moisture.
- **Q: How can I make the kit lighter?**
- **A:** Focus on multi-use items, like a multi-tool, and limit the number of single-purpose items. Evaluate the necessity of each item.

Difficulty Rating: ★★☆☆☆

Variations:
- For colder climates, add hand warmers and a thermal bivvy.
- Customize the first aid kit based on personal medical needs or specific activities (e.g., hiking, boating).
- Include a solar charger for electronic devices if the kit will be used in remote areas or for extended periods.

Troubleshooting:

- If your flashlight won't turn on, check the batteries and ensure they are installed correctly
- If your multi-tool is stuck, apply a lubricant to the joints and work it back and forth gently
- If your first aid supplies are missing, create a checklist to ensure all necessary items are included
- If your fire starter isn't igniting, check the fuel source and ensure it is dry and functional
- If your emergency radio isn't receiving signals, verify the batteries and antenna position
- If your water purification system is not working, inspect the filters for clogs and replace them if necessary
- If your emergency blanket is torn, consider patching it with duct tape for temporary use
- If your whistle is not producing sound, check for obstructions and clean it thoroughly

BOOK 8: ADVANCED SURVIVAL COMMUNICATION

In the realm of advanced survival communication, the ability to set up and use shortwave and ham radios stands as a critical skill for ensuring connectivity during emergencies. These radios offer a lifeline to the outside world, providing updates, weather alerts, and the means to call for help when traditional communication systems fail. The first step in harnessing this powerful tool is understanding the equipment needed and the basic setup required to establish a reliable communication channel.

Starting with shortwave radios, these devices can pick up international broadcasts across long distances, making them invaluable in a survival scenario for receiving news and information from outside your immediate area. To begin, select a shortwave radio that is both portable and has a wide frequency range. The Tecsun PL880 Portable Digital PLL Dual Conversion Shortwave Radio is a recommended choice due to its exceptional sensitivity, selectivity, and built-in antenna, which can be further extended with an external wire antenna for improved reception. For optimal performance, place the radio near a window and extend the antenna fully, adjusting its direction for the clearest signal. It's crucial to familiarize yourself with the frequency bands used for emergency broadcasts in your region and to practice tuning into these frequencies before an emergency arises.

Ham radios, or amateur radios, require more preparation but offer more direct communication capabilities, including two-way conversations with other operators. Before you can legally operate a ham radio, you must obtain a license from the Federal Communications Commission (FCC). The process involves passing an examination that covers basic regulations, operating practices, and electronics theory. Once licensed, you can set up your ham radio station. Start with a basic transceiver, such as the Yaesu FT-60R Dual Band Handheld 5W VHF / UHF Amateur Radio Transceiver, known for its reliability and ease of use. Alongside the transceiver, you'll need a power source, typically a 12-volt battery or a power supply unit, and an antenna. For beginners, a simple magnetic mount VHF/UHF antenna can significantly enhance your ability to communicate over local frequencies. Place the antenna as high as possible, ideally on a metal surface for a ground plane, to maximize your transmission range.

Both shortwave and ham radios rely heavily on their antennas, which are the key to successful transmission and reception. For shortwave radios, an external long wire antenna, made from a length of insulated wire approximately 23 feet long, can dramatically improve your ability to receive distant broadcasts. This wire should be strung outside, away from obstructions, and as high as possible. For ham radios, the antenna needs vary based on the frequencies you plan to use. A dual-band VHF/UHF antenna covers most needs for local and regional communication. For global communication, consider investing in a high-frequency (HF) antenna, which requires more space but allows you to reach other continents using shortwave frequencies.

Understanding the basics of radio operation is also essential. This includes learning how to adjust the squelch control to eliminate background noise, setting the volume at a level where transmissions are clear, and mastering the use of the tuning dial to locate and fine-tune frequencies. Regular practice with your equipment, including participating in local radio clubs or emergency preparedness drills, will enhance your proficiency and confidence in using these communication tools.

In addition to the technical setup, developing a communication plan is crucial. This plan should outline which frequencies to monitor for news and updates, the schedule for checking in with family or community members, and emergency protocols for seeking help. It's also wise to compile a list of emergency frequencies, such as the National Weather Service and local emergency services, as well as frequencies used by amateur radio emergency services in your area.

Building on the foundation of shortwave and ham radio operations, it's imperative to delve into the nuances of signal propagation and how environmental factors can affect communication. Understanding the principles of radio wave travel—such as the differences between ground wave, sky wave, and line-of-sight propagation—can significantly impact your ability to send and receive messages effectively. For instance, during the day, higher frequency bands may offer better reach due to the ionospheric conditions, while at night, lower frequencies might provide more reliable communication over long distances. Experimenting with your radio during different times and weather conditions will give you a practical sense of how propagation changes and what frequencies are most reliable under specific circumstances.

Another critical aspect of advanced survival communication is encryption and secure messaging. In situations where privacy is paramount, knowing how to encrypt your communications can prevent unauthorized access to sensitive information. While encryption might seem complex, there are accessible methods for amateur radio operators, such as using digital modes like PSK31 or JT65, which can encode messages into a format that's not easily decipherable without the proper decoding software. Additionally, consider leveraging amateur radio email services, such as Winlink, which allows sending and receiving encrypted emails over radio frequencies. These services require setup and practice to use effectively, so integrating them into your regular communication drills is advisable.

The integration of alternative power sources to ensure your communication equipment remains operational during extended outages is another layer of preparedness. Solar panels, hand-crank generators, and battery banks can all serve as lifelines for your radio gear. For example, a portable solar panel kit, capable of generating at least 50 watts, can keep a small transceiver and a laptop charged in most situations. Pairing this with a charge controller featuring Maximum Power Point Tracking (MPPT) technology ensures you're getting the most efficient charge to your battery bank, which should consist of deep-cycle batteries designed for prolonged use.

Maintenance and troubleshooting of your communication equipment are skills as vital as operating them. Regularly inspecting connections for corrosion, testing battery life and capacity, and verifying the operational status of your antennas can prevent failures when you least expect them. Learning to diagnose common issues, such as high SWR (Standing Wave Ratio) readings or intermittent signal loss, will enable you to perform repairs or adjustments in the field, ensuring your ability to communicate does not falter in critical moments.

Lastly, the role of community in advanced survival communication cannot be overstated. Building a network of reliable contacts—both locally and internationally—can provide you with a wealth of resources and information. Participating in net check-ins, radio contests, and emergency drills not only hones your skills but also establishes your presence in the amateur radio community. This network can be invaluable during crises, offering assistance, relayed messages, or simply the reassurance of a friendly voice in challenging times.

By embracing these advanced concepts and integrating them into your survival communication plan, you equip yourself with the knowledge and skills to maintain connectivity in the most adverse conditions. Remember, the key to effective survival communication lies not only in the equipment and technologies you employ but also in your continuous commitment to learning, practicing, and adapting to the ever-changing landscape of emergency preparedness.

CHAPTER 1: SEAL COMMUNICATION IN CRISIS

In the high-stakes scenarios where Navy SEALs operate, effective communication can mean the difference between success and failure, life and death. This principle holds true in survival situations as well, where establishing and maintaining communication can significantly impact your ability to navigate crises. One of the most effective ways to ensure you can communicate during emergencies is by setting up a shortwave and ham radio station. This section will guide you through the process of selecting the right equipment, setting up your station, and operating it effectively, even under duress.

Selecting the right equipment starts with choosing a shortwave radio. Look for a model that is known for its durability, battery life, and range of frequencies it can access. The Kaito KA500 Voyager is an excellent choice, as it not only meets these criteria but also features a solar panel and a hand crank for alternative charging methods, ensuring operability even when power sources are scarce. It's crucial to have a radio that can receive a wide range of frequencies, from international broadcasts to local emergency channels, providing you with vital information during a crisis.

For ham radio, the Yaesu FT-4XR Dual Band VHF/UHF Handheld Transceiver stands out for its compact size, robust build, and ease of use, making it suitable for both beginners and experienced operators. Before purchasing, ensure you understand the licensing requirements set by the Federal Communications Commission (FCC) and prepare to obtain your license, which is a critical step in legally operating a ham radio.

Setting up your station requires careful consideration of location and antenna placement. For shortwave radios, an indoor setup near a window may suffice, but for ham radios, outdoor antenna placement will significantly enhance your ability to transmit and receive signals. A simple but effective antenna for beginners is the Nagoya NA-771 VHF/UHF handheld antenna, which offers a good balance between range and ease of installation. When installing any antenna, aim to place it as high as possible, clear of obstructions, to maximize signal strength and range.

Operating your radio effectively under crisis conditions demands familiarity with your equipment and a clear communication plan. Begin by familiarizing yourself with the basic functions of your radios, such as tuning, adjusting volume, and switching between bands. Practice tuning into emergency frequencies and local ham radio repeaters, which will be your lifelines in an emergency. Develop a communication plan that includes regular check-ins with family or community members, monitoring specific frequencies for emergency broadcasts, and a protocol for calling for help.

In addition to technical proficiency, psychological readiness is crucial. High-stress situations can impair cognitive functions, making simple tasks seem daunting. Regularly practice operating your radio under various conditions to build muscle memory and confidence. This includes running drills where you simulate emergency scenarios, such as power outages, natural disasters, or situations where you need to rapidly evacuate.

Lastly, integrate your communication setup with your overall emergency preparedness plan. This means ensuring you have backup power sources, such as solar chargers or battery packs, and keeping a physical list of essential frequencies and contacts. Remember, in a crisis, your ability to communicate effectively can provide not only a means of rescue but also comfort and psychological support to yourself and others.

By meticulously selecting your equipment, setting up your station with attention to detail, and practicing operation and communication protocols, you equip yourself with the skills to maintain a critical lifeline during emergencies. This approach, inspired by the rigorous standards and adaptability of Navy SEALs, prepares you to face crisis situations with confidence and resilience, ensuring that you can protect yourself and your loved ones when it matters most.

Shortwave and Ham Radios for Emergencies

When it comes to setting up and using shortwave and ham radios for emergencies, the first step is selecting the right equipment. For shortwave radios, a model like the Tecsun PL880 stands out due to its portability, wide frequency range, and the inclusion of a built-in antenna that can be enhanced with an external wire antenna for improved reception. This wire antenna should be made from a length of insulated wire, ideally 23 feet long, to optimize the ability to receive distant broadcasts. To set this up, attach one end of the wire to the external antenna jack of the radio and elevate the wire as much as possible outdoors, away from obstructions, to maximize signal reception. The orientation of the wire may need adjustment to find the best signal for specific frequencies or stations.

For ham radios, the process begins with obtaining a license from the Federal Communications Commission (FCC), which involves passing an examination that covers basic regulations, operating practices, and electronics theory. After securing a license, a good starting point for equipment is a reliable transceiver like the Yaesu FT-60R, which is known for its durability and ease of use. This dual-band handheld transceiver will require a power source, such as a 12-volt battery or a power supply unit, and an antenna. A simple yet effective choice for beginners is a magnetic mount VHF/UHF antenna, which can be placed on a metal surface to act as a ground plane and elevate the antenna for better signal transmission and reception.

The antenna setup for ham radios is critical for effective communication. For VHF/UHF operations, the antenna should be positioned as high as possible to extend the line-of-sight range. If space allows, a high-frequency (HF) antenna can enable global communication capabilities. This might involve more complex installations like a dipole or vertical antenna, which should be placed clear of obstructions and as high as feasible to enhance transmission capabilities over longer distances.

Operating these radios effectively in emergencies requires familiarity with their functions and the development of a communication plan. This plan should detail which frequencies to monitor for updates, schedule check-ins with family or community members, and outline emergency protocols for seeking help. For shortwave radios, practice tuning into various international and local emergency broadcast frequencies to understand how to access critical information during different times of the day, as signal propagation can change with atmospheric conditions. For ham radios, joining local nets and participating in emergency preparedness drills can improve operational skills and integrate you into the amateur radio community, which can be a vital resource in emergencies.

Powering your communication equipment during an extended outage is another consideration. Solar panels, hand-crank generators, and battery banks can ensure your radios remain operational. A portable solar panel kit, capable of generating at least 50 watts, paired with a charge controller featuring Maximum Power Point Tracking (MPPT) technology, can efficiently charge a battery bank consisting of deep-cycle batteries. This setup ensures a sustainable power source for your radio equipment, allowing for continuous operation during prolonged emergencies.

Maintenance and troubleshooting are also essential skills. Regular checks for corrosion on connections, battery life and capacity testing, and antenna inspections can prevent equipment failure when it's needed most. Learning to diagnose and fix common issues, such as adjusting the squelch control to reduce background noise or resolving high SWR readings, will ensure reliable communication capabilities.

By meticulously selecting and setting up the appropriate equipment, developing a comprehensive communication plan, and ensuring a sustainable power source, you can establish a reliable means of emergency communication. This preparation, combined with regular practice and maintenance, will equip you with the skills to use shortwave and ham radios effectively in any crisis situation, maintaining a critical lifeline that can make a significant difference in emergency scenarios.

Backup Communication Networks

Establishing backup communication networks is a critical step in ensuring you have reliable means to reach out for help, coordinate with family or community members, and receive vital information during emergencies when primary systems might fail. To set up a robust backup communication network, follow these detailed steps focusing on redundancy, simplicity, and adaptability to various scenarios.

1. **Identify Multiple Communication Methods**: Start by listing all possible communication methods available to you. This includes landline phones, cell phones, internet-based communication apps (like WhatsApp, Skype, or email), satellite phones, and radio systems such as CB (Citizens Band), GMRS (General Mobile Radio Service), and amateur (ham) radios. Each of these methods has its strengths and weaknesses depending on the situation, such as power outages, network overloads, or infrastructure damage.

2. **Invest in Hand-Crank and Solar-Powered Radios**: For immediate news updates and emergency broadcasts, a hand-crank or solar-powered radio is indispensable. These radios do not rely on electricity or batteries and can receive AM/FM and NOAA weather alerts. The Eton FRX5-BT Emergency Weather Radio is a recommended model due to its multiple charging options (hand crank, solar, and rechargeable battery), ensuring you stay informed even when power is scarce.

3. **Set Up a Ham Radio Station**: Ham radio is renowned for its reliability in disaster scenarios. To operate a ham radio, one must pass an FCC exam to obtain a license. Once licensed, setting up a station requires a transceiver, a power source, and an antenna. The Yaesu FT-60R handheld transceiver is a solid choice for beginners, offering dual-band capabilities and robust construction. For the antenna, a Nagoya NA-771 whip antenna enhances signal reach. Power the setup with a 12-volt deep-cycle battery, and incorporate a solar panel charging system to ensure operability during extended outages.

4. **Create a Communication Plan**: Document a clear communication plan that includes contact information, primary and secondary meeting points, and scheduled check-in times. Use waterproof, tear-resistant paper to print copies for each family member. The plan should detail which communication methods to use in various scenarios, emphasizing the use of text messages and social media for non-urgent communications to conserve bandwidth for emergency services.

5. **Leverage Text-Based Alert Systems**: Register for local and national emergency alert systems that send warnings via text message. These systems provide real-time information about severe weather, natural disasters, and other emergencies. Ensure all family members are registered to receive these alerts.

6. **Utilize Satellite Messengers for Remote Areas**: In situations where cellular networks are down or when in remote locations, satellite messengers like the Garmin inReach Mini provide a lifeline to the outside world. These devices allow for two-way messaging, SOS alerts, and location sharing via satellite, independent of cell towers or internet access. They require a subscription service but are invaluable in true off-grid scenarios.

7. **Practice Regularly**: Regular drills that simulate different emergency scenarios are crucial. Practice using each communication method, ensuring everyone knows how to operate the equipment and understands the communication plan. Include scenarios where primary methods fail, forcing the use of backup options.

8. **Join a Local Emergency Communication Group**: Many communities have amateur radio clubs or emergency communication groups that conduct regular drills and offer training. Joining such a group connects you with experienced operators who can provide assistance and relay messages during widespread emergencies.

9. **Backup Power Solutions**: Ensure all communication devices have backup power options. For battery-operated devices, maintain a stock of batteries in various sizes. For rechargeable devices, invest in portable solar chargers and power banks. The Anker PowerCore 10000 is a compact, high-capacity power bank that can recharge phones and other small devices multiple times.

10. **Secure and Waterproof Your Equipment**: Store all communication equipment in a waterproof, easily accessible location. Use dry bags or waterproof cases like those from Pelican to protect devices from moisture and dust. Label each item clearly and include quick reference guides for operation.

By meticulously implementing these steps, you establish a comprehensive backup communication network that enhances your resilience in facing emergencies. This network, built on the principles of redundancy, reliability, and readiness, ensures that you and your loved ones remain connected and informed, no matter the circumstances.

Encrypted Communication Channels

Creating encrypted communication channels for secure messaging is a critical component of maintaining privacy and security during crises. Encryption transforms readable data into a coded format that can only be decoded with the right key, ensuring that sensitive information remains confidential. To set up encrypted communication channels, follow these detailed steps:

1. **Select Encryption Software**: Choose software that is widely recognized for its strong encryption standards. Signal and Telegram are two examples that offer end-to-end encryption for messages and calls. These apps use algorithms like AES-256, which is the gold standard for encrypting data, ensuring that only the sender and the recipient can read the messages.

2. **Install on Secure Devices**: Ensure that the devices you plan to use for communication are secure and free from malware. Install antivirus and anti-malware software on your computer or smartphone before downloading the encryption software. For smartphones, consider factory resetting the device to remove any potential threats before installing the encryption app.

3. **Create Strong Passwords**: When setting up your account on the encryption software, use a strong, unique password that combines letters, numbers, and symbols. Consider using a password manager to generate and store your passwords securely. This adds an additional layer of security, preventing unauthorized access to your encrypted communication channels.

4. **Verify Contacts**: Most encrypted messaging apps offer a way to verify the identity of the people you are communicating with, such as scanning a QR code or comparing a verification code. Take the time to perform these verifications to ensure that your messages are not being intercepted by a third party.

5. **Regularly Update Software**: Keep your encryption software and all related applications up to date. Developers regularly release updates that patch vulnerabilities, which could be exploited by attackers to bypass encryption. Enable automatic updates on your device to ensure you're always using the latest, most secure version of the software.

6. **Use Secure Networks**: Avoid using public Wi-Fi networks when sending encrypted messages. These networks are often unsecured and can be a haven for attackers looking to intercept data. Use a virtual private network (VPN) to encrypt your internet connection, adding an extra layer of security to your communications.

7. **Educate Your Contacts**: Encrypted communication is only effective if both the sender and the recipient understand how to use it properly. Take the time to educate your family, friends, or team members on the importance of encryption and how to use the chosen software. This includes understanding the risks of malware, the importance of software updates, and the need for strong passwords.

8. **Backup Communication Plans**: In the event that your primary encrypted communication channel becomes compromised or unavailable, have a backup plan in place. This could involve using a different encrypted messaging app or switching to another secure method of communication. Ensure that all parties involved in your communication network are aware of and understand how to switch to the backup plan if necessary.

9. **Physical Security Measures**: Remember that encryption protects your digital communications, but physical security is also crucial. Keep devices in a secure location when not in use and consider using biometric locks (fingerprint or facial recognition) for added security. In high-risk situations, be aware of your surroundings to prevent shoulder surfing or other methods that could compromise your secure messaging.

By meticulously following these steps, you can establish a robust encrypted communication channel that safeguards your messages from unauthorized access, ensuring that your sensitive information remains confidential during crises. This approach, rooted in the principles of operational security and privacy, is essential for anyone looking to protect their communications in today's digital age.

CHAPTER 2: SECURING COMMUNICATION SYSTEMS

Implementing encryption protocols to protect your data is a critical step in securing your communication systems, especially in scenarios where privacy and security are paramount. Encryption is the process of encoding messages or information in such a way that only authorized parties can access it. Here's how to set up basic encryption protocols for your communication devices, ensuring that your messages remain confidential and secure from unauthorized access.

1. **Choose Encryption Software**: Start by selecting reputable encryption software for your communication devices. Look for software that offers end-to-end encryption, meaning that your messages are encrypted on your device and only decrypted by the recipient's device. Popular choices include Signal for instant messaging and Tutanota or ProtonMail for email. These services are known for their strong encryption standards and commitment to user privacy.

2. **Install and Set Up**: Follow the installation instructions provided by the encryption software. This typically involves downloading the application to your device, creating an account, and setting a strong, unique password. For email encryption, you may need to generate a public and private key pair. Your public key can be shared with others to encrypt messages to you, while your private key, which is never shared, is used to decrypt messages sent to you.

3. **Verify Contacts**: When using encryption software, it's important to verify the identity of your contacts. Many encrypted messaging apps provide a way to verify the contacts through a special code or a QR code. This step ensures that you are communicating with the intended person and not an imposter.

4. **Regularly Update Software**: Encryption software, like all software, can have vulnerabilities. Regular updates are crucial as they often contain patches for security vulnerabilities that have been discovered since the last version. Enable automatic updates if available, or make it a habit to check for updates regularly.

5. **Use Secure Wi-Fi Connections**: When sending or receiving encrypted messages, ensure you are using a secure Wi-Fi connection. Public Wi-Fi networks can be insecure, making it easier for hackers to intercept your data. Consider using a virtual private network (VPN) to secure your internet connection, especially when on public Wi-Fi.

6. **Backup Encryption Keys**: For email encryption, back up your encryption keys. Losing your private key can result in losing access to your encrypted emails. Store the backup in a secure location, such as an encrypted external hard drive or a secure cloud storage service.

7. **Educate Your Contacts**: Encourage and educate your contacts on using encryption for their communications with you. The strength of encrypted communication is only as strong as the weakest link. If your contacts are not using encryption, your communications with them are not fully protected.

By following these steps, you can significantly enhance the security of your communication systems, protecting your messages from eavesdropping and ensuring that your communications remain confidential. Remember, the goal of encryption is not just to protect the content of your messages but also to preserve your privacy and the privacy of those you communicate with.

Encryption Protocols for Data Protection

Implementing encryption protocols to protect your data involves a series of steps that ensure your communication remains secure and inaccessible to unauthorized parties. The first step in this process is to identify the specific needs of your communication system. Consider what type of data you will be encrypting, whether it's text messages, emails, or files, and the level of security required. For text messaging and emails, applications that provide end-to-end encryption are essential. For files, consider using encryption software that can encrypt files on your hard drive or before uploading them to cloud storage.

Once you've identified your needs, select encryption tools that match these requirements. For messaging, Signal and WhatsApp offer strong end-to-end encryption, ensuring that only you and the recipient can read what is sent. For emails, ProtonMail and Tutanota offer encrypted email services with user-friendly interfaces. For file encryption, VeraCrypt is a reliable tool that allows you to create encrypted volumes on your hard drive or USB sticks.

After selecting the appropriate tools, the next step is to install and configure them according to the best security practices. When setting up encrypted messaging apps, make sure to verify your identity and enable all available security settings, such as two-factor authentication. For email encryption, you'll need to create a pair of cryptographic keys – a public key that others can use to encrypt messages to you, and a private key that you use to decrypt messages you receive. Store your private key in a secure location and never share it with anyone.

For file encryption with tools like VeraCrypt, create a strong password that you will remember but is difficult for others to guess. The password should be a mix of letters, numbers, and symbols, and be at least 12 characters long. When creating an encrypted volume, choose a size that fits your needs, keeping in mind that larger volumes take longer to encrypt and decrypt.

Regularly updating your encryption software is crucial to protect against newly discovered vulnerabilities. Set your software to update automatically or manually check for updates at least once a month. Additionally, be cautious when using public Wi-Fi networks for sending or receiving encrypted messages. Use a trusted virtual private network (VPN) to secure your connection and protect your data from potential eavesdroppers.

Finally, educate yourself and your contacts on the importance of encryption and secure communication practices. Share knowledge on verifying identities, using secure passwords, and the dangers of phishing attacks. The more informed you and your network are, the stronger your collective security will be.

By meticulously selecting, installing, and maintaining encryption software, and by following best practices for secure communication, you can significantly enhance the privacy and security of your data. Remember, the strength of your encryption is not just in the technology but in how you use it.

Powering communication devices off-grid with solar or battery backups

Project Introduction (Description - Benefits - Challenges): This project outlines how to set up a system for powering communication devices using solar panels and battery backups, ensuring connectivity in off-grid scenarios. Benefits include independence from the grid, renewable energy use, and emergency preparedness. Challenges involve understanding solar power basics, the initial setup cost, and maintaining the system.

Required Matcrials:
- Solar panels (100-watt, 12-volt panels recommended for small setups)
- Deep cycle batteries (12-volt, AGM or Lithium recommended for efficiency and durability)
- Charge controller (MPPT type for maximum efficiency)
- Inverter (Pure sine wave inverter, at least 300 watts)
- Wiring and connectors (UV-resistant cables suitable for outdoor use, MC4 connectors)
- Mounting hardware (for securing solar panels in an optimal sun-exposure location)
- Battery box (to protect the batteries from environmental conditions)

Required Tools:
- Drill with various bits (for mounting hardware installation)

- Wire cutters and strippers (for preparing electrical connections)
- Multimeter (for testing voltage and current)
- Screwdriver set (for securing connections and mounting hardware)
- Safety equipment (gloves, safety glasses)

Detailed Instructions:
1. **Select an Optimal Location:** Identify a location that receives maximum sunlight throughout the day, ideally south-facing with minimal shading.
2. **Install Solar Panels:** Use the mounting hardware to secure the solar panels in the chosen location. Ensure they are angled to capture the most sunlight, considering your geographic location.
3. **Set Up the Battery Bank:** Place the deep cycle batteries in the battery box to protect them from environmental elements. Position the box in a cool, dry place to extend battery life.
4. **Wire the Solar Panels to the Charge Controller:** Connect the solar panels' positive and negative terminals to the corresponding inputs on the charge controller using UV-resistant cables. Ensure a proper seal with MC4 connectors to prevent moisture ingress.
5. **Connect the Charge Controller to the Battery Bank:** Use suitable gauge wires to connect the charge controller's output to the battery bank, ensuring correct polarity and secure connections.
6. **Install the Inverter:** Connect the inverter to the battery bank, converting DC power stored in the batteries to AC power suitable for most communication devices.
7. **Final Connections and Testing:** Connect your communication devices to the inverter. Use the multimeter to test the system's output and ensure it matches the devices' requirements.

Safety:
- Always disconnect the batteries before making any changes to the system to prevent electrical shocks.
- Wear safety glasses and gloves when handling electrical components.
- Ensure all outdoor installations are weatherproof to prevent water damage.

Cost of the Project: Approximately $500-$1000, depending on the quality of components and the scale of the system.

Preparation Time: 1-2 days for gathering materials and installation.

Maintenance and Care:
- Regularly clean the solar panels to remove dust and debris that could reduce efficiency.
- Check battery voltage monthly to ensure they are properly charged.
- Inspect all wiring and connections periodically for signs of wear or damage.

FAQ or Common Issues:
- **Q: What if my solar panels aren't generating enough power?**
- **A:** Ensure there's no shading on the panels, especially during peak sun hours. Consider adding more panels if power needs increase.
- **Q: How do I know if my battery is fully charged?**
- **A:** Use a multimeter to check the battery voltage. A fully charged 12-volt battery should read around 12.7 volts or higher when not under load.

Difficulty Rating: ★★★☆☆

Variations:
- For larger power needs, increase the number and capacity of solar panels and batteries accordingly.
- Integrate a wind turbine for additional power generation, especially useful in areas with less consistent sunlight but adequate wind.
- Consider a dual charging system that can also connect to a vehicle's alternator, providing an alternative charging method while on the move.

Troubleshooting:

- Check all connections to ensure they are secure and properly attached
- Verify that the solar panels are clean and free from debris that could block sunlight
- Inspect the battery for any signs of damage or corrosion
- Ensure that the charge controller is functioning correctly and displaying the appropriate readings
- Test the inverter to confirm it is converting DC to AC power as expected
- Monitor the output voltage to ensure it meets the requirements of your devices
- If using a generator, check the fuel levels and ensure it is in good working condition
- Review the user manuals for all devices to troubleshoot specific issues related to them
- Consider environmental factors such as extreme temperatures that may affect performance
- If problems persist, consult with a professional for further assistance

CHAPTER 3: FAMILY COMMUNICATION PLANS

In the face of a crisis, establishing a robust family communication plan is paramount. This plan ensures that every family member knows exactly what to do, who to contact, and where to go, minimizing confusion and enhancing safety during emergencies. The following steps will guide you through setting up an effective family communication plan tailored to various scenarios, from natural disasters to unforeseen emergencies.

1. **Identify Emergency Contacts**: Start by selecting primary and secondary emergency contacts outside your immediate family. These should be trusted individuals who live in different geographical areas, ensuring that at least one contact is likely reachable in any given situation. Include local emergency numbers and contacts for family members in a laminated list. Each family member should carry a copy in their wallet, backpack, or purse.

2. **Choose Family Rally Points**: Designate two meeting places where your family can regroup in case of an emergency: one close to your home, such as a neighborhood park, and another further away, in case the neighborhood is inaccessible. Ensure every family member is familiar with these locations.

3. **Create a Communication Tree**: A communication tree is a structured system where each person is assigned a specific individual to contact. This prevents the overload of communication lines and ensures messages are systematically relayed. For example, the youngest child might contact an older sibling, who then contacts a parent, who then reaches out to the designated emergency contact.

4. **Utilize Technology**: In today's digital age, leveraging technology can significantly enhance your family communication plan. Encourage the use of group messaging apps that allow for the sharing of real-time location and status updates. Apps like WhatsApp, Telegram, or Signal can provide encrypted communication, ensuring privacy and security. Additionally, consider using a shared family cloud storage where copies of important documents can be safely stored and accessed by any family member when needed.

5. **Implement Safe Words**: Establish a set of safe words that can be used to convey complex messages quickly and discreetly. These words can indicate the level of danger, specific types of emergencies, or even whether to enact the family communication plan silently.

6. **Practice Digital Detox**: In an era where digital devices are omnipresent, it's crucial to prepare for scenarios where these devices might not be available. Encourage regular "digital detox" periods where family members practice navigating without smartphones or GPS, using physical maps and compasses instead. This ensures that in the event of a power outage or network failure, your family remains confident and capable of navigating and communicating through traditional means.

7. **Emergency Drills**: Conduct regular family emergency drills that include practicing evacuation routes, meeting at rally points, and using alternative communication methods. These drills should cover various scenarios, including fires, natural disasters, and home invasions, to ensure preparedness for any situation.

8. **Document and Distribute the Plan**: Once your family communication plan is established, document it in detail. This document should include emergency contacts, rally points, the communication tree, and any other relevant information. Distribute copies to each family member and discuss the plan in detail, ensuring everyone understands their role and responsibilities.

9. **Review and Update Regularly**: Circumstances change, and so should your family communication plan. Review the plan at least twice a year, updating contact information, rally points, and any other elements that

might have changed. This is also an excellent opportunity to discuss any concerns and adjust the plan based on recent experiences or new family dynamics.

By meticulously crafting a family communication plan and ensuring each member understands and can execute their role within it, you significantly increase your family's resilience in the face of emergencies. This proactive approach not only fosters a sense of security but also empowers each family member, regardless of age, with the knowledge and skills needed to navigate crises effectively.

Family Communication in Crisis

Identifying emergency contacts is the first critical step in establishing a family communication protocol for separation during crises. Begin by selecting at least two trusted individuals outside your immediate family circle who live in different geographical areas. This diversity ensures that at least one contact remains accessible under various circumstances, such as regional disasters or network outages. For each contact, include full names, relationship to the family, and multiple ways to reach them—landline numbers, mobile phone numbers, email addresses, and physical addresses. Store this information in waterproof, durable forms such as laminated cards or engraved tags, ensuring every family member carries a copy in their personal belongings at all times.

Choosing family rally points involves designating two safe locations where family members can meet if separated during a crisis. The first location should be nearby, such as a community park or a local landmark, easily accessible on foot. The second should be farther away, accounting for situations where the immediate neighborhood might be unsafe or unreachable. It's essential to physically visit these rally points with all family members, discussing the safest routes to each location from home, school, work, and other frequently visited places.

Creating a communication tree is a structured approach to streamline communication and prevent overwhelming any single family member or communication line. Start with the head of the household at the top, followed by the next responsible adult, and then children in descending order of age or responsibility. Assign each person a primary and secondary individual to contact, ensuring they have physical and digital copies of contact information. This method ensures information is relayed efficiently and everyone is accounted for without clogging communication channels.

Utilizing technology to enhance your family communication plan involves leveraging encrypted messaging apps such as WhatsApp, Telegram, or Signal. These platforms offer end-to-end encryption, ensuring that messages remain confidential and secure. Encourage family members to share real-time locations and status updates during emergencies. Additionally, establish a shared family cloud storage space for digital copies of important documents—birth certificates, passports, medical records, and insurance policies—that can be accessed remotely by any family member when necessary.

Implementing safe words within your family communication protocol allows for the conveyance of complex messages or instructions succinctly and discreetly. Choose words or phrases that are easy to remember but unlikely to be used in regular conversation. Each safe word should have a specific meaning, such as indicating a particular type of emergency, signaling the severity of a situation, or instructing family members to silently initiate the communication plan.

Practicing digital detox periods prepares family members for scenarios where digital communication tools might not be available. Regularly schedule times where all family members forego the use of smartphones, computers, and GPS, relying instead on physical maps, compasses, and face-to-face communication. This practice not only reduces dependency on digital devices but also enhances each member's navigational skills and situational awareness.

Conducting emergency drills that simulate various crisis scenarios is crucial for ensuring that all family members understand their roles and responsibilities within the communication plan. These drills should include practicing evacuation routes, meeting at rally points, and executing the communication tree. Tailor drills to cover a range of potential emergencies, such as natural disasters, home invasions, or public incidents, to build confidence and familiarity with the plan under different conditions.

Documenting and distributing the plan is the final step in establishing your family communication protocol. Compile all information—emergency contacts, rally points, the communication tree, safe words, and digital detox practices—into a comprehensive document. Make sure each family member receives a copy and understands its contents. Hold regular family meetings to discuss the plan, address any questions, and make necessary adjustments based on feedback or changes in circumstances.

Reviewing and updating the family communication plan at least twice a year ensures that it remains relevant and effective. Update contact information, discuss new potential threats, and refine rally points and safe words as needed. These regular reviews keep the plan front of mind for family members and adapt to any changes in the family structure, such as new members, moves, or changes in employment and schooling.

By following these detailed steps, families can establish a robust communication protocol that maximizes safety and minimizes confusion during crises. This proactive approach empowers each family member, ensuring they have the knowledge, skills, and confidence to navigate emergencies effectively.

Neighborhood Support Network

Building a neighborhood support and communication network is a critical step in enhancing the resilience and safety of your community during crises. This network serves as a vital link among neighbors, ensuring that everyone can receive assistance and information when it's most needed. Here's how to establish and maintain an effective neighborhood support and communication network:

1. **Identify Community Leaders and Volunteers**: Start by identifying individuals in your neighborhood who are willing to take on leadership roles or volunteer. Look for those with skills or backgrounds in emergency response, communication, medical fields, or organization. These individuals can help coordinate efforts and disseminate information effectively.

2. **Organize a Neighborhood Meeting**: Arrange an initial meeting with your neighbors to discuss the importance of a support and communication network. This can be done at a community center, local park, or someone's home. The goal is to share ideas, concerns, and resources, and to gauge the interest and skills of participants.

3. **Create a Contact List**: Compile a comprehensive contact list of all the households in your neighborhood. This list should include names, addresses, phone numbers, and email addresses. With permission, include any special skills or resources each household can contribute, such as medical expertise, power generators, or food storage.

4. **Establish Communication Channels**: Decide on the primary and secondary means of communication for your network. This could include a private online group, such as a Facebook group or a Nextdoor community, walkie-talkies for immediate local communication, or a simple phone tree. Ensure everyone understands how to use these channels effectively.

5. **Develop an Emergency Plan**: Work together to develop a neighborhood emergency plan. This plan should outline specific actions to take in various scenarios, such as natural disasters, power outages, or other emergencies. Include evacuation routes, emergency shelter locations, and a system for checking on vulnerable neighbors.

6. **Distribute Emergency Kits**: Encourage each household to prepare or update their emergency kits. Offer workshops or share resources on what to include in these kits, such as water, food, first aid supplies, and important documents. Consider creating communal emergency supplies stored in a central location for neighborhood use.

7. **Conduct Regular Drills and Meetings**: Schedule regular drills to practice your emergency plan and keep the communication lines active. Regular meetings can help to update the contact list, refine the emergency plan, and share new resources or information. This also helps to strengthen community bonds and trust among neighbors.

8. **Leverage Technology for Monitoring and Alerts**: Utilize technology to monitor weather alerts, emergency notifications, and local news. Share this information promptly with your network through your established communication channels. Consider setting up a system where neighbors can signal if they need help or if they are safe during an emergency.

9. **Create a Resource Inventory**: Develop an inventory of resources available within the neighborhood that can be useful in an emergency. This could include tools, generators, medical supplies, or skills like CPR certification. Make this inventory accessible to all network members, ensuring privacy and security are maintained.

10. **Foster a Culture of Preparedness and Cooperation**: Beyond the logistical aspects of building a support and communication network, fostering a culture of preparedness, cooperation, and mutual aid is essential. Encourage neighbors to look out for each other, share resources, and offer support when needed. This culture strengthens the network's effectiveness and resilience.

By following these steps, you can build a robust neighborhood support and communication network that enhances the safety, preparedness, and resilience of your community. This network not only serves as a critical resource during emergencies but also strengthens the social fabric of the neighborhood, creating a more connected and supportive community.

DIY COMMUNICATION PROJECTS

Building a basic ham radio setup for reliable communication in emergencies is a critical skill that can keep you connected when modern communication infrastructures fail. Ham radio, or amateur radio, allows you to communicate across distances without the need for the internet or cellular networks. Here's a step-by-step guide to setting up your own ham radio station, ensuring you can reach out for help, information, or coordination with others during crises.

1. **Obtain Your Ham Radio License**: Before you can legally operate a ham radio, you must obtain a license from the Federal Communications Commission (FCC). This involves passing an examination that covers basic regulations, operating practices, and electronics theory. Study materials are widely available online or through local amateur radio clubs.

2. **Selecting Your Equipment**: For beginners, a dual-band VHF/UHF handheld transceiver is a good starting point. These radios are relatively inexpensive, portable, and easy to use. The Yaesu FT-60R and the Baofeng UV-5R are popular choices among new operators for their balance of features, reliability, and cost.

3. **Setting Up an Antenna**: The effectiveness of your ham radio largely depends on your antenna setup. For a handheld transceiver, consider purchasing a high-gain antenna to replace the standard one that comes with the radio. This can significantly improve your ability to send and receive signals. For home stations, an outdoor antenna mounted as high as possible will provide the best performance. A simple 1/4 wavelength ground plane antenna for VHF and UHF bands is a good start. This requires a metal rod or tube for the vertical element and four equally long metal rods for the ground elements, all connected to a central hub and mounted on a mast.

4. **Powering Your Radio**: Handheld transceivers come with rechargeable batteries. For extended use, especially in emergencies, consider having a solar charger or a manual crank charger compatible with your radio's battery. For home-based setups, a reliable power source is crucial. A 12-volt deep-cycle battery, similar to those used in boats or RVs, can power your station. Connect this to a solar panel setup with a charge controller to keep your battery charged without access to the grid.

5. **Learning to Operate Your Radio**: Familiarize yourself with your radio's operations. Practice tuning into various frequencies, and listen to broadcasts to get a feel for amateur radio communications. Most ham radios have a scan function that allows you to find active frequencies easily. Joining a local amateur radio club can provide valuable hands-on learning and mentorship from experienced operators.

6. **Programming Your Radio**: Program your radio with local repeater frequencies to extend your communication range. Repeaters are setups by amateur radio clubs and enthusiasts that receive signals on one frequency and rebroadcast them on another, allowing for communication over hundreds of miles. Websites like RepeaterBook provide listings of repeaters by location.

7. **Emergency Communication Practices**: In an emergency, clear and concise communication is vital. Learn the phonetic alphabet to spell out critical information, and familiarize yourself with common ham radio emergency frequencies, also known as calling frequencies. Practice participating in net check-ins, organized meetings on a specific frequency where operators can practice emergency communication protocols.

8. **Maintaining Your Equipment**: Regularly check your equipment for wear and tear, especially antenna connections and power supply units. Ensure batteries are charged and that you have backup power options available. For antennas, especially those outdoors, inspect them for damage after severe weather conditions.

By following these detailed steps, you can establish a basic but effective ham radio setup that will serve as a lifeline during emergencies. This setup not only enables you to communicate locally but also, with the right equipment and conditions, globally, connecting you with a vast network of amateur radio operators ready to provide assistance and information in times of need.

Building a basic ham radio setup for reliable communication

Project Introduction (Description - Benefits - Challenges): Setting up a basic ham radio system offers a reliable communication method during emergencies when traditional networks may fail. Benefits include long-range communication capabilities, access to a wide network of amateur radio operators, and the ability to receive emergency broadcasts. Challenges involve understanding radio operation principles, obtaining the necessary license, and setting up the equipment correctly.

Required Materials:
- Ham radio transceiver (VHF/UHF for local communication, HF for long-distance)
- Power supply (12V, capable of handling the transceiver's power requirements)
- Antenna (specific to the band you plan to operate on, e.g., a dual-band VHF/UHF antenna for local, or a wire dipole for HF long-distance)
- Coaxial cable (50-ohm, appropriate length to connect the transceiver to the antenna)
- Antenna tuner (for HF bands, to match the antenna system to the transceiver)
- SWR (Standing Wave Ratio) meter (to measure the efficiency of the antenna system)
- Grounding equipment (copper grounding rod and wire for safety and noise reduction)

Required Tools:
- Screwdriver set (for assembling and adjusting components)
- Wire cutters and strippers (for coaxial cable preparation)
- Soldering iron and solder (for antenna or cable assembly)
- Drill (for mounting antennas or grounding rod installation)
- Multimeter (for testing power supply and connections)

Detailed Instructions:
1. **Obtain a License:** Before operating a ham radio, acquire the necessary amateur radio license from the Federal Communications Commission (FCC). Study materials and exam schedules are available online.
2. **Select a Location for the Radio and Antenna:** Choose an area with minimal electrical interference and a clear path for the antenna. An elevated position is preferable for antennas to ensure a broader communication range.
3. **Install the Antenna:** Depending on the type, mount the antenna as high as possible. For HF antennas, ensure they are clear of obstructions and at least a half-wavelength above the ground for the frequency of operation. VHF/UHF antennas should be mounted on the roof or high pole.
4. **Ground the System:** Drive a copper grounding rod into the ground near the radio setup. Connect the grounding rod to the radio and any other equipment using heavy gauge copper wire to protect against electrical surges and reduce noise.
5. **Connect the Transceiver to the Antenna:** Use the coaxial cable to connect the antenna to the transceiver. If using an HF band, include an antenna tuner in the setup to match the antenna system to the transceiver, minimizing SWR.
6. **Set Up the Power Supply:** Connect the transceiver to the power supply, ensuring it meets the radio's voltage and current requirements. Use a multimeter to verify the correct power settings.
7. **Test the SWR:** With the SWR meter, check the standing wave ratio to ensure the antenna system is efficiently transmitting the radio signals. Adjust the antenna tuner as necessary to achieve the lowest SWR reading.
8. **Program Frequencies and Begin Operation:** Program local repeater frequencies and any other frequencies of interest into the transceiver. Begin listening to gain familiarity with radio operations and protocols before transmitting.

Safety:
- Always disconnect the power supply before making adjustments to the radio equipment.
- Use proper grounding techniques to protect against electrical shocks and lightning strikes.
- Follow FCC regulations strictly to avoid interference with other communications and emergency services.

Cost of the Project: Approximately $300-$1000, depending on the quality of the transceiver and accessories.

Preparation Time: 1-2 days for studying, obtaining a license, and setting up the equipment.

Maintenance and Care:
- Regularly check antenna connections and coaxial cables for wear or damage.
- Inspect the grounding system periodically to ensure it remains effective.
- Keep the transceiver and other equipment clean and dust-free.

FAQ or Common Issues:
- **Q: What if I experience high SWR readings?**
- **A:** Adjust the antenna tuner, check for proper antenna installation, and ensure there are no obstructions or damage to the antenna or coaxial cable.
- **Q: Can I operate a ham radio without a license?**
- **A:** No, operating a ham radio without the appropriate FCC license is illegal and can result in fines.

Difficulty Rating: ★★★☆☆

Variations:
- Integrate a digital interface to explore digital modes of communication, such as FT8 or PSK31, for enhanced experience and global communication.
- Add a portable setup with a battery pack and a mobile antenna for ham radio operations on the go.
- Experiment with different antenna designs to find the best combination for your specific location and communication needs.

Troubleshooting:

- Check all connections to ensure they are secure and properly seated
- Verify that the power supply is functioning and providing the correct voltage
- Ensure the antenna is properly installed and positioned for optimal reception
- Test the radio on different frequencies to rule out issues with specific channels
- Inspect the radio for any visible damage or wear that may affect performance
- Confirm that the correct settings are selected for the type of communication you are attempting
- If using a battery, check its charge level and replace if necessary
- Consult the user manual for specific error codes or troubleshooting steps related to your model
- If problems persist, consider reaching out to a professional for assistance or further diagnosis

Assembling a DIY shortwave radio emergency kit

Project Introduction (Description - Benefits - Challenges)

Creating a DIY shortwave radio emergency kit equips you with a powerful tool for global communication, especially in scenarios where conventional communication networks are down. The benefits of this project include the ability to receive news and information from around the world, connect with amateur radio communities, and maintain a line of communication in emergencies. Challenges include mastering the technical aspects of shortwave radio operation and the initial setup of the equipment.

Required Materials

- Shortwave radio receiver capable of SSB (Single Side Band) reception
- Telescopic antenna or external wire antenna for improved reception
- Power source: AA batteries or rechargeable battery pack with charger
- Protective case: Waterproof and shockproof to safeguard the equipment
- Headphones or earbuds for private listening
- Frequency guidebook or chart for shortwave bands and stations

Required Tools

- Screwdriver set for assembling and adjusting components
- Soldering iron and solder, if modifications or repairs are needed
- Wire cutters and strippers for antenna setup
- Multimeter for testing electrical connections

Detailed Instructions

1. **Select a Shortwave Radio Receiver:** Choose a receiver that covers a wide range of frequencies and includes SSB mode, essential for listening to amateur radio transmissions, maritime, and aviation frequencies.

2. **Assemble the Antenna:** For a telescopic antenna, attach it directly to the radio. If using an external wire antenna, find a high point to mount it, such as a tree or a pole, and connect it to the radio using a coaxial cable or directly to the antenna input.

3. **Power Source Preparation:** Insert AA batteries into the radio or charge the battery pack. Ensure you have spare batteries or a backup power source.

4. **Protective Case Setup:** Place the radio and its accessories in the waterproof and shockproof case. Arrange the items so that the radio is cushioned and protected from impact.

5. **Headphones or Earbuds:** Pack headphones or earbuds to use with the radio. This allows for private listening and can help conserve battery life.

6. **Frequency Guidebook:** Include a guidebook or chart of shortwave bands and stations. This will assist in finding broadcasts and understanding the shortwave frequency spectrum.

Safety

- When installing an external antenna, ensure it's well away from power lines or any electrical hazards.
- Use the soldering iron with caution, following safety guidelines to prevent burns or other injuries.
- Handle batteries and electrical components carefully to avoid short circuits or other electrical hazards.

Cost of the Project

Approximately $100-$300, depending on the quality of the radio receiver and accessories chosen.

Preparation Time

2-3 hours for gathering materials, assembly, and initial setup.

Maintenance and Care

- Regularly check the condition of the antenna and connections for wear or damage.
- Keep the radio and its components dry and clean. Remove batteries if the radio will not be used for an extended period to prevent corrosion.

- Test the radio and recharge or replace batteries as needed to ensure readiness.

FAQ or Common Issues

- Q: What if I can't receive any signals?
- **A:** Check the antenna connections and ensure it's properly extended or installed. Experiment with different locations and times of day, as signal strength can vary.

- Q: How can I improve reception?
- **A:** Use an external wire antenna and place it as high as possible. Avoid using the radio near large metal objects or electronic devices that can cause interference.

Difficulty Rating

★★★☆☆

Variations

- Add a solar charger to recharge the battery pack, making the kit more sustainable for long-term use.
- Include a signal booster or preamplifier for the antenna to enhance reception in areas with weak signals.
- Assemble a portable kit with a foldable antenna and a lightweight, durable radio for use while hiking or camping.

Troubleshooting:

- Ensure all connections are secure and properly seated
- Check the power source; replace batteries or ensure the power adapter is functioning
- Verify that the antenna is correctly installed and extended for optimal reception
- Tune the radio to the correct frequency; consult the frequency guide for emergency channels
- Inspect the radio for any physical damage or signs of wear
- Test the radio in different locations to rule out interference from nearby electronics
- If using a solar charger, ensure it is receiving adequate sunlight and is functioning properly
- Reset the radio to factory settings if it continues to malfunction
- Consult the user manual for specific troubleshooting steps related to your model

BOOK 9: MEDICAL PREPAREDNESS AND HYGIENE

Ensuring your family has access to clean, safe water for drinking, cooking, and hygiene is paramount in any crisis situation. Contaminated water can lead to serious health issues, including gastrointestinal infections, cholera, and other waterborne diseases. To mitigate these risks, setting up a DIY water filtration and purification unit is a critical step in your home preparedness plan. Here's how to create an effective water purification system using readily available materials and simple techniques.

First, gather the necessary materials. You will need two food-grade buckets or containers, a ceramic water filter, a spigot, plumbing tape, a drill with various bits, and two lids. Ensure the ceramic filter you choose is capable of removing bacteria, protozoa, and other pathogens. Some filters are also impregnated with silver, which helps to kill or inhibit the growth of microbes.

Begin by drilling a hole in the bottom of the first bucket, which will serve as the top section of your filtration unit. The size of the hole should match the diameter of the ceramic filter's threaded end. Carefully screw the filter into this hole from the inside of the bucket, ensuring a snug fit. If your filter came with a wing nut or similar securing device, use it on the outside of the bucket to firmly attach the filter. Apply plumbing tape around the threads before securing to ensure a watertight seal.

Next, drill a hole in the lid of the second bucket, which will be the bottom section where the filtered water collects. The hole should be large enough to accommodate the spigot. Install the spigot using the manufacturer's instructions, typically involving inserting the spigot into the hole from the outside and securing it with a washer and nut from the inside. Again, use plumbing tape to ensure a watertight seal around the spigot.

Place the second bucket (the one with the spigot) on a sturdy, elevated surface, such as a table or a stack of bricks. This elevation is necessary to use gravity to push the water through the filter and out the spigot. Then, place the first bucket (the one with the filter) on top of the lid of the second bucket. If your buckets did not come with lids, you could use a clean, heavy cloth or a piece of wood as a makeshift lid to prevent contamination.

To use your DIY water filtration system, simply pour water into the top bucket. It will seep through the ceramic filter, where pathogens and impurities are removed, and drip into the bottom bucket as clean, potable water. Depending on the size of your filter and the volume of water, filtration can take several hours. Always start with the clearest water possible to extend the life of your filter, and pre-filter murky water through a cloth or coffee filter to remove large particulates.

It's crucial to regularly clean the ceramic filter according to the manufacturer's instructions, usually by gently scrubbing its surface with a brush under running water. Avoid using soap or detergents, as they can damage the filter's effectiveness. Additionally, periodically check all connections for leaks and tighten or reseal as necessary.

This simple, cost-effective DIY water filtration and purification unit can be a lifesaver in emergency situations, providing your family with a continuous supply of clean water. Remember, while this system is effective for removing many pathogens and impurities, it may not remove viruses or chemical contaminants. For complete safety, consider combining this system with water purification tablets or boiling water before consumption if you suspect viral or chemical contamination.

CHAPTER 1: SEAL-GRADE MEDICAL KIT ASSEMBLY

When assembling a SEAL-grade medical kit, it's crucial to prioritize items that address a wide range of medical scenarios, from minor injuries to life-threatening situations. The goal is to prepare a kit that is both comprehensive and compact, ensuring you can respond effectively to any health emergency that might arise, especially in situations where professional medical help is not immediately available. Here's a step-by-step guide to assembling your kit with specific recommendations for materials, tools, and techniques to ensure you're fully prepared.

1. **Select a Durable, Waterproof Container**: Begin with a rugged, waterproof case like the Pelican 1400 Case. Its hard shell and watertight seal protect contents from moisture and damage, while its compact size makes it portable and easy to store. The case should be large enough to hold all your supplies but small enough to be easily carried in a backpack or stored in a vehicle.

2. **Organize Supplies Using Modular Pouches**: Use clear, waterproof pouches or vacuum-sealed bags to organize supplies into categories such as wound care, medications, tools, and personal protection. This not only keeps your kit organized but also ensures items remain sterile and are easy to access quickly. Label each pouch with a permanent marker for easy identification.

3. **Wound Care Essentials**: Stock your kit with a variety of bandages, including adhesive bandages in multiple sizes, gauze pads, and roll gauze for dressing wounds. Include a roll of medical tape, such as 3M Durapore Surgical Tape, for securing dressings. Add butterfly closures and steri-strips for closing small lacerations, and a pack of transparent film dressings like Tegaderm to protect wounds from water and dirt.

4. **Tools for Treatment**: Essential tools include a pair of medical-grade scissors, such as the Leatherman Raptor Shears, for cutting clothing or bandages, and a pair of precision tweezers for removing debris from wounds. A digital thermometer for monitoring fever and a manual blood pressure cuff with a stethoscope for checking vital signs are also important. Ensure you have a quality tourniquet, like the CAT Tourniquet, for controlling severe bleeding and a CPR mask for safe resuscitation efforts.

5. **Medications and Topical Treatments**: Assemble a selection of over-the-counter medications, including pain relievers like ibuprofen and acetaminophen, antihistamines for allergic reactions, and loperamide for diarrhea. Include topical treatments such as antibiotic ointment, hydrocortisone cream for rashes and itching, and burn gel for minor burns. Remember to check expiration dates regularly and replace any used or expired items.

6. **Splinting and Immobilization Supplies**: For sprains, fractures, or dislocations, include a SAM splint, which is lightweight and moldable to support any limb. Elastic bandages and triangular bandages can be used for wrapping and immobilizing injuries.

7. **Personal Protection and Hygiene**: Pack nitrile gloves to prevent contamination when treating wounds, and a small bottle of hand sanitizer for cleaning hands before and after providing care. Include a pack of face masks to protect against the transmission of airborne illnesses.

8. **Specialized Items**: Depending on your specific needs or concerns, consider adding specialized items such as an epinephrine auto-injector for severe allergic reactions, glucose gel for low blood sugar, or naloxone for opioid overdose. Consult with a healthcare professional to determine what specialized items are appropriate for your kit.

9. **Instructional Material**: Include a compact, waterproof first aid guide that covers basic treatment procedures for common injuries and illnesses. This can be invaluable in stressful situations when clear thinking is difficult.

10. **Regular Review and Practice**: Familiarize yourself with the contents of your medical kit and how to use each item. Regularly review and update your kit as needed, and consider taking a first aid course to enhance your skills and confidence in using the kit effectively.

By meticulously assembling your SEAL-grade medical kit with these detailed steps, you ensure that you are prepared to handle a wide range of medical emergencies with confidence. This kit, combined with the knowledge of how to use it, becomes an indispensable tool for ensuring the safety and well-being of yourself and those around you in any situation.

Essential Medical Supplies for First Aid Kits

When assembling a first aid kit with the rigor of a Navy SEAL, the selection of essential medical supplies is paramount to ensure readiness for any situation. The foundation of a SEAL-grade medical kit is its comprehensiveness and adaptability to various emergencies, from minor injuries to potentially life-threatening situations. The following items are indispensable in creating a kit that meets these criteria:

1. **Adhesive Bandages**: Include a variety of sizes and shapes, such as standard strips, butterfly closures for deeper cuts, and knuckle bandages. Opt for waterproof and fabric options for durability and flexibility.

2. **Sterile Gauze Pads and Rolls**: Choose multiple sizes of gauze pads (2x2 inches, 4x4 inches) for dressing wounds and gauze rolls for securing dressings or creating pressure bandages. Ensure the gauze is sterile to minimize infection risk.

3. **Medical Tape**: Select a hypoallergenic and easy-to-tear tape for securing gauze and bandages. A width of 1 inch is versatile for various applications.

4. **Antiseptic Wipes or Solution**: Pack antiseptic wipes for cleaning wounds or skin around injuries. An iodine solution or hydrogen peroxide can also be included for wound disinfection.

5. **Antibiotic Ointment**: Tubes of antibiotic ointment are crucial for preventing infection in cuts, scrapes, and burns. Single-use packets can also be useful for portability and hygiene.

6. **Pain Relievers**: Include over-the-counter pain relievers such as ibuprofen, acetaminophen, and aspirin. Consider individual packets to maintain dosage accuracy and shelf life.

7. **Tweezers and Scissors**: Choose medical-grade tweezers for splinter or debris removal and a pair of rounded-tip scissors for cutting tape, gauze, or clothing without causing injury.

8. **Elastic Bandages**: For sprains or strains, elastic bandages (such as ACE bandages) are essential. They provide support and reduce swelling when applied correctly.

9. **Thermal Blanket**: A compact, reflective thermal blanket can prevent hypothermia in shock cases or provide shade in heat-related emergencies.

10. **Nitrile Gloves**: Pack several pairs of nitrile gloves to protect against bloodborne pathogens and maintain hygiene during first aid administration.

11. **CPR Mask**: A pocket-sized CPR mask with a one-way valve ensures safety while performing CPR, protecting against the transfer of fluids.

12. **Instant Cold Packs**: For reducing swelling or numbing pain, instant cold packs that activate without refrigeration are invaluable.

13. **Saline Solution**: A small bottle of sterile saline solution is useful for flushing out eye injuries or cleaning wounds when clean water isn't available.

14. **Allergy Medication**: Antihistamines, both oral and topical, can be life-saving for allergic reactions. Consider including an epinephrine auto-injector if prescribed.

15. **Tourniquet**: A commercial-grade tourniquet is recommended for controlling severe bleeding that can't be stopped with direct pressure. Familiarize yourself with its use and limitations.

16. **Burn Gel or Cream**: Include a soothing burn treatment for minor burns. Look for products that contain aloe vera or lidocaine for pain relief.

17. **Emergency Contact Information**: A waterproof card with emergency contacts, allergies, and medical conditions should be included for each family member.

18. **Instruction Booklet**: A compact first aid guide or instructions for using specific items in the kit can be invaluable, especially under stress.

Each item in your first aid kit should be checked regularly for expiration dates and replenished as necessary. Customizing your kit based on personal or family medical needs, activities, and potential risks in your environment ensures you are as prepared as possible for any situation. Remember, the goal of your first aid kit is not just to respond to emergencies but to do so with the confidence and efficiency of a Navy SEAL.

Stockpiling Medications for Long-Term Health

When considering the stockpiling of medications for long-term health management, it's crucial to approach this with the same precision and foresight as assembling your SEAL-grade medical kit. The objective is to ensure you and your family have access to necessary medications during extended periods of crisis or when access to medical facilities and pharmacies may be restricted. Here's how to effectively stockpile medications:

1. **Inventory Current Medications**: Begin by creating a comprehensive list of medications currently prescribed to all family members. This list should include medication names, dosages, frequency of use, and the prescribing doctor's contact information. Don't forget to include over-the-counter medications that are regularly used, such as antihistamines, antacids, and pain relievers.

2. **Consult Healthcare Providers**: With your list in hand, consult with your healthcare providers about obtaining a surplus supply of prescribed medications. Explain your intent to prepare for emergencies and ask for prescriptions that cover an extended period, typically 3 to 6 months. Some providers may have suggestions for alternative, longer-lasting medications in case specific ones are hard to stockpile.

3. **Understand Medication Shelf Life**: Research the shelf life of each medication you plan to stockpile. Most medications have a shelf life of 1 to 5 years from the date of manufacture, but this can vary. It's essential to understand how the efficacy of medication can change over time and under different storage conditions.

4. **Optimal Storage Conditions**: Medications should be stored in a cool, dry place away from sunlight. The bathroom medicine cabinet is not ideal due to humidity. Instead, choose a dedicated storage area in a closet or a drawer in a climate-controlled room. Use airtight containers to protect medications from moisture and pests. Label each container with the medication name, dosage, and expiration date for easy reference.

5. **Rotate Stock**: Just like food stockpiles, medication supplies should be rotated to ensure nothing expires before it's used. Use the oldest stock first and replace it with new supplies. Regularly check expiration dates and remove any medications that are past their effective date.

6. **Special Considerations for Controlled Substances**: If you or a family member requires controlled substances, be aware that regulations may limit how much you can stockpile. Work closely with your healthcare provider to understand what is permissible and to document the necessity for these medications.

7. **Alternative Remedies and Supplements**: In addition to prescription medications, consider stockpiling vitamins and supplements that support overall health, such as Vitamin C, Vitamin D, and Zinc. Herbal remedies and essential oils can also be useful, but ensure you understand their use and any potential interactions with prescription medications.

8. **Emergency Prescription Information**: Alongside your medication stockpile, maintain an up-to-date list of all prescriptions, including digital copies if possible. This list should include medication names, dosages, prescribing doctors, and pharmacy contact information. In an emergency, this list can be invaluable for medical personnel or if you need to replenish supplies.

9. **Legal and Ethical Considerations**: Always follow legal guidelines when stockpiling medications. Never share prescription medications with others, and ensure that all prescriptions are obtained through proper medical consultation.

By meticulously planning and managing your medication stockpile, you can ensure that you and your family maintain access to essential medications during extended crises. This preparation, much like the training and readiness of a Navy SEAL, can significantly impact your ability to navigate health challenges with resilience and foresight.

CHAPTER 2: SELF-RELIANT HEALTH MANAGEMENT

In the realm of managing health without outside help, it's imperative to have a solid understanding of how to provide emergency medical care for common injuries. This knowledge can be a lifeline in situations where professional medical assistance is not immediately available. The first step in this process is recognizing and appropriately responding to various types of injuries that one might encounter. Let's delve into the specifics of treating some common injuries, ensuring you're prepared to act decisively and effectively.

Starting with cuts and lacerations, the priority is to control bleeding and prevent infection. For minor cuts, clean the wound thoroughly with soap and water or an antiseptic wipe to remove any debris or bacteria. Apply gentle pressure with a sterile gauze pad to stop the bleeding. Once the bleeding has ceased, cover the wound with a sterile bandage or adhesive bandage. For deeper cuts that don't stop bleeding with direct pressure or are gaping, seeking professional medical attention is necessary as stitches may be required.

Moving on to burns, which can range from mild to severe, the initial step is to cool the burn. Run cool (not cold) water over the affected area for several minutes to reduce the temperature of the skin and underlying tissues. Avoid using ice as it can cause further damage to the burn site. After cooling, cover the burn with a sterile, non-adhesive bandage or clean cloth. Do not apply creams, ointments, or butter to burns as these can trap heat and worsen the injury. For burns that cover a large area of the body, are on the face, hands, or feet, or appear to be third-degree burns, it's crucial to seek medical attention immediately.

Sprains and strains are also common injuries that can be managed at home with the RICE method: Rest, Ice, Compression, and Elevation. Rest the injured limb to prevent further injury. Apply ice wrapped in a cloth to the affected area for 20 minutes every two hours to reduce swelling and pain. Use a compression bandage to wrap the area snugly, but not so tight as to cut off circulation. Finally, elevate the injured limb above the level of the heart to decrease swelling. It's important to monitor the injury for signs of more serious damage, such as inability to bear weight, deformity, or severe pain, which would necessitate a visit to a healthcare provider.

In cases of suspected fractures or dislocations, immobilization of the affected area is key. Use splints made from available materials to stabilize the injury and prevent movement. Splints can be fashioned from cardboard, magazines, or pieces of wood, and should extend beyond the joints above and below the injury. Secure the splint with bandages or cloth strips, ensuring it's tight enough to hold the limb in place but not so tight as to impede circulation. Seek medical attention as soon as possible for X-rays and proper treatment.

Each of these procedures underscores the importance of having a well-stocked first aid kit and the knowledge to use it effectively. Remember, the goal is to stabilize the injured person and prevent further harm until professional medical care can be obtained. In the next section, we will continue exploring how to manage health issues without outside help, focusing on handling illnesses and other medical conditions in the absence of immediate professional medical assistance.

Handling illnesses without access to professional medical care requires a proactive and informed approach. Begin by assessing symptoms to determine the severity of the condition. For common illnesses like colds or flu, supportive care can be effective. This includes staying hydrated, resting, and using over-the-counter medications to relieve symptoms such as fever, cough, and congestion. It's crucial to monitor the illness for signs of worsening conditions, such as difficulty breathing, high fever, or persistent pain, which indicate the need for medical intervention.

For gastrointestinal issues such as diarrhea or vomiting, maintaining hydration is paramount. Oral rehydration solutions, which can be homemade using clean water, salt, and sugar, are essential for replacing lost fluids and electrolytes. Avoid solid foods until vomiting has stopped, and then gradually reintroduce bland foods like rice, bananas, and toast. If symptoms persist for more than 24 hours or are accompanied by severe abdominal pain, dehydration, or blood in vomit or stool, seek medical attention as these may be signs of a more serious condition.

In the event of an allergic reaction, identifying and removing the allergen is the first step. For mild reactions, antihistamines can reduce symptoms such as itching, swelling, and hives. However, severe reactions, known as anaphylaxis, characterized by difficulty breathing, swelling of the throat, or a sudden drop in blood pressure, require immediate use of an epinephrine auto-injector if available, followed by urgent medical care. It's important for individuals with known severe allergies to have an emergency action plan and to carry an epinephrine auto-injector at all times.

Managing chronic conditions without regular access to healthcare providers demands careful planning and education. For those with conditions like diabetes, hypertension, or asthma, it's essential to understand how to monitor and manage the illness, recognize signs of complications, and know when and how to adjust medications. Regular monitoring of blood sugar levels for diabetics, blood pressure for those with hypertension, and peak flow for asthma patients can help prevent complications. Stockpiling necessary medications and supplies, understanding how to adjust dosages based on symptoms or test results, and having a clear plan for seeking emergency care when needed are all critical components of self-reliant health management.

Mental health is another crucial aspect of managing health without outside help. Stress, anxiety, and depression can exacerbate physical health issues and make managing chronic conditions more challenging. Techniques such as mindfulness, meditation, regular physical activity, and maintaining a routine can help manage stress and improve mental well-being. Establishing a support network, even if it's virtual, can provide emotional support and reduce feelings of isolation.

In conclusion, managing health without immediate access to professional medical care requires a comprehensive approach that includes understanding how to treat common injuries and illnesses, managing chronic conditions, and maintaining mental health. A well-stocked first aid kit, knowledge of basic medical procedures, and a proactive approach to health management can empower individuals and families to care for their health with confidence, even in challenging circumstances.

Emergency Medical Care for Common Injuries

When faced with a nosebleed, a common yet sometimes alarming injury, the first step is to ensure the injured person is seated upright, leaning slightly forward. This position prevents the blood from flowing down the throat, which can lead to nausea or vomiting. Pinch the soft part of the nose just above the nostrils with a firm, steady pressure for about 10 to 15 minutes. It's crucial to resist the urge to check if the bleeding has stopped before this time, as this could disrupt the clotting process. If available, a cold compress or an ice pack wrapped in a cloth can be applied to the bridge of the nose to help constrict the blood vessels and reduce the bleeding. Avoid packing the nostrils with tissues or cotton, as this can cause further irritation. If the bleeding persists beyond 20 minutes or is the result of a severe injury, seek medical attention immediately.

In the event of a tooth being knocked out, time is of the essence. First, locate the tooth and pick it up by the crown, avoiding touching the root to minimize damage. If the tooth is dirty, gently rinse it with milk or saline solution—never use tap water, as this can damage the root cells. Attempt to reinsert the tooth into the socket, ensuring it is facing the correct way. If reinsertion is not possible, the tooth should be kept moist at all times. Place it in a container of milk, saline solution, or even the injured person's saliva. Avoid storing the tooth in water. Seek dental or medical assistance immediately, as the chances of saving the tooth decrease significantly after 30 minutes.

For a choking individual, it's vital to assess whether they can breathe, talk, or cough. If the person is unable to do any of these, stand behind them and wrap your arms around their waist. Make a fist with one hand and place it just above the person's navel, grabbing the fist with your other hand. Perform a quick, upward thrust to attempt to dislodge the object. This maneuver, known as the Heimlich maneuver, may need to be repeated several times. For pregnant or obese individuals, the fist should be placed at the base of the breastbone, just above the joining of the lowest ribs. If the person becomes unconscious, lay them down on their back and begin CPR, checking periodically for any dislodged objects in their mouth. Immediate medical attention is required if the object is not expelled quickly.

Dealing with a sprained ankle involves the RICE protocol—Rest, Ice, Compression, and Elevation. Rest the injured ankle to prevent further injury. Apply ice wrapped in a cloth to the affected area for 20 minutes every two hours to reduce swelling and pain. Use a compression bandage to wrap the area snugly, but not so tight as to cut off circulation. Finally, elevate the injured limb above the level of the heart to decrease swelling. Over-the-counter pain relievers can be used to manage pain. It's important to monitor the injury for signs of more serious damage, such as inability to bear weight, deformity, or severe pain, which would necessitate a visit to a healthcare provider.

By following these detailed steps for managing common injuries, individuals can provide effective emergency medical care in a variety of situations. Each method emphasizes the importance of quick, calm action and proper technique to minimize harm and promote healing, reflecting the adaptability and preparedness central to Navy SEAL training.

Handling Illnesses Without Medical Help

When facing illnesses without access to medical professionals, it's crucial to have a well-prepared plan and the necessary knowledge to manage symptoms and provide care. This section delves into the specifics of handling common illnesses, focusing on practical steps and remedies that can be administered at home. The goal is to equip you with the skills and confidence needed to care for yourself and your loved ones in situations where professional medical help is not immediately available.

1. **Fever Management**: Fever is a common symptom of many illnesses and can often be managed at home. Start by monitoring the sick person's temperature using a digital thermometer. If the fever is above 100.4°F (38°C), you can use over-the-counter medications like acetaminophen or ibuprofen, following the dosage instructions on the package. Ensure the patient stays hydrated by drinking plenty of fluids, such as water, herbal teas, or electrolyte solutions. Dress them in lightweight clothing and use a light blanket if necessary. Keep the room well-ventilated and slightly cool to help reduce body temperature. If the fever persists for more than three days or is accompanied by severe symptoms like difficulty breathing, confusion, or persistent vomiting, seek medical attention as soon as possible.

2. **Dealing with Diarrhea and Vomiting**: These symptoms can lead to dehydration quickly, especially in children and the elderly. The priority is to keep the patient hydrated. Oral rehydration solutions (ORS) are highly effective and can be made at home by dissolving six level teaspoons of sugar and half a teaspoon of salt in one liter of clean, boiled water, cooled to room temperature. Encourage the patient to sip the ORS slowly throughout the day. Avoid giving solid foods until vomiting has stopped for at least six hours. Once vomiting subsides, introduce bland foods gradually, such as bananas, rice, applesauce, and toast (the BRAT diet).

3. **Soothing Sore Throats**: A sore throat can be incredibly painful and is often the first sign of a cold. Gargling with warm salt water can help reduce swelling and discomfort; dissolve one teaspoon of salt in a glass of warm water and gargle several times a day. Honey, mixed with warm tea or lemon water, is an effective natural remedy for soothing sore throats and coughs. However, honey should not be given to children under one year old due to the risk of botulism.

4. **Managing Coughs and Colds**: Increase fluid intake to help loosen congestion and stay hydrated. Warm broths, teas, and clear soups are comforting and can ease congestion. A cool-mist humidifier in the patient's room can also help by adding moisture to the air, which eases breathing. For cough relief, a spoonful of honey can be as effective as over-the-counter cough syrups. If the patient is congested, saline nasal drops or sprays can help relieve nasal congestion. Elevate the head with extra pillows at night to make breathing easier.

5. **Controlling Asthma Flare-Ups**: For those with asthma, ensure that the patient has access to their prescribed rescue inhaler. Monitor their breathing and encourage them to use a peak flow meter if they have one, to assess the severity of the flare-up. Follow the asthma action plan if one has been developed with a healthcare provider. Avoid triggers like smoke, pet dander, or pollen, and ensure the patient remains calm, as panic can exacerbate symptoms.

6. **Reducing Fever in Children**: Children are particularly susceptible to fevers, which can sometimes spike quickly. Use lukewarm sponge baths to help lower body temperature, in addition to administering pediatric doses of fever-reducing medications as per the product's instructions. Keep children hydrated with frequent sips of water, breast milk, or formula, and monitor their temperature regularly. Avoid bundling children in too many layers of clothing or blankets.

7. **Herbal Remedies and Supplements**: Certain herbal remedies and supplements can support the immune system and alleviate symptoms of common illnesses. Echinacea, vitamin C, and zinc supplements may reduce the duration and severity of colds, though it's important to consult with a healthcare provider before starting any new supplement, especially for individuals with pre-existing health conditions or those taking other medications.

Remember, while many illnesses can be managed at home, it's important to recognize when professional medical help is needed. If the patient experiences severe symptoms such as shortness of breath, chest pain, severe headache, stiff neck, or confusion, seek emergency medical care immediately. By being prepared and knowledgeable, you can provide effective care for common illnesses, ensuring the well-being of yourself and your loved ones even when professional medical help is not within immediate reach.

SEAL Trauma Management Techniques

When dealing with severe injuries, time and precision are of the essence. The SEAL-approved trauma management techniques focus on immediate actions that can be the difference between life and death. The first step in managing severe trauma is to ensure personal safety and then proceed with the assessment and application of first aid measures. Here's a detailed breakdown of how to manage severe injuries using SEAL-endorsed techniques:

1. **Rapid Assessment**: Quickly assess the severity of the injury. Look for signs of heavy bleeding, impaired breathing, or shock. This initial assessment should take no more than 10 seconds, as immediate action may be required to save the injured person's life.

2. **Stop Heavy Bleeding**: If the injury involves significant blood loss, immediate action is required to control the bleeding. Use a clean cloth or gauze and apply direct pressure to the wound. If bleeding does not stop, consider applying a tourniquet above the injury site. For a tourniquet, use a commercial-grade product or improvise with a band and a rigid item for twisting (like a sturdy pen). Tighten until the bleeding stops. Mark the time when the tourniquet was applied. Remember, tourniquets are for limb injuries only and should not be used on the neck or torso.

3. **Ensure Airway is Clear**: For unconscious individuals or those with facial injuries, ensure that the airway is clear. Tilt the head back slightly and lift the chin to open the airway. Check for any obstructions. If the person is conscious but struggling to breathe, encourage them to sit in a position that makes breathing easier.

4. **Breathing Support**: If the person is not breathing, begin rescue breathing or CPR if you are trained to do so. Place a CPR mask over their mouth and nose, if available, to prevent direct contact and provide rescue breaths or chest compressions as necessary.

5. **Prevent Shock**: Shock is a life-threatening condition that can follow severe injury. Lay the person down and elevate their legs if possible, unless you suspect spinal injuries. Cover them with a blanket to maintain body heat. Do not give them anything to eat or drink.

6. **Immobilization**: If you suspect a fracture, immobilize the injured area. Use splints made from rigid materials like wood or magazines, ensuring they extend beyond the joints above and below the injury. Secure the splints with bandages or cloth strips, but not so tightly that circulation is cut off. Check for warmth and color beyond the injury to ensure good blood flow.

7. **Rapid Evacuation**: Once immediate first aid measures are in place, evaluate the need for rapid evacuation to a medical facility. If the injuries are beyond first aid treatment, call emergency services or transport the injured person to the nearest hospital as quickly as safety allows.

8. **Continuous Monitoring**: While waiting for professional medical help, continuously monitor the injured person's vital signs—breathing, consciousness, and pulse. Be prepared to administer additional first aid as their condition changes.

9. **Documentation**: If time and situation allow, document the injury, any first aid measures taken, and the time those measures were applied. This information can be invaluable to emergency responders and medical personnel upon their arrival.

10. **Mental Support**: Offer calm reassurance to the injured person. Keeping them calm can prevent the onset of shock and makes it easier to manage their injuries.

Materials and tools for managing severe injuries should be part of your first aid kit, including sterile gauze, medical tape, a commercial-grade tourniquet, CPR mask, splinting materials, and a blanket for shock prevention. Regularly review and practice these techniques to ensure readiness in case of an emergency. Remember, the goal of these SEAL-approved techniques is to stabilize the injured person until professional medical help can be obtained, potentially saving a life.

CHAPTER 3: HYGIENE IN CRISIS SITUATIONS

Maintaining hygiene during crisis situations is paramount to preventing illness and ensuring the well-being of yourself and your family. In environments where traditional facilities and resources are scarce, innovative and practical solutions become necessary. Here we delve into strategies for sustaining personal and environmental cleanliness when conventional means are not available.

For personal hygiene, start with water conservation techniques for bathing. If water supply is limited, consider sponge baths using a small amount of water mixed with a few drops of biodegradable soap. Focus on cleaning the face, underarms, and groin area to control odor and reduce the risk of infection. Use a clean cloth for each person to avoid cross-contamination. For hair washing, dry shampoo or even cornstarch can be an effective alternative to conserve water and maintain scalp health.

Dental care remains crucial, yet it may be overlooked in crisis conditions. Continue brushing teeth at least twice a day using a fluoride toothpaste. If water is scarce, spit the toothpaste out without rinsing or use a damp cloth to wipe the mouth. In extreme situations, baking soda can substitute for toothpaste, and a clean piece of cloth can replace a toothbrush. Flossing should not be neglected, as dental health significantly impacts overall health.

Handwashing is a critical practice for preventing the spread of germs. When running water is not available, use hand sanitizer with at least 60% alcohol. For a more sustainable option, prepare a handwashing station by filling a container with soapy water and placing it on a raised surface. Poke small holes in the cap or use a spigot to control the flow. Place another container below to catch the used water, which can then be repurposed for flushing toilets or watering plants.

Toilet hygiene must be adapted to the situation. If the water supply is interrupted, a portable camping toilet or a DIY latrine can be set up. For the latter, dig a hole at least 6-8 inches deep and away from water sources to prevent contamination. After use, cover with soil or sawdust to reduce odors and deter flies. For solid waste disposal, securely bag and seal waste before disposing of it in a designated trash collection area.

Menstrual hygiene can be challenging without access to disposable products. Reusable menstrual cups or cloth pads offer a sustainable alternative, requiring minimal water for cleaning. If these are not available, improvise with clean, soft fabric cut into strips and folded for absorbency. Ensure these homemade pads are washed thoroughly with soap and water, then dried in the sun for natural disinfection.

Clothing and bedding should be kept clean to prevent skin infections and pest infestations. Wash clothes and linens by hand using a bucket or basin, scrubbing with soap and rinsing thoroughly. If possible, boil clothes for disinfection before hanging them to dry in direct sunlight, which has natural sanitizing properties.

In managing waste, separate organic from inorganic materials to reduce odors and pests. Organic waste can be composted to create nutrient-rich soil for gardening, while inorganic waste should be recycled or disposed of properly. Ensure all waste containers are securely covered to prevent attracting animals and insects.

By implementing these hygiene practices, you can maintain a healthy and safe environment for your family even in the most challenging circumstances. Each step, from water conservation methods to waste management, contributes to the overall resilience and well-being of individuals facing crisis situations.

Sanitation in Water Scarcity

In environments where water is scarce, maintaining sanitation becomes a critical challenge that demands innovative and practical solutions to prevent disease. The key to effective sanitation under these conditions lies in maximizing the use of limited water resources while ensuring that hygiene practices are not compromised. Here are detailed steps and recommendations to achieve this:

1. **Hand Washing with Minimal Water**: Hand washing is paramount in preventing the spread of germs. When water is scarce, use a spray bottle filled with a mixture of water and a small amount of soap to wet your hands. Rub your hands together vigorously to create a lather, covering all surfaces of your hands and fingers. Rinse with a minimal amount of water or use a damp cloth to remove the soap. Dry your hands thoroughly with a clean towel or air dry them. This method significantly reduces water usage compared to traditional hand washing.

2. **Dry Sanitation Systems**: Consider the implementation of dry toilets, which do not require water for flushing. Composting toilets are an excellent option, transforming human waste into compost through aerobic decomposition. Ensure the composting toilet is well-ventilated to speed up the composting process and minimize odors. For urine, divert it separately using a urine-diverting dry toilet (UDDT) to reduce moisture and facilitate the composting of solid waste. This not only conserves water but also recycles waste into valuable resources for gardening.

3. **Sanitizing Surfaces with Homemade Solutions**: Create a sanitizing solution by mixing 1 part bleach with 9 parts water in a spray bottle. Use this solution to disinfect surfaces, especially in the kitchen and bathroom. Spray the solution on surfaces and let it sit for at least 1 minute before wiping it off with a clean cloth. This method ensures effective sanitation without the need for running water.

4. **Waterless Hand Sanitizers**: Use alcohol-based hand sanitizers that contain at least 60% alcohol as an alternative to hand washing when water is not available. Apply a generous amount to the palm of one hand and rub your hands together, covering all surfaces until they feel dry. This is an effective way to kill germs and maintain hand hygiene without using water.

5. **Waste Management Practices**: Proper disposal of waste is crucial in preventing disease. Double-bag waste using sturdy garbage bags and seal them tightly before disposal. If regular waste collection services are not available, designate a secure area away from living spaces to store the waste until it can be properly disposed of. Regularly disinfect the storage area to prevent the attraction of pests.

6. **Greywater Recycling for Flushing Toilets**: If you have access to a limited amount of water, consider setting up a greywater recycling system. Greywater from sinks, showers, and washing machines can be collected and used for flushing toilets. Use a simple filtration system, such as a bucket filled with gravel and sand, to remove particles from the greywater before using it to flush. This conserves fresh water for more critical uses like drinking and cooking.

7. **Personal Hygiene Practices**: In the absence of showers, use no-rinse bathing wipes or baby wipes for personal hygiene. Focus on cleaning the armpits, groin, and face to control body odor and reduce the risk of skin infections. For oral hygiene, minimize water usage by wetting your toothbrush with a small amount of water and using a cup to rinse your mouth instead of running tap water.

By adopting these detailed sanitation practices, you can effectively prevent disease even when water is scarce. Each step is designed to minimize water usage while maintaining a high standard of hygiene, ensuring the health and safety of individuals and communities in water-limited environments.

DIY Hygiene Without Traditional Facilities

In situations where traditional hygiene facilities are unavailable, creating effective DIY solutions becomes essential for maintaining health and preventing disease. One of the most critical aspects of hygiene is handwashing, especially in crisis situations where access to running water might be compromised. Here's how to set up a simple, effective handwashing station using minimal resources:

1. **Materials Needed**: Secure a clean 5-gallon bucket with a lid, a small plastic container (like a detergent bottle) with a push-pull cap, a nail or drill, non-toxic soap, clean water, and paper towels or clean cloths.

2. **Preparing the Water Container**: Take the small plastic container and clean it thoroughly. Using a nail or drill, create a small hole near the cap. This will be used to control the flow of water for handwashing. Fill this container with clean water and tighten the cap.

3. **Soap Dispenser**: Place a bar of non-toxic soap in a mesh bag or an old sock. Tie this near the handwashing station for easy access. Alternatively, if liquid soap is available, it can be placed in another small container next to the water.

4. **Setting Up the Station**: Position the 5-gallon bucket under the water container to catch used water. This greywater can later be used for flushing toilets or watering plants, ensuring no wastage.

5. **Usage Instructions**: To wash hands, tilt the water container slightly to let water flow out through the hole created. Wet hands, use the soap, then rinse thoroughly under the water flow. It's crucial to ensure that hands are dried completely after washing, using paper towels or a clean cloth, which should be washed regularly.

6. **Maintenance**: Regularly check the water level in the container and refill as needed with clean water. The soap and drying materials should also be kept clean and replenished to ensure the station remains hygienic.

For dental hygiene, when traditional toothpaste is not available, baking soda can be a viable alternative. Here's how to use it:

1. **Materials Needed**: Baking soda, a small cup or container, and a toothbrush.

2. **Preparing the Paste**: Mix a small amount of baking soda with water in a cup or container to create a paste. The consistency should be similar to that of regular toothpaste.

3. **Brushing**: Apply the baking soda paste to the toothbrush and brush teeth thoroughly for two minutes. Ensure to reach all surfaces of the teeth and gums.

4. **Rinsing**: After brushing, rinse the mouth with clean water. This method is effective for cleaning teeth and neutralizing acids in the mouth.

For bathing without running water, a sponge bath can be an efficient method to maintain cleanliness:

1. **Materials Needed**: Clean water, a basin or large bowl, a clean sponge or washcloth, and mild soap.

2. **Preparing the Bath**: Warm the water if possible and pour it into the basin. Add a small amount of mild soap to create a soapy solution.

3. **Bathing**: Dip the sponge or washcloth into the soapy water and wring out excess. Clean the body one section at a time, starting from the face and moving downwards, ensuring to clean all areas thoroughly.

4. **Rinsing**: After soaping, rinse the sponge or washcloth with clean water and wipe off the soap from the body. It may require several rinses to remove all soap residue.

5. **Drying**: Use a clean towel to dry the body completely, paying special attention to areas where moisture can accumulate, such as underarms and between toes.

These DIY hygiene solutions are practical and can be implemented with minimal resources, ensuring that even in the absence of traditional facilities, personal cleanliness and health are maintained.

Managing Waste in Survival Scenarios

Managing waste safely in long-term survival scenarios requires meticulous planning and execution to prevent health hazards and maintain hygiene. The process involves segregating waste at the source, ensuring proper disposal, and considering composting and recycling options. Here's a detailed guide on how to manage waste efficiently and safely.

1. **Segregate Waste**: Start by categorizing waste into biodegradable, recyclable, and hazardous. Use separate containers for each category. Label them clearly to avoid confusion. For biodegradable waste, use a container with a tight-fitting lid to minimize odors and deter pests. Recyclables should be cleaned to prevent attracting insects or rodents. Hazardous waste, including batteries, medical sharps, and chemicals, requires special handling to avoid contamination and injury.

2. **Biodegradable Waste Management**: Designate an area away from your living space for composting. A simple compost pit can be made by digging a hole approximately 3 feet deep. Add your biodegradable waste here and cover it with soil or dry leaves. This layering process aids in the decomposition and minimizes odors. Over time, this organic matter turns into compost that can enrich the soil for growing food, completing a sustainable cycle.

3. **Recyclable Waste Handling**: Collect recyclables and store them separately. Metals, plastics, and glass can be repurposed or reused for various needs around your safe haven. For instance, clean plastic bottles can be cut and used as planters for small herbs or vegetables. Glass jars make excellent containers for storing food or water. Metals can be repurposed with basic tools to create utensils or tools.

4. **Hazardous Waste Disposal**: Hazardous waste poses a significant risk and must be handled with care. Store hazardous materials in well-marked, durable containers to prevent leakage. If possible, identify a safe disposal site far from your living area and water sources. Regularly check local guidelines for disposal of such materials, as improper handling can lead to soil and water contamination.

5. **Sanitation Practices**: After handling waste, always wash your hands with soap and water to prevent the spread of germs. In the absence of running water, use the handwashing station setup described earlier, ensuring you maintain high hygiene standards.

6. **Waste Reduction Strategies**: Minimize waste generation by repurposing items and reducing reliance on disposable products. Opt for reusable goods and repair broken items instead of discarding them. This not only reduces the amount of waste needing management but also conserves resources.

7. **Regular Monitoring and Maintenance**: Inspect your waste management areas regularly for signs of pests or leakage, especially in the case of hazardous waste. Ensure that compost pits and recyclable storage do not become sources of contamination or attract unwanted wildlife.

8. **Community Involvement**: In a long-term survival scenario, collaborating with your community can enhance waste management efforts. Share resources like composting sites or organize collective hazardous waste disposal to ensure a clean and safe environment for everyone.

By implementing these detailed steps, you can manage waste safely and effectively, ensuring your survival haven remains hygienic and sustainable. This approach not only protects your health and that of your family but also contributes to the overall well-being of the environment, even in challenging long-term survival scenarios.

BOOK 10: CRISIS ADAPTATION AND LEADERSHIP

In the face of a crisis, the ability to adapt and lead can mean the difference between chaos and order, fear and calm. Drawing from the principles of Navy SEAL training, this guide will delve into the essential leadership qualities and adaptive strategies necessary for managing emergencies effectively. Leadership in crisis situations requires a unique blend of decisiveness, empathy, and strategic thinking. The first step towards effective leadership is establishing clear communication channels within your family or group. This involves not only the ability to convey instructions clearly but also the willingness to listen and incorporate feedback from all members.

1. **Establish Clear Roles and Responsibilities**: Begin by assigning specific roles and responsibilities to each member of your household or group, tailored to their strengths and capabilities. For instance, one person might be in charge of medical supplies, while another handles food storage and preparation. This division of labor ensures that critical tasks are managed efficiently and reduces the burden on any single individual.

2. **Develop a Decision-Making Framework**: In a crisis, time is of the essence. Create a decision-making framework that allows for quick and informed decisions. This could involve setting up a hierarchy of command or establishing a consensus-based approach, depending on the size and dynamics of your group. The key is to have a system in place that everyone understands and respects.

3. **Practice Situational Awareness**: Teach and practice the skill of situational awareness with your group. This means being observant of your surroundings, understanding how they might change, and anticipating potential threats before they arise. Regularly assess your environment for new risks and adjust your plans accordingly.

4. **Conduct Regular Training and Drills**: Just as Navy SEALs undergo rigorous training to prepare for any scenario, your group should regularly practice emergency drills. This could include evacuation drills, first aid training, and scenarios that simulate the loss of utilities or communication. These exercises not only build skills but also help to identify any gaps in your plans.

5. **Foster Resilience and Mental Toughness**: Encourage a mindset of resilience and mental toughness within your group. This involves focusing on solutions rather than problems and viewing challenges as opportunities to learn and grow. Share stories of survival and resilience to inspire and motivate each other.

6. **Adaptability**: The core of SEAL leadership lies in adaptability—the ability to adjust strategies and tactics in response to changing conditions. Encourage an environment where innovative thinking and flexibility are valued. This means being open to altering plans as new information becomes available or as situations evolve.

7. **Empathy and Support**: Effective leadership also requires empathy. Recognize the emotional and psychological needs of your group members, especially during prolonged crises. Providing support, whether through listening or helping to alleviate fears, can strengthen group cohesion and morale.

8. **Strategic Planning for Long-Term Survival**: Beyond immediate crisis response, focus on strategic planning for long-term survival. This involves considering sustainable food and water sources, energy needs, and security measures. Engage your group in brainstorming sessions to identify creative solutions for long-term challenges.

By incorporating these leadership principles and strategies, you can create a cohesive, resilient group capable of navigating the complexities of any crisis. Leadership in such times is not just about survival; it's about emerging stronger and more united in the face of adversity.

9. **Leverage Technology and Information**: In today's digital age, access to information can significantly enhance your group's ability to adapt and respond to crises. Utilize online resources, apps, and communication tools to stay informed about local threats, weather conditions, and emergency services. Equip your group with basic knowledge on how to use these technologies effectively for information gathering and sharing.

10. **Resource Management**: Efficient management of resources plays a crucial role in crisis adaptation. Conduct regular audits of your supplies, from medical kits to food reserves and water sources. Implement a system for tracking usage and replenishing stocks. This not only ensures your group's needs are met but also minimizes waste and maximizes the utility of available resources.

11. **Conflict Resolution Skills**: In high-stress environments, conflicts are inevitable. Develop and practice conflict resolution skills within your group to address disagreements constructively. This could involve mediation techniques, active listening exercises, and establishing clear guidelines for communication. Resolving conflicts swiftly and fairly can prevent them from escalating and undermining group cohesion.

12. **Continuous Learning and Improvement**: Adopt a mindset of continuous learning and improvement. After each drill or real-life crisis situation, debrief as a group to discuss what went well and what could be improved. Encourage feedback and constructive criticism. This process not only enhances your group's capabilities but also fosters a culture of trust and mutual respect.

13. **Health and Wellness**: Prioritize the physical and mental health of your group members. Stress and anxiety can take a toll, particularly in prolonged crisis situations. Incorporate activities that promote wellness, such as regular exercise, meditation, or group discussions. A healthy group is more resilient and better equipped to face challenges.

14. **Community Engagement**: Extend your leadership and crisis adaptation strategies beyond your immediate group by engaging with the wider community. Building relationships with neighbors and local organizations can create a support network that enhances security, resource sharing, and collective knowledge. Participate in community preparedness programs and contribute your group's skills and resources where possible.

15. **Innovative Problem-Solving**: Encourage innovative thinking and problem-solving within your group. Challenges during a crisis can be unique and complex, requiring creative solutions. Facilitate brainstorming sessions where all members can contribute ideas, no matter how unconventional. This not only helps in finding effective solutions but also empowers each member, reinforcing their value to the group.

16. **Documenting and Sharing Knowledge**: Keep detailed records of your group's plans, resources, training schedules, and lessons learned. This documentation can be invaluable for onboarding new members, adapting strategies over time, and sharing knowledge with other groups or communities. Consider creating manuals, guides, or even digital content based on your experiences.

By integrating these strategies into your leadership approach, you can build a group that is not only prepared to face any crisis but also capable of thriving in the aftermath. The resilience, adaptability, and unity fostered through these practices will serve as your group's greatest assets, ensuring that you can navigate the uncertainties of the future with confidence and strength.

CHAPTER 1: LEADING YOUR FAMILY IN A CRISIS

When a crisis strikes, the immediate response and leadership provided within the family unit can significantly impact the outcome. The first step in leading your family through a crisis is to ensure that everyone is on the same page regarding the emergency plan. This involves detailed discussions about what to do, where to go, and how to communicate should the usual channels become unavailable. It's crucial that these plans are revisited and practiced regularly, not just created and forgotten. For instance, if the plan involves evacuating to a specific location, make sure every family member knows the address, the route, and alternative routes in case the primary path is blocked.

Communication is the backbone of effective crisis management. Equip your family with multiple ways to stay in touch. This could mean investing in walkie-talkies that don't rely on cell service, establishing a family group chat on a secure messaging app that can work over minimal internet connections, or setting up a physical meeting point in case digital communication fails. It's also wise to teach every family member how to send a distress signal, whether digitally or through traditional methods like signal fires or flares, depending on the nature of the crisis.

In addition to communication, assigning roles is a critical step in crisis leadership. Each family member should have a specific role that plays to their strengths. For example, someone with medical training or first aid knowledge should be in charge of the family's medical kit and be the primary caregiver in case of injury. Someone with a knack for mechanics could be responsible for ensuring the family vehicle is in good condition or managing any equipment that might be needed. Children, too, can have roles, such as being in charge of the family pet or carrying their own emergency backpack. Assigning roles not only distributes the workload but also gives each person a sense of purpose and responsibility, which can be psychologically beneficial during stressful situations.

Training is another key element. Just as a Navy SEAL undergoes continuous, rigorous training to prepare for any scenario, your family should also engage in regular training sessions. This could involve first aid workshops, fire safety drills, or even survival skills camping trips. The goal is to ensure that when faced with a crisis, every family member knows how to react swiftly and efficiently, minimizing panic and confusion.

Preparation extends to physical resources as well. Ensure your home is stocked with emergency supplies, including water, non-perishable food, medical supplies, flashlights, batteries, and other essentials. Each family member should know where these supplies are stored and how to use them. Consider creating individual emergency kits for each family member that they can grab quickly if evacuation is necessary. These kits should include personal items, a change of clothes, essential documents, and personal care items, in addition to basic survival supplies.

Lastly, mental preparedness is as crucial as physical preparedness. Cultivating a mindset of resilience and adaptability in the face of adversity can significantly influence your family's ability to cope with and recover from a crisis. Discuss potential scenarios and encourage open conversations about fears and concerns. This not only helps in mentally preparing for the unexpected but also strengthens the emotional bonds within the family, creating a solid support system to rely on during tough times.

By taking these steps, you lay a strong foundation for leading your family through any crisis with confidence and competence. Remember, the goal is not just to survive but to emerge from the crisis as intact and unscathed as possible, both physically and emotionally.

Ensuring your family understands the importance of mental preparedness alongside the physical and logistical preparations is vital. This involves regular discussions about the emotional and psychological aspects of dealing with emergencies. Encourage family members to express their feelings and concerns about different scenarios, and work together to address these worries constructively. This could include stress-relief techniques such as deep breathing exercises, meditation, or even role-playing different crisis scenarios to build confidence and reduce anxiety.

Incorporating scenario-based learning into your family's preparation can significantly enhance their ability to respond to various crises. For instance, simulate a power outage scenario where your family must manage without electricity for an extended period. This not only tests your preparedness in terms of supplies and equipment but also helps identify areas for improvement in your family's emotional and psychological readiness. Such exercises should be conducted with sensitivity to each family member's comfort level, gradually building up to more challenging scenarios to prevent overwhelming anyone.

Another critical aspect of leading your family through a crisis is the continuous evaluation and adaptation of your emergency plans. As situations change and family members grow and evolve, so too should your strategies for dealing with potential emergencies. Regularly review and update your plans, incorporating new skills learned, feedback from drills, and any changes in your living situation. This might include updating emergency contact information, revising evacuation routes, or incorporating new technology into your communication plans.

Building a network of support with neighbors and local community members can also enhance your family's crisis resilience. Establish connections with those living nearby who you can rely on for mutual assistance during emergencies. This could involve sharing resources like tools, skills, or even creating a neighborhood watch program. Engaging in community emergency response training programs can also provide valuable knowledge and skills that benefit not only your family but also those around you.

Fostering a culture of preparedness within your family means integrating these practices into your daily life, not just as occasional activities. This could be as simple as discussing current events and how they might affect your family, to more involved projects like building a rainwater collection system together. The key is to make preparedness a regular part of your family's routine, which in turn normalizes the behaviors and attitudes necessary for effectively dealing with crises.

Finally, remember to celebrate your family's achievements in building their crisis management skills. Acknowledge the progress made during drills, the acquisition of new skills, or the successful implementation of a preparedness project. Positive reinforcement not only boosts morale but also reinforces the value of being prepared, encouraging ongoing participation and engagement in these crucial activities.

By integrating these strategies into your family's routine, you create a dynamic and adaptable approach to crisis management. This not only prepares your family for a wide range of scenarios but also strengthens the bonds between you, fostering a sense of unity and shared purpose. With each member playing a vital role and contributing their unique strengths, your family can face challenges with confidence, knowing that together, you are resilient and prepared to overcome whatever crises may come your way.

SEAL Leadership in High-Pressure Scenarios

Leading effectively in high-pressure scenarios, much like a Navy SEAL, requires a blend of strategic thinking, emotional intelligence, and unwavering discipline. When a crisis hits, the ability to maintain composure and lead with confidence is paramount. Here, we delve into the SEAL leadership principles that can be applied to ensure your family navigates through crises with strength and unity.

Firstly, establish a clear chain of command within your family unit. This doesn't mean enforcing a rigid military hierarchy but rather clarifying who makes critical decisions during an emergency. For instance, the person with the most medical knowledge might take the lead during health-related emergencies, while someone with expertise in mechanics could spearhead technical or equipment-related decisions. This approach ensures decisions are made swiftly and by the most knowledgeable individual in that domain.

Communication is the cornerstone of effective leadership. Equip your family with the skills and tools necessary for clear, concise, and direct communication. This includes both verbal and non-verbal cues. In high-stress situations, it's often the non-verbal signals that can either escalate or de-escalate a situation. Practice clear signaling methods, such as hand signals or coded messages, that can be understood by all family members, even in the chaos of a crisis.

Develop and nurture situational awareness within your family. This means training each member to be constantly aware of their environment and to anticipate and react to changes. For example, if you're in a situation where you need to evacuate your home, each member should be trained to quickly identify exits, potential hazards, and gather essential supplies without needing explicit instructions. This kind of awareness can significantly improve your family's response time and safety during emergencies.

Resilience and adaptability are traits that SEALs are renowned for, and fostering these within your family is crucial. Encourage a mindset that views challenges as opportunities for growth and learning. This can be achieved through regular family meetings to discuss potential crisis scenarios and brainstorm solutions. Such exercises not only prepare your family for various emergencies but also help build a resilient mindset that thrives on overcoming obstacles.

Empathy and emotional intelligence are as important as tactical skills. Recognize and validate the fears and concerns of each family member, ensuring they feel heard and supported. This builds trust and strengthens the emotional bonds within the family, which are invaluable during times of crisis. For instance, after a stressful drill or real emergency, take the time to debrief as a family, allowing each member to express how they felt during the situation and what could be done better next time.

Finally, continuous training and improvement are vital. Navy SEALs undergo constant training to refine their skills, and adopting this principle can significantly benefit your family's preparedness. Regularly review and update your emergency plans, conduct drills, and stay informed about the latest in crisis management and survival strategies. Encourage each family member to learn new skills that could be beneficial in a crisis, such as first aid, self-defense, or emergency signaling.

By integrating these SEAL leadership principles into your family's crisis management plan, you empower each member to act decisively, communicate effectively, and adapt swiftly to changing situations. This not only enhances your family's ability to navigate through crises but also fosters a sense of confidence, unity, and resilience that will serve well beyond emergency situations.

Crisis-Ready Family Training and Planning

Building a crisis-ready family unit requires a strategic approach that combines training with meticulous planning. The foundation of this process is to ensure that every family member is equipped with the knowledge and skills necessary to respond effectively in various emergency situations. This begins with a comprehensive assessment of potential risks specific to your geographical location and living situation. Whether it's natural disasters like floods, earthquakes, and hurricanes, or man-made crises such as power outages or civil unrest, understanding the threats you are most likely to face is the first step in preparation.

Once the potential risks are identified, the next step involves creating a detailed emergency plan tailored to address each scenario. This plan should include evacuation routes, meeting points outside the home, and methods of communication should the family be separated during a crisis. It's crucial that this plan is written down, and a copy is given to each family member. Additionally, designate a safe, easily accessible place in the home where this plan along with other important documents can be stored.

Training plays a critical role in ensuring that when faced with a crisis, every family member knows what to do. This training should cover basic first aid, including how to treat minor injuries, recognize signs of serious health issues, and when to seek medical attention. CPR certification is another valuable skill that can be life-saving in emergencies. Local community centers and health organizations often offer courses on first aid and CPR, making it accessible for family members to gain these essential skills.

Another aspect of training involves familiarizing each family member with the emergency supplies kit. This kit should include items such as water, non-perishable food, flashlights, batteries, a first aid kit, and other essentials. Regularly review the contents of this kit together, ensuring that everyone knows how to use each item. For example, conduct a practical demonstration on how to use a hand-crank radio or water purification tablets. This hands-on approach not only reinforces the learning but also helps to alleviate anxiety by providing a sense of control and preparedness.

Practicing evacuation drills is another critical component of building a crisis-ready family unit. These drills should simulate different scenarios, including fires, natural disasters, and other emergencies that require quick evacuation from the home. Assign specific responsibilities to each family member during these drills, such as who is responsible for grabbing the emergency kit, who should ensure that all family members are accounted for, and who will be in charge of pets. These roles should be based on each individual's strengths and abilities, and it's important to rotate responsibilities periodically so that each family member becomes comfortable with multiple roles.

In addition to physical preparedness, psychological readiness is equally important. Discussing potential emergencies in a calm and factual manner can help reduce fear and anxiety. Encourage family members to express their concerns and questions, and address them with clear, reassuring information. This open line of communication fosters a supportive environment where family members feel safe and understood.

As part of the ongoing preparation, it's also beneficial to engage in community preparedness activities. Many communities have local emergency response teams and offer training programs. Participating in these programs not only enhances your family's preparedness but also strengthens community ties, which can be invaluable during and after a crisis.

In building a crisis-ready family unit, the emphasis should be on continuous learning and adaptation. The landscape of potential threats can change, as can the dynamics of the family. Regularly revisiting and updating your emergency plan, conducting drills, and refreshing training ensures that your family remains prepared for whatever challenges may arise. This proactive approach to crisis management empowers each family member, building a resilient unit that can confidently face emergencies together.

Ensuring that your family is well-versed in survival skills is another cornerstone of building a crisis-ready unit. This includes teaching children and adults alike how to signal for help, basic navigation skills using a compass or maps, and understanding how to find and purify water if stranded or in a situation where the water supply is compromised. Workshops and outdoor adventure groups often offer courses in these skills, providing a practical and engaging way for family members to learn and practice together. Incorporating these lessons into family hiking trips or camping excursions can turn them into enjoyable learning experiences that reinforce important survival skills.

Technology can also play a significant role in crisis preparedness. Familiarize your family with apps and devices that can provide critical information during emergencies, such as weather alerts, GPS tracking, and emergency communication apps that work without cellular service. Assign someone the responsibility of keeping devices charged and ensuring portable chargers or solar chargers are included in your emergency kit. This person should also be tasked with regularly updating any apps and checking the functionality of devices to ensure they're ready for use when needed.

Creating a home safety audit is an effective way to identify potential hazards and make necessary adjustments to mitigate risks. This involves checking the structural integrity of your home, ensuring that heavy furniture is secured to prevent tipping during earthquakes, verifying that smoke and carbon monoxide detectors are functioning and properly placed, and ensuring that fire extinguishers are accessible and all family members know how to use them. Conducting this audit annually, or as the family situation changes, helps maintain a safe living environment that can withstand or mitigate the impacts of various crises.

Financial preparedness is an often overlooked aspect of crisis readiness. Establishing an emergency fund that can cover several months of living expenses provides a financial buffer that can be crucial during extended power outages, natural disasters, or other situations that might disrupt income or access to banking services. Teach family members about the importance of financial planning and involve them in discussions about budgeting for emergencies. This not only prepares them for potential crises but also instills valuable financial management skills.

Incorporating self-defense training and situational awareness can significantly enhance your family's security during a crisis. Self-defense classes designed for various age groups and physical abilities can provide family members with the confidence and skills to protect themselves if faced with danger. Additionally, teaching situational awareness — the practice of being mindful of your environment and recognizing potential threats before they escalate — can be a valuable skill in avoiding or safely navigating dangerous situations.

Lastly, the emotional and psychological well-being of your family cannot be underestimated in crisis situations. Establishing routines that include stress-relieving activities, such as exercise, meditation, or family game nights, can help maintain a sense of normalcy and reduce anxiety. Additionally, consider creating a "comfort kit" for each family member that includes personal items that can provide emotional support and comfort during stressful times, such as a favorite book, photos, a comforting blanket, or a small toy for children.

By taking a comprehensive and proactive approach to crisis preparedness, you can build a family unit that is not only equipped to handle emergencies but also resilient in the face of challenges. This involves not just planning and training but also fostering a supportive and communicative family environment where each member feels valued, understood, and confident in their ability to contribute to the family's safety and well-being. Through continuous learning, adaptation, and a focus on both physical and emotional preparedness, your family can stand strong together, ready to face whatever the future may hold with confidence and resilience.

Roles and Responsibilities in Crisis Management

Assigning roles and responsibilities within your family or group for efficient crisis management begins with a clear understanding of each member's strengths, skills, and limitations. This process is crucial for ensuring that when a crisis strikes, everyone knows exactly what their job is, reducing confusion and maximizing the effectiveness of your collective response. The first step in this process is to gather your family or group for a detailed discussion about the various scenarios you might face and the specific tasks that would need to be managed in each case.

1. **Inventory of Skills and Interests**: Start by making an inventory of each member's skills, interests, and physical capabilities. This could include medical training, cooking skills, mechanical aptitude, or even a calm demeanor under pressure which can be invaluable for tasks requiring a steady hand or clear thinking. Don't overlook the younger members of the family; they can be responsible for tasks such as gathering pet supplies or ensuring all family members have a flashlight and whistle in their emergency kit.

2. **Assigning Primary and Secondary Roles**: Once you have a clear picture of each person's capabilities, begin assigning primary and secondary roles. For example, the person with medical training might take the lead on assembling and maintaining the first aid kit, as well as being the primary caregiver in the event of an injury. However, it's also important to designate a secondary person for each critical role, ensuring that someone else can step in should the primary person be unable to fulfill their duties.

3. **Creating a Communication Plan**: Effective communication is the backbone of efficient crisis management. Assign someone the role of communication officer, responsible for maintaining all devices in working order, knowing emergency contacts by heart, and understanding how to operate any backup communication systems you have in place, such as two-way radios or a satellite phone. This person should also be tasked with teaching these skills to at least one other member of the group.

4. **Logistics and Supplies Management**: Assign a logistics officer responsible for managing supplies, including food, water, and fuel. This involves not only stockpiling but also rotating supplies to ensure nothing expires, as well as knowing how to ration supplies if the situation calls for it. They should be detail-oriented, able to maintain clear records of inventory levels, and plan for replenishments.

5. **Security and Safety**: Depending on your location and the nature of the crisis, security can be a significant concern. Assign someone to oversee the physical security of your home or shelter, including checking locks, reinforcing entry points, and monitoring any security systems. This role requires someone who is detail-oriented and has a good understanding of basic home defense principles. Additionally, designate a safety officer responsible for ensuring that the family or group adheres to safety protocols, such as fire safety rules, and that everyone knows what to do in case of different types of emergencies, from natural disasters to home invasions.

6. **Education and Training Coordinator**: Continuous education and training are vital for keeping your family or group prepared. Assign someone the role of organizing regular drills and educational sessions. This could include first aid refreshers, evacuation drills, or sessions on how to purify water. The ideal person for this role is not only knowledgeable in various survival skills but also a good teacher, capable of engaging and motivating others to participate and learn.

7. **Well-being and Morale Officer**: Never underestimate the importance of mental health and morale during a crisis. Assign someone the role of monitoring the group's emotional well-being, organizing activities to relieve stress, and ensuring that any signs of mental health strain are addressed promptly. This role is best suited to someone with empathy, good listening skills, and the ability to remain positive and encouraging under challenging circumstances.

By carefully considering each member's skills and interests, you can assign roles and responsibilities that not only ensure the efficient management of any crisis but also help each person feel valued and integral to the group's survival. This initial assignment of roles is just the beginning. Regular reviews and adjustments based on evolving situations, new skills acquired, or changes in your group's composition will ensure that your crisis management plan remains robust and effective.

8. **Health and Nutrition Overseer**: In a crisis, maintaining proper nutrition and monitoring health becomes even more critical. Assign someone the responsibility of planning meals that are nutritionally balanced from your stockpiled supplies, taking into account any dietary restrictions or health conditions within the group. This person should have a good understanding of basic nutrition and be able to create meal plans that conserve resources while ensuring everyone remains healthy. They should also keep track of health issues, such as monitoring for signs of malnutrition or illness, and coordinating with the medical officer for any necessary treatment.

9. **Technical and Mechanical Specialist**: In many crisis situations, the ability to repair tools, maintain generators, or even set up a solar power system can be invaluable. Assign someone with mechanical skills and technical knowledge to this role. They would be responsible for maintaining and repairing any equipment, from vehicles to power generators, and ensuring that everything is in working order. This role requires someone who is resourceful, with a strong problem-solving ability, and who has a basic understanding of mechanics and electronics.

10. **Environmental Monitor**: Assign someone the task of monitoring the environment and weather conditions, especially if your crisis plan involves staying in place for an extended period. This person should be familiar with using the internet and other resources to track weather patterns, potential hazards, and any changes in the local environment that could affect your group's safety. They would be responsible for advising on any necessary adjustments to your plans, such as reinforcing your shelter before a storm or planning evacuation routes in case of a wildfire.

11. **Child and Elder Care Coordinator**: If your group includes children, elderly members, or individuals with special needs, assign someone to focus on their care. This role involves planning activities to keep

children engaged and safe, ensuring that elderly members have their needs met, and making any necessary adjustments to the living situation to accommodate those with special needs. This person should be patient, compassionate, and creative, with a good understanding of the care requirements for different age groups and abilities.

12. **Resource Acquisition Specialist**: Depending on the length and nature of the crisis, you may need to acquire additional resources. Assign someone the role of identifying and obtaining these resources, whether it's through bartering with neighbors, foraging, or other means. This person needs to be diplomatic, with good negotiation skills, and have an understanding of what resources are most valuable and necessary for your group's survival.

13. **Documentation and Records Keeper**: Keeping detailed records can be crucial in a crisis. Assign someone the task of documenting strategies, inventory levels, medical records, and any incidents that occur. This role is vital for maintaining organization and ensuring that valuable information is not lost. This person should be meticulous, with good organizational skills, and ideally, have some experience with record-keeping or administration.

14. **Community Liaison**: Building and maintaining relationships with the surrounding community can be a lifeline in a crisis. Assign someone to act as a liaison with other groups, whether it's neighbors, local government, or relief organizations. This role involves communication and diplomacy, as well as the ability to represent your group's interests while fostering cooperative relationships.

By assigning these roles, you create a structured response team within your family or group, each member bringing their unique skills and strengths to the table. This not only ensures a comprehensive approach to crisis management but also empowers each individual, giving them a clear purpose and responsibility. Regular meetings to discuss roles, responsibilities, and any adjustments based on current needs or situations will keep your group coordinated and ready to face whatever challenges come your way. Remember, flexibility and the willingness to adapt roles as needed are key to effective crisis management and survival.

CHAPTER 2: ADAPTING TO NEW THREATS

Adapting to new threats in a crisis scenario requires a proactive and dynamic approach, focusing on anticipation, preparation, and execution. The landscape of potential dangers is ever-evolving, with each new challenge demanding a unique strategy and set of responses. To effectively adapt, it's crucial to understand the nature of these threats, which can range from natural disasters to technological failures, and from pandemics to social unrest. Each type of threat requires a specific set of preparations and responses, tailored to mitigate risks and protect your family or group.

1. **Anticipation and Continuous Learning**: Stay informed about potential threats by regularly consulting reliable news sources, government alerts, and updates from local authorities. This continuous learning process involves not just understanding the nature of different threats but also recognizing the signs that may precede them. For instance, if you're in an area prone to hurricanes, understanding meteorological patterns and warnings can give you a crucial head start in preparations.

2. **Scenario Planning**: Develop detailed plans for a variety of potential threats. This involves creating specific action plans that include evacuation routes, communication protocols, and emergency supplies tailored to each scenario. For example, an earthquake preparedness plan would include securing heavy furniture and appliances to walls, practicing "Drop, Cover, and Hold On" drills, and ensuring easy access to emergency supplies like water, food, and first aid kits.

3. **Skill Development**: Equip your family or group with the skills necessary to respond to various threats. This could include first aid training, self-defense classes, survival skills workshops, and technical skills for managing utilities or machinery. For instance, knowing how to purify water using household bleach or iodine tablets is a vital skill in scenarios where the water supply is compromised.

4. **Supply Stockpiling and Rotation**: Maintain a well-stocked supply of food, water, medical supplies, and other essentials, with careful attention to expiration dates and storage conditions. For example, store at least one gallon of water per person per day for at least three days, and rotate supplies to ensure they remain fresh. Include supplies specific to different threats, such as N95 masks for air quality issues or sandbags for flooding.

5. **Home Fortification and Safety Measures**: Implement safety measures tailored to anticipated threats. This could involve reinforcing your home's structure against earthquakes, installing storm shutters for hurricane protection, or creating a firebreak if you live in a wildfire-prone area. Regularly inspect and maintain these defenses to ensure they remain effective.

6. **Communication Systems**: Establish robust communication systems that can function in various scenarios. This includes having battery-powered or hand-crank radios for receiving information when the power is out, as well as establishing a family communication plan that outlines how to stay in touch if separated. Consider alternative communication methods, such as satellite phones or two-way radios, especially in scenarios where cellular networks might be down.

7. **Emergency Drills and Training**: Regularly conduct drills to practice your response to different threats. This not only helps to ensure everyone knows what to do but also helps to identify any weaknesses in your plans. For instance, conduct evacuation drills to practice leaving your home quickly and safely, and simulate scenarios where you must stay indoors for extended periods.

8. **Adapting to Technological and Cyber Threats**: In our increasingly digital world, being prepared for cyber threats is as important as physical threats. Ensure your family understands basic cyber hygiene, such

as not sharing personal information online and using strong, unique passwords for online accounts. Keep digital copies of important documents in a secure, encrypted format and consider backup power options for maintaining communication and information access during power outages.

9. **Mental Health and Resilience Building**: Foster a mindset of resilience and adaptability within your family or group. Encourage open discussions about fears and concerns regarding potential threats, and work together to build a supportive environment that promotes mental well-being. This can involve stress-relief practices such as mindfulness or meditation, which can be vital in maintaining clarity and calm in high-pressure situations.

10. **Community Engagement and Support Networks**: Build relationships with neighbors and local community organizations to create a support network that can offer assistance and resources during crises. Participate in community preparedness programs and consider how you can contribute to collective safety and resilience, such as volunteering for local emergency response teams.

By taking these steps, you can create a comprehensive strategy for adapting to new threats, ensuring that you and your family or group are not just reactive but proactive in facing whatever challenges may arise. The key is to remain vigilant, flexible, and prepared to adjust your plans as new information and threats emerge, always prioritizing the safety and well-being of your group.

SEAL Threat Assessment Techniques

In the dynamic landscape of crisis management, the ability to accurately assess threats as they evolve is paramount. This skill, honed by Navy SEALs in the most unpredictable environments, is critical for ensuring the safety and security of your home and family during emergencies. The SEAL approach to threat assessment in evolving situations involves a systematic process that includes observation, orientation, decision, and action, often referred to as the OODA Loop. Here's how you can apply these techniques to adapt to new threats effectively.

1. **Observation**: The first step is to gather as much information as possible about the changing situation. This means keeping a vigilant watch over news sources, social media, and local community alerts for any signs of emerging threats. Equip your home with a reliable shortwave radio and maintain a charged battery pack to ensure you can receive updates even during power outages. Regularly check the functionality of your communication devices and ensure all family members know how to access and interpret the information.

2. **Orientation**: Once you have observed and gathered data, the next step is to orient yourself to the new information. This involves understanding how the evolving threat impacts your immediate environment and safety plans. For instance, if a natural disaster is changing course and heading towards your area, reassess your home's fortifications against the specific type of disaster. If you have previously prepared for flooding but are now facing a wildfire threat, you might need to clear flammable materials from around your property and check the integrity of firebreaks.

3. **Decision**: After orienting yourself to the new threat, decide on the best course of action. This decision should be based on the severity of the threat, its immediacy, and the resources you have at hand. For example, if an imminent threat requires evacuation, your decision process should include selecting the safest route, deciding what supplies to take, and determining the best time to leave to avoid traffic or other hazards. Keep a pre-packed "go bag" for each family member, including essential items such as water, non-perishable food, first aid supplies, personal identification, and communication devices.

4. **Action**: The final step in the SEAL threat assessment technique is taking action based on your decision. This could involve implementing your evacuation plan, fortifying your home, or executing a lockdown procedure. Actions should be swift, decisive, and well-coordinated among all family members. Regularly practice evacuation drills, lockdown procedures, and other emergency actions to ensure everyone knows their role and can perform it under stress.

Throughout this process, maintain clear and calm communication with your family and your community. Establishing and utilizing a neighborhood watch or community-based defense network can provide additional layers of information and security. Share insights and resources with neighbors, as collective vigilance can often detect threats more quickly and accurately.

By adopting these SEAL threat assessment techniques, you can enhance your ability to adapt to evolving situations with the precision and calm required for effective crisis management.

Remember, the key to successful adaptation is not just in the initial preparation but in the continuous reassessment and readiness to act as situations change.

Mental Flexibility for Shifting Challenges

Mental flexibility, the ability to adapt thoughts and behaviors quickly in response to changing circumstances, is a cornerstone of Navy SEAL training and a vital skill for effective crisis management. This skill enables individuals and families to pivot strategies, make rapid decisions, and implement actions that could be lifesaving in evolving threat scenarios. To cultivate mental flexibility in the face of shifting challenges, it's essential to develop a mindset that embraces change, practices problem-solving, and encourages creative thinking.

Firstly, fostering a mindset that views change as an opportunity rather than a threat is crucial. This perspective can be nurtured by regularly engaging in exercises that push you out of your comfort zone. For example, try altering your daily routines in small ways, such as taking a different route during your morning jog or experimenting with unfamiliar tasks that require adaptability. These practices help build a mental resilience that is invaluable when faced with unexpected situations.

Secondly, honing problem-solving skills is fundamental. Begin by identifying potential threats or challenges that could arise in your environment. Once identified, brainstorm various strategies to mitigate these risks. For instance, if you live in an area prone to natural disasters, develop multiple evacuation routes and contingency plans for each type of disaster. Engage your family in these exercises, encouraging them to think critically and offer solutions. This collaborative approach not only strengthens collective problem-solving skills but also ensures that everyone is mentally prepared to adapt to changes swiftly.

Thirdly, creative thinking is a powerful tool in adapting to new challenges. Encourage this by setting aside time for brainstorming sessions where no idea is considered too outlandish. Use scenarios to stimulate thinking, such as how to communicate if the power grid fails or ways to purify water without traditional means. Creativity in problem-solving can lead to innovative solutions that might be crucial in a crisis.

Additionally, practicing stress management techniques is essential for maintaining mental flexibility under pressure. Techniques such as deep breathing, meditation, and physical exercise can help keep the mind clear and focused, enabling better decision-making when it counts. Incorporate these practices into your daily routine to ensure they become second nature.

Lastly, continuous learning plays a significant role in mental flexibility. Stay informed about new survival strategies, technologies, and resources. Regularly update your knowledge base and be open to integrating new information into your existing plans. This could involve taking courses in first aid, emergency preparedness, or even attending workshops on innovative survival techniques.

By integrating these strategies into your daily life, you and your family can develop the mental flexibility required to navigate the complexities of evolving threats. Remember, the goal is not to predict every change but to be so well-prepared and adaptable that you can confidently face whatever comes your way.

CHAPTER 3: TRAINING FOR ONGOING READINESS

Training for ongoing readiness requires a structured approach, blending physical preparedness with mental agility to ensure you and your family can respond effectively to any crisis. This part of your training focuses on establishing a routine that encompasses physical fitness, skill development, and scenario-based practice, all designed to keep your readiness at its peak.

Start by setting a weekly schedule that dedicates specific days to different aspects of readiness training. For instance, Mondays and Wednesdays could focus on physical fitness, incorporating exercises that build strength, endurance, and flexibility. Emphasize functional fitness exercises such as push-ups, pull-ups, squats, and lunges, which mimic movements you might need in a survival situation. Include cardiovascular training like running or cycling to improve endurance. Remember, the goal is to prepare your body to handle the physical demands of a crisis, so tailor your fitness routine to simulate these conditions as closely as possible.

Tuesdays and Thursdays can be reserved for skill development. This includes first aid training, learning to use a ham radio, practicing knot tying, or any other skill that enhances your survival capabilities. Consider enrolling in local classes or workshops that offer hands-on experience in these areas. Online resources can also be valuable, providing step-by-step guides and tutorials. The key is consistent practice; skills like these can diminish without regular use, so incorporate them into your routine in a way that feels engaging and relevant.

Fridays could be dedicated to scenario-based practice. This involves creating simulations of potential crises your family might face, such as power outages, natural disasters, or home invasions. Use these drills to practice everything from evacuation procedures to communication protocols. Each scenario should be treated as real as possible, with roles assigned to each family member to ensure everyone knows their responsibilities. After each drill, hold a debriefing session to discuss what went well and what could be improved. This feedback loop is crucial for refining your family's response to different situations.

In addition to these structured training sessions, incorporate readiness into your daily life. This could mean discussing a different survival topic at dinner each night or playing "what if" games that challenge your family to think through their responses to hypothetical scenarios. The goal is to weave preparedness into the fabric of your daily existence, making it second nature rather than something that feels like a chore.

Remember, the landscape of potential threats is ever-changing, and your training should adapt accordingly. Stay informed about new survival strategies and technologies, and be prepared to integrate them into your training regimen. This might mean updating your first aid kit with the latest medical supplies or learning to use a new communication device that could be critical in an emergency.

By following this structured yet adaptable approach to training, you'll ensure that you and your family remain ready to face whatever challenges come your way. Keep in mind that readiness is not a destination but a continuous journey, requiring ongoing commitment and adaptation.

Ensuring that your training remains relevant and effective also means incorporating regular assessments and updates to your emergency plans. As situations evolve, so too should your strategies for dealing with them. This could involve revisiting your evacuation routes quarterly to account for changes in the local environment or infrastructure. It also means testing your emergency supplies, such as rotating stored water and food supplies to ensure they remain fresh and usable. Regularly check the expiration dates on medical supplies and batteries, replacing them as necessary. This not only ensures your readiness but also familiarizes you with the contents and organization of your emergency kits, making it easier to find items under stress.

Engagement with your broader community can also enhance your preparedness. Participating in local emergency response drills or joining a neighborhood watch program can provide valuable insights into larger-scale coordination efforts and introduce you to resources you might not have known were available. These connections can be invaluable during a crisis, offering mutual support and sharing of information.

Incorporating technology into your readiness training offers another layer of preparation. Utilize apps and online platforms that provide real-time alerts for weather and other emergencies. Familiarize yourself with the functionality of these tools, ensuring you can quickly access vital information. Additionally, consider investing in portable solar chargers to keep electronic devices powered in the absence of electricity, and practice using these devices to ensure you're comfortable with their operation.

Adaptability extends to the psychological aspects of crisis management as well. Cultivating a mindset that remains calm and focused under pressure can significantly impact your ability to navigate emergencies. Practice mindfulness or meditation to improve your stress response, and engage in regular discussions with family members about fears and concerns, addressing them constructively. This emotional preparedness is as crucial as physical readiness, enabling you to make clear-headed decisions when faced with challenges.

Finally, celebrate your progress and milestones in readiness training. Acknowledging the efforts and improvements made by each family member not only boosts morale but also reinforces the importance of preparedness in everyone's minds. Whether it's mastering a new skill, completing a challenging drill, or simply maintaining the discipline of regular training, recognition of these achievements fosters a positive and proactive approach to readiness.

By weaving these elements together—physical fitness, skill development, scenario-based practice, regular assessments, community engagement, technological integration, psychological preparedness, and celebration of achievements—you create a comprehensive and dynamic readiness training program. This approach ensures that you and your family are not just prepared to face emergencies but are also continuously enhancing your ability to adapt and thrive in any situation.

SEAL Continuous Training for Survival

To implement SEAL continuous training strategies for long-term survival, it's essential to start with a foundational understanding that readiness is not a static state but a dynamic process. This approach requires a commitment to regular updates and improvements to your skills, equipment, and plans based on new information, technology, and potential threats. The first step in this ongoing process is to establish a baseline of essential survival skills and knowledge for you and your family. This includes basic first aid, emergency communication methods, navigation, and self-defense techniques. Each family member should be proficient in these areas to ensure collective resilience in various crisis scenarios.

Once the baseline skills are established, the next phase involves integrating advanced skills and knowledge. This might include specialized training such as advanced first aid techniques, including CPR and trauma care, ham radio operation for emergency communication, and advanced navigation skills that could be vital in an evacuation scenario. It's beneficial to engage in regular training sessions led by experts in these fields, which could be facilitated through local community centers, online courses, or by inviting professionals to conduct private sessions.

In parallel with skill development, it's crucial to continuously assess and upgrade your emergency kits and supplies. This involves not only checking the expiration dates on food and medical supplies but also evaluating the relevance of each item in your kit. Technology evolves rapidly, and what was considered the best communication device or the most efficient water purification method a year ago might have been surpassed by newer, more effective solutions. Regularly researching and investing in these advancements ensures that your equipment stays at the cutting edge, enhancing your family's survivability in a crisis.

Another key aspect of SEAL continuous training strategy is physical fitness. Physical readiness is as important as mental preparedness in survival situations. Establishing a regular, comprehensive fitness regimen that includes strength, endurance, and flexibility training ensures that each family member can withstand the physical demands of a crisis. Tailor these routines to mimic real-world survival scenarios, such as carrying heavy packs over uneven terrain or sprinting short distances to seek shelter. Incorporating these practical exercises into your weekly schedule not only builds physical resilience but also reinforces the mindset of readiness and adaptability.

To truly embrace the SEAL continuous training strategy, scenario-based drills should be a regular part of your routine. These drills go beyond basic fire drills or evacuation plans; they should simulate as closely as possible the conditions and decisions you might face in a real emergency. Scenarios can range from natural disasters to home invasions, with each drill designed to test and improve both your physical readiness and decision-making under stress. After each drill, conduct a thorough debrief to identify strengths and areas for improvement. This feedback loop is vital for refining your family's response capabilities and ensuring that lessons learned are integrated into future training sessions.

Engagement with the broader community is also a crucial element of ongoing readiness. Building relationships with neighbors and local emergency responders can provide additional layers of support and information during a crisis. Participate in community emergency preparedness programs, share knowledge and resources, and collaborate on training exercises when possible. This not only strengthens your immediate support network but also contributes to the resilience of the wider community.

Incorporating these elements into a continuous training program requires dedication and discipline, but the benefits to your family's safety and security are immeasurable. By adopting a SEAL-inspired approach to training, you ensure that your preparedness is comprehensive, current, and capable of adapting to whatever challenges the future may hold.

Maintaining a state of readiness also involves the strategic use of technology to enhance your family's ability to respond to emergencies. For instance, leveraging apps that provide real-time weather alerts, GPS navigation, and emergency communication channels can significantly improve your situational awareness and response time. It's crucial to familiarize yourself and your family members with these technologies before a crisis occurs. Practice using these apps during your scenario-based drills to ensure everyone is comfortable and proficient with their functionalities. This could involve setting up mock scenarios where family members must use a GPS app to navigate to a predetermined safe location or using a weather alert app to decide on the best course of action during a simulated natural disaster.

Another critical component of SEAL continuous training is the development of self-sufficiency skills. This includes learning how to grow your own food, purify water, and generate power. These skills not only prepare you for long-term survival scenarios but also promote a sustainable lifestyle that can benefit your family even in times of stability. Consider setting up a small garden to practice growing vegetables or installing a rainwater collection system to learn about water purification. These projects not only enhance your self-sufficiency but also serve as practical, hands-on learning experiences for the entire family.

The psychological aspect of readiness cannot be overlooked. Developing a resilient mindset is essential for enduring the stress and uncertainty of crisis situations. This involves regular mental conditioning, such as practicing mindfulness, visualization, and stress-relief techniques. Encourage family members to engage in these practices together, creating a supportive environment that fosters mental well-being. Additionally, discussing potential fears and anxieties openly can help mitigate the psychological impact of a crisis, ensuring that each family member feels heard and supported.

Regularly revisiting and revising your family's emergency plan is another key element of the SEAL continuous training strategy. As your skills, resources, and circumstances evolve, so too should your plan. This might involve updating evacuation routes, reassigning roles based on newly acquired skills, or incorporating new technologies into your communication and response strategies. Make this review process a regular event, such as every six months, to ensure that your plan remains relevant and effective.

Finally, integrating community service and leadership into your training regimen can provide invaluable experience and insights. Volunteering with local emergency response teams or disaster relief organizations not only contributes to the well-being of your community but also offers practical experience in crisis management and leadership. These experiences can deepen your understanding of effective response strategies and enhance your ability to lead and make decisions under pressure.

By weaving these advanced strategies into your family's continuous training program, you create a comprehensive and dynamic approach to readiness that prepares you for a wide range of scenarios. This holistic approach, inspired by the rigor and adaptability of Navy SEAL training, ensures that your family is not only prepared to survive but to thrive in the face of any challenge.

Family Preparedness Drills

Running family drills to maintain preparedness is a critical component of ensuring your family's safety and readiness in the face of potential crises. These drills are designed to simulate real-life emergency scenarios, allowing each family member to practice their roles and responses in a controlled, safe environment. The goal is to engrain these procedures so deeply that they become second nature, enabling swift, efficient action when faced with actual emergencies. To begin, it's essential to establish a clear, comprehensive plan that outlines the specific steps and actions each family member should take during different types of emergencies, such as natural disasters, home invasions, or medical emergencies.

The first step in running effective family drills involves selecting the scenarios you'll practice. It's important to tailor these scenarios to the most likely threats you may face, based on your geographical location and personal circumstances. For instance, if you live in an area prone to hurricanes, your drills should focus on evacuation procedures, securing the home, and communication strategies during the storm. Alternatively, if you're in an urban setting where home invasions might be a concern, drills should focus on lockdown procedures, silent alarms, and safe rooms.

Once you've identified the scenarios, the next step is to develop a detailed script for each drill. This script should outline the sequence of events, the expected actions of each family member, and the location of all necessary equipment and supplies, such as emergency kits, flashlights, and first aid supplies. It's crucial to assign specific roles to each family member, taking into account their age, physical ability, and skill level. For example, an adult might be responsible for securing the home and communicating with emergency services, while a child's role might be to gather pets and move to a predetermined safe location.

To ensure the drills are as realistic and beneficial as possible, incorporate realistic elements such as time constraints, simulated weather conditions, and the use of actual emergency supplies. For instance, if you're conducting a drill for a power outage, turn off the main power supply to simulate the lack of electricity. Use flashlights or headlamps to navigate your home and gather at the designated safe spot. This not only tests your preparedness but also familiarizes everyone with the experience of moving and acting in the dark, which can be disorienting during an actual emergency.

Communication is another critical aspect of running family drills. Establish a clear communication plan that includes both internal communication among family members and external communication with emergency services, neighbors, or relatives outside the immediate area. Practice using walkie-talkies or a family group chat on mobile devices to convey messages and updates during the drill. This practice will help identify any gaps in your communication plan, such as dead zones in your home where mobile phones may not have signal or the need for backup communication methods if primary systems fail.

After each drill, gather the family for a debriefing session to discuss what went well and what areas need improvement. This is a crucial step in the learning process, as it allows for constructive feedback and the opportunity to refine your emergency plans based on real-life practice. Encourage open, honest communication during these sessions, and make sure to address any concerns or fears, especially those expressed by children. The debriefing is also an excellent time to review the contents of your emergency kits, ensuring that all supplies are up to date and replenished as necessary.

In addition to these structured drills, it's beneficial to incorporate impromptu, unannounced drills to simulate the unexpected nature of real emergencies. These surprise drills can provide valuable insights into your family's readiness to respond without prior warning, highlighting areas where further practice or adjustments are needed. Remember, the primary goal of running family drills is not to instill fear but to empower each family member with the knowledge and skills needed to act confidently and effectively in an emergency. By making these drills a regular part of your family's routine, you'll build a strong foundation of preparedness that can significantly enhance your resilience in the face of any crisis.

To maximize the effectiveness of your family drills, it's essential to vary the scenarios and conditions under which you practice. This means not only focusing on different types of emergencies but also varying the time of day and weather conditions during which you conduct your drills. Practicing an evacuation plan at night, for example, can present unique challenges compared to daylight hours, such as reduced visibility and the need for additional safety measures. Similarly, conducting a drill during adverse weather conditions, such as heavy rain or snow, can help your family adapt to the added complexities these elements bring to an emergency situation.

Incorporating non-family members into your drills can also provide valuable learning opportunities. Inviting neighbors to participate or observe can foster a sense of community preparedness and may highlight additional resources or strategies you hadn't considered. It also prepares your family to work with others in a crisis, an essential skill in community-wide emergencies.

Technology can play a significant role in enhancing your family drills. Utilize apps and online resources that simulate emergency alerts or provide scenario-based challenges. These tools can add a layer of realism to your drills and introduce your family to the types of notifications and information they might receive in an actual emergency. Additionally, consider using video recording to capture your drills. Reviewing the footage can offer insights into your family's response and help identify areas for improvement that may not be apparent in the moment.

Setting measurable goals for each drill can also contribute to a more focused and effective training session. Establish clear objectives, such as reducing the time it takes for your family to gather at a safe location or improving the accuracy of communication under stress. Tracking your progress over time can be incredibly motivating and can provide tangible evidence of your family's increasing competence and confidence in handling emergencies.

Remember, the ultimate aim of these drills is not just to practice the physical actions required during different scenarios but also to cultivate a mindset of preparedness and adaptability. This mindset, characterized by calmness, decisiveness, and resilience, can be as crucial to your family's safety as any physical skill or piece of equipment. Encourage reflection after each drill, asking family members to share not only what they did but also what they were thinking and feeling during the exercise. This reflection can help identify emotional and psychological strengths and vulnerabilities, allowing you to address them constructively.

Finally, integrating fun and positive reinforcement into your drills can significantly enhance engagement, especially among younger family members. Consider incorporating elements of gamification, such as rewards for achieving goals or friendly competitions between family members. Celebrating successes and milestones, no matter how small, can reinforce the value of preparedness and encourage ongoing participation.

By adopting a comprehensive and dynamic approach to running family drills, you ensure that your family not only develops the necessary skills and knowledge to face emergencies but also strengthens the bonds of trust and cooperation that are invaluable in any crisis. Through consistent practice, open communication, and a focus on both physical and psychological readiness, your family can achieve a level of preparedness that brings peace of mind and, ultimately, could make all the difference when faced with the unexpected.

Updating Emergency Plans Regularly

Regular updates to your emergency plans and systems are crucial to ensure they remain effective in the face of new challenges and evolving situations. The process of updating your emergency plans should be systematic and thorough, involving every member of your household to ensure that all perspectives and potential risks are considered. Here's how to approach this vital task with precision and attention to detail.

First, schedule a regular review session for your emergency plans. This could be every six months or annually, depending on your specific circumstances and the frequency of changes in your environment. Mark this on your calendar as a non-negotiable appointment, treating it with the same importance as a medical check-up or vehicle maintenance. During this session, gather all household members for a comprehensive review of your current emergency plans and systems.

Begin by assessing any changes in your living situation that might impact your emergency response. This includes changes in household composition, such as the addition of new family members or pets, which may require adjustments to evacuation plans or emergency supplies. Also, consider any physical changes to your home, such as renovations or the addition of new security features, which could alter your strategies for sheltering in place or defending your home.

Next, review the emergency scenarios outlined in your plan. Evaluate whether these scenarios are still relevant or if new threats have emerged that need to be addressed. For example, if your area has recently experienced extreme weather events not previously considered a risk, incorporate plans to deal with these situations. This step ensures that your emergency plans are aligned with the most current risk assessment for your area.

Examine the effectiveness of your communication plan. Check that all contact information is up to date and consider any new communication tools or apps that could enhance your ability to stay connected during an emergency. Technology evolves rapidly, and what was state-of-the-art a year ago may now be outdated. Ensure that your communication plan includes redundancies, such as backup power sources for charging devices, to maintain connectivity even when conventional power sources fail.

Review your emergency supplies and kits. Check expiration dates on food, water, medications, and batteries, replacing any items that are no longer viable. Consider any new needs that have arisen since your last review and add supplies accordingly. For instance, if a family member has developed a new medical condition, ensure that your first aid kit includes the necessary medications and supplies to manage it.

Evaluate your training and preparedness activities. Reflect on any drills or training exercises you have conducted since the last review. Identify areas where performance could be improved and plan additional training sessions to address these gaps. This might include first aid training, fire evacuation drills, or practice using emergency communication equipment.

Incorporate feedback from family members about their comfort and confidence levels with the current plan. This feedback is invaluable for identifying areas that may need clarification or additional focus. For example, if children are unsure of their role during an evacuation, provide targeted instruction and practice to build their confidence and ensure they know what to do.

Finally, document any changes made to your emergency plans and ensure that all family members have access to the updated information. Consider creating a digital copy of your plan that can be accessed from smartphones or tablets, in addition to a physical copy stored in a secure, easily accessible location.

By following these detailed steps, you can ensure that your emergency plans and systems remain robust, relevant, and ready to activate. Regular updates are not just about revising documents but about reinforcing your family's readiness to face whatever challenges may come. This proactive approach to emergency preparedness empowers each family member, building a resilient and adaptable unit capable of navigating crises with confidence and competence.

Made in the USA
Las Vegas, NV
23 January 2025

16776746R00109